Mediating Interpersonal Conflicts:

A Pathway to Peace

By
Mark Umbreit, Ph.D.

Center for Restorative Justice and Mediation
School of Social Work
University of Minnesota, St. Paul

Foreword by
Melinda Smith, Executive Director
New Mexico Center for Dispute Resolution

Mediating Interpersonal Conflicts:
A Pathway to Peace

by Mark Umbreit, Ph.D.

Published by
CPI Publishing
West Concord, Minnesota

Cover design: Greg Wimmer, Rochester, MN

ISBN 1-881111-04-0

Printed in the United States of America.

1 2 3 4 5 6 7 8 9

TABLE OF CONTENTS

I. OVERVIEW

II. MEDIATION APPLICATIONS

Dedication

This book is dedicated to my life partner, Alexa, and our two daughters, Jenni and Laura, all of whom represent the source of my strength, joy and growth as a person.

FOREWORD

Mediation practitioners in the thick of developing mediation programs and tending to the day-to-day demands of busy agencies rarely have the time to document their work or create a record for others. Mark Umbreit has done a great service to new and experienced practitioners and students of mediation by creating a valuable handbook which presents the full richness of mediation across multiple settings.

Umbreit's book provides historical and descriptive summaries of all of the major areas in the mediation field: community mediation, school mediation, divorce mediation, parent/child mediation, victim offender mediation, and workplace mediation. To my knowledge, this is the first book in the field to provide such a broad and comprehensive review of the theory and practice of mediation for these types of interpersonal disputes. As such, it serves as an excellent resource for practitioners and students who seek an overview of the mediation field in the last 20 years. It also incorporates the major theories, principles, and models in the field and weaves them into the narrative in a clear and lucid way.

The areas that Umbreit addresses in the book, with the possible exception of divorce mediation, are the province of community mediation agencies, which have proliferated throughout North America in the last two decades. Despite this growth, these centers need to diversify programs and funding sources not only to expand but to survive. Mediating Interpersonal Conflicts offers the community mediation practitioner critical information about each potential program area - including rationale, process, key issues, and research summaries - which can assist community mediation centers in building rationales and making informed decisions for new program initiatives.

Umbreit also offers an analysis of what he calls the

"humanistic mediation model," which reminds us of the interpersonal and transformational outcomes of mediation vs. the settlement driven processes that are often found in court-annexed programs. While some readers may not agree with all of Umbreit's prescriptions for how to achieve these outcomes, he has offered us a framework for discussion and debate as the field begins to focus on the healing potential of mediation.

In the summer of 1988, I had occasion to hear Mark Umbreit for the first time at a gathering of victim offender mediation practitioners near Toronto. He presented the results of his preliminary research on victim offender mediation and I was struck by how useful the results were, not only for researchers, but also for program directors and mediators. As both an academic and a practicing mediator and trainer, Umbreit continues to bridge the unfortunate gap between these areas.

Since our first meeting, Mark has become a friend, a mentor and a colleague. We have collaborated on many projects including research, training, and the early development of the Victim Offender Mediation Association. Mark's ability to create bridges between the victim offender field and the larger community mediation field has provided leadership which has strengthened both areas. <u>Mediating Interpersonal Conflicts: A Pathway to Peace</u> will serve to strengthen the connections among the different areas of mediation. I predict this publication will be an often used resource in colleges, community mediation centers and human service agencies for a long time to come.

Melinda Smith, Executive Director
New Mexico Center for Dispute Resolution
Co-Chair, National Association for Community
    Mediation

Preface

MEDIATING INTERPERSONAL CONFLICTS: A PATHWAY TO PEACE

Mark Umbreit, Ph.D.

The preparation of this book has been grounded in my own personal journey over the past twenty-five years of dealing with conflict in the family, community, workplace, and criminal justice system. After a great deal of stumbling and learning from my mistakes, I have grown to fully embrace the power of good communication and conflict resolution skills in bringing a more healthy closure, if not peace, to even the most intense conflicts. Through my work as a mediator, a trainer, a friend, a parent, and a husband, I have come to believe that it is through the constructive resolution of interpersonal conflict that we become enriched and grow as individuals. I have also come to believe that the highest expression of mediation and conflict resolution is not based on the paradigm of problem solving alone, with its focus on settlement agreements. Rather, it is based on what Lois Gold calls the paradigm of healing and "the preference for peace" which resides in all of us. It is the intrinsic healing and transformative power of mediation which can lead to embracing our common humanity and building a greater sense of social harmony.

Many have contributed to the preparation of this book. A special thanks is due to those students, colleagues and friends who reviewed the manuscript and offered helpful feedback. These include: Terry Amsler, Bill Bradshaw, Kathy Bradshaw, Jerry Becker, Richard Cohen, Tom Christian, Jeff Edleson, Marilyn McKnight Erickson, Burt Galaway, Lois Gold, Dane Jorento, Jim Levin, Rachel Lipkin, Dean Peachey, Alice Phalan, Kay Pranis, Janet Schmidt, Melinda Smith, and Mark Toogood. Without the valuable contributions made by these individuals, publication of this book would not have been possible. The support of my life partner, Alexa, was invaluable. The challenges we faced in co-parenting our two teen-age daughters, Jenni and Laura, put the themes of this book in a very personal, and at times, painful perspective, but one in which the four of us have grown enormously. Jenni and Laura have become trained peer mediators. We are all now trying to consistently practice the art of conflict resolution and peacemaking in the many dimensions of our lives.

1
RESOLVING CONFLICT: A JOURNEY OF THE HEART

*The key of conflict management is
the belief that conflict is a natural and
inevitable part of life, and the realization
that it is our reaction or responses to the
conflict that make a conflict situation
constructive or destructive.[1]*

Conflict is an unavoidable part of life. We are faced almost daily with disputes, arguments, or misunderstandings within our families, communities, or jobs. For some of us, conflict is very uncomfortable and to be avoided. Often we tend to deny that conflict is even present or, at the other extreme, we may rush to a quick, if not false, sense of resolution, without ever addressing the underlying emotional issues present in all conflict.

Fortunately, a growing number of people are learning to recognize and talk about conflict. Once a conflict has been named, it then has the potential to be discussed in a direct and respectful manner that can lead to eventual resolution. Instead of denial and avoidance, conflict can be embraced as a necessary step in the journey of individual

1. Mediation Services, 1993.

or organizational growth and development.

We do not have the power to eliminate the uncomfortable presence of conflict in our lives, but every individual has the capacity to choose how he or she deals with conflict, and that choice contributes greatly to whether the conflict is destructive or constructive. In choosing how to respond to conflict, many people engage in power struggles and coercion in an attempt to force their positions on other persons. This book, however, emphasizes the choice of mediation and negotiation, which can lead to more collaborative solutions that contribute to a greater sense of social harmony and peace.

Mediation involves a neutral third party who assists in a discussion of the conflict among the involved people, so that their concerns can be expressed and important issues resolved. A written agreement is often negotiated. The full power of mediation embraces the hope of repairing relationships through expressing and understanding the emotional context of the conflict. Taken as a whole, the mediation process offers an opportunity to resolve interpersonal conflicts through empowering people to create their own best solutions.

Resolving interpersonal conflict through effective communication skills, negotiation, and mediation has grown enormously in North America and Europe over the past two decades. Today hundreds of mediation programs are being used in families, communities, schools, and criminal justice systems. Mediation is highly effective in resolving conflicts between parents and children, spouses or partners, co-workers, neighbors, criminals and their victims, and among students in elementary and secondary schools. In the haste to develop mediation as a credible and efficient alternative to the courts, it has become increasingly settlement--or solution--driven. The "technology" of conflict resolution through effective communication skills--such as active listening, assertiveness, and problem solving--has been so heavily emphasized in training and mediation practice that the underlying spirit of the field is often lost. Repairing relationships through taking the time required for expressing and understanding the emotional context of the conflict is often of secondary concern; the fullest benefits of mediation thereby go unrealized.

Resolution of painful and dysfunctional interpersonal conflict requires far more than the technical application of skills, far more than the mechanics of mediation. It very often requires a journey of the heart, as well as the head, through dialogue and mutual aid. It requires the recognition that despite conflict we remain fellow human beings. Although a settlement agreement is often desirable, the full power of mediation in important relationships can be achieved by viewing it as a growth and healing process that addresses the emotional context of the conflict. This process enables people in disputes to own up to their contribution to the conflict.

The practice of mediation has spread to many settings, but most books and articles tend to address the topic from only one area of application, such as divorce mediation or community mediation, thereby diminishing recognition of the full richness of mediation and its broad range of applications. In addition, much of mediation literature has been dominated by a legal perspective. The goal of this book is to provide a broad understanding of the many applications of mediation and to particularly emphasize the important contribution that staff and volunteers with human services and social work training can make to the field. Emphasis will be on recognizing that long-term effective conflict resolution in relationships that we care about is ultimately a journey of the heart characterized by openness and transformation, rather than the periodic exercise of communication techniques and behavioral manipulation.

A brief description of mediation is useful here, along with a review of the dynamics of conflict and of important communication skills. A far more extensive discussion of the mediation model and its many implications is provided in Chapter 2.

Throughout the book, the terms dispute and conflict are used. They are not meant to be interchangeable; instead, they should be understood as being placed along a continuum of conflict. A dispute is a lower-intensity conflict, usually involving less emotional baggage.

What Is Mediation?

The process of mediation involves a neutral third party who assists disputants to talk about their conflict and negotiate a plan for resolving it. When people get "stuck" in their efforts to directly talk and negotiate with each other, an impartial mediator can assist the parties to continue to discuss the conflict and explore possible ways to resolve it. Mediators do not impose any binding decisions but instead work on empowering the parties in conflict to construct their own settlement, which they considered to be fair.

It is important to distinguish mediation from negotiation and arbitration. Negotiation occurs directly between the disputants without an impartial third party involved, whereas mediation essentially is a discussion and negotiation that is facilitated by a third party that is not involved in the conflict. Arbitration, like mediation, involves an impartial third party listening to the disputants, however, in arbitration the third party, with limited client input, decides how to resolve the conflict. In some respects, mediation and arbitration look similar, although arbitration is essentially an informal process of adjudication, as the parties themselves do not negotiate the agreement.

Mediation is becoming increasingly central to the delivery of human services due to its empowering nature, effectiveness in conflict resolution, and diverse applications of the various mediation styles. Mediation is grounded in an empowerment and strengths perspective: disputants are viewed as having untapped reserves of physical, mental, and emotional resources that can be drawn upon to help manage and resolve even the most severe conflicts. The effectiveness of mediation in conflict resolution stems from an emphasis that focuses on the inner strengths of the disputants to engage in a future oriented process of negotiated problem solving, not on individual pathology or dysfunctional relationships. There are two distinct mediation styles: bargaining, which tends to be more directive and controlling, and therapeutic, which tends to be nondirective and more empowering.[1]

1. Umbreit, 1988; Sibley & Merry, 1986.

Depending upon the situation and the participants involved, either or both styles may be used. Mediation is multidisciplinary in nature, and there has been an increasing effort to emphasize quality control. For example, in recognition of the increasing role that social workers are playing in the field of mediation, the National Association of Social Workers developed the Standards of Practice for Social Worker Mediators in 1991 (Appendix 5).

Understanding Conflict

The important issue is not whether there will be conflict, which is normal and predictable, but how we respond to it. Of equal importance are the communication skills that we use in clarifying the conflict and defining the resolution.

Conflict can be destructive when the disputing parties fail to talk directly with each other, share their feelings, and negotiate some form of resolution. Not confronting the conflict and avoiding the person at whom one is angry preclude resolving the problem through development of a mutually satisfactory agreement. If one talks to others about the person who is the object of anger, escalation is likely. That person may become demonized. The cause of the conflict may become understood as a personal attack rather than inappropriate behavior. Without confronting the source of the conflict, one's perceptions and judgments can become distorted. Destructive conflict can become a painful and life-consuming journey characterized by heightened emotions, increased polarity of positions, and possibly unethical behavior.

A quite different experience occurs when conflict is addressed directly. Even when one is involved in an extended, painful, and intense conflict, a constructive process of resolution can take place. By treating the other person respectfully instead of angrily, one can turn him or her into a partner in a collaborative problem-solving process. In effect, one needs to be tough on the specific behavior but gentle on the person responsible for that behavior. When our negative or defensive emotions have been triggered, showing respect is difficult. Many people tend to take criticism personally and respond by attacking the critic; rather than considering the criticism rationally, they redefine the problem as the person. One of the most fundamental strategies of managing conflict is to separate the problem from the person. This requires a recognition that despite our anger toward another person, we are all human and have more in common with each other—such as loved ones, hopes, fears and dreams—than we have differences. This does not minimize the issues that lead to a conflict, but does place the problem behavior in a larger context which enhances our ability to separate the undesired behavior from the person.

Constructive use of conflict can actually preserve and enhance relationships. Because the involved parties are treated with respect, in that specific behaviors are focused on, personal attacks or put-downs are avoided and they are far less likely to respond defensively. The expectations of a relationship can be clarified, the influence of each party in the relationship can be more appropriately balanced, and entirely new options can be considered. Without addressing conflict directly, individuals and organizations are less likely to grow in positive ways. Our choice of how to respond to a conflict determines the nature of its eventual impact on our lives.

Responding To Conflict

Conflict can be understood as having two dimensions: assertiveness and cooperativeness.[1] The assertiveness dimension reflects the degree to which we promote our own needs and interests, with little concern for maintaining positive relationships. The cooperativeness dimension reflects the degree to which we focus on meeting others' needs and interests along with our own. This dimension places a high value on maintaining positive relationships. Combining the assertiveness and cooperativeness dimensions yields five styles of conflict management, each reflective of its relative placement along the two dimensions (Table 1.1).

Persons who are high on assertiveness and low on cooperativeness tend to use a competing style of conflict management. This is a win-or-lose style in which one person forces his or her perspective upon others. Here conflict is managed through power and domination, and goals are achieved at the expense of the relationship. This is a very aggressive and pushy style. For example, a parent may force his or her desire to go to a ball game upon the entire family, triggering a major conflict because no one else in the family has an interest in doing so. Although a competing style may harm long-term relationships, it may be appropriate in an emergency situation or when dealing with trivial issues.

1. Thomas & Kilmann, 1974.

Table 1.1
Conflict Management Styles

The avoiding style of conflict management is used by persons who deny that a problem exists. Such persons are neither assertive nor cooperative; they simply tune out a discussion of the conflict. For example, your administrative assistant may be irritated by something you communicated to him. Rather than further expressing your concerns or taking the time to listen to him, you simply leave. Such avoidance can be an appropriate conflict-management style when the issue is unimportant, the timing is not right for addressing it, or a cooling-off period is desirable in order to deal with it more suitably.

Persons with an accommodating style are high on cooperativeness-they want to meet the needs of others-but low on assertiveness. They may be great listeners but are not likely to put their own interests and concerns forward. They tend to want to please other persons and suppress their own needs. An actual conflict situation is often minimized to maintain the appearance of harmony. This style can often be found in friendships. Your friend is upset about something you said. Instead of responding defensively, you take the time to listen to your friend and do everything possible to please her, even though you don't wholly agree with her perception of the conflict. Accommodation is appropriate when the most important consideration is to preserve the relationship, or when the issue that triggered the conflict is not very important.

A compromising style of conflict management stands at midpoint along the two dimensions of assertiveness and cooperativeness. The parties involved are concerned about achieving some of the task goals and not damaging the relationship. Each gives up something in order to settle the conflict. For example, you may be in conflict with your neighbors over placement of a new fence. You prefer no fence. Your neighbor plans on erecting an eight-foot fence along a line that you believe is two feet into your property. The two of you talk and agree to a lower fence along a line acceptable to both of you. Compromising is a partial-win and partial-lose style of conflict management that is appropriate when cooperation is important and the time or resources required for more intense collaboration is limited, or when there exists a danger of getting locked into polar positions.

In a collaborating style of conflict management, the parties are very assertive and very cooperative. Each party's needs are clearly and persuasively presented, and each is open to hearing the other's needs. Rather than focusing on the initial positions expressed, the parties work at understanding the underlying values, interests, and needs of both. An example of collaboration is when both parties begin a negotiation with clear positions, such as "Either I get a raise or I'm going to quit," but after identifying each other's underlying interests and needs, agree to something quite different, such as the employee's receiving several nonsalary benefits and perks because of the company's current fiscal straits. A collaborative style requires more energy and time than the other styles of responding to conflict. It is a win/win strategy in which the interests of both parties are fully addressed in any final resolution. Collaboration is particularly appropriate for managing conflict when the relationship and the concerns are very significant to the parties and when a commitment can be made to take the required time for resolution.

All five conflict management styles have an appropriate use, depending on the specific context of the conflict. Collaboration is clearly the most desirable style when important relationships are at stake. But because it requires a good deal of energy and time, it is simply not realistic in many other lesser conflicts. Most people make use of all five styles to some degree, although a dominant style tends to be present in everyone.

Communication Skills

Effective conflict resolution through negotiation or mediation rests upon good communication skills. The quality of the skills employed can dictate whether a conflict will become a constructive or destructive experience for the parties involved. These skills are important for both individuals in conflict and the mediators who are invited to help them. A review of communication skills will be useful in understanding mediation in its many aspects.

Five important communication skills are information sharing, reflective listening, assertion, conflict management, and problem solving. Application of a specific skill depends on the needs of the parties and the emotional energy present (see Table 1.2).

Information sharing is the skill used in normal communication, as culturally defined, between two people. The emotional energy in each party is moderate. When one person has a pressing need and his or her emotional energy is high, reflective listening is the most helpful skill. When one party is agitated and has an intense need to communicate, assertion is the best skill. When both parties have pressing needs and high emotional energy the skill of conflict management is required, which entails a continual back-and-forth use of reflective listening and assertion until the emotional energy is diminished and the conflict has de-escalated. Once the emotional energy of both parties has moderated, the skill of problem solving can be brought into play to negotiate a mutually satisfactory agreement. Effective problem solving seldom occurs until the heightened emotional energy in both parties is discharged. Allowing expression of intense feelings is integral to the conflict-resolution process. When the anger felt by the parties is ignored or down-played and they quickly move to problem solving, a false sense of peace and harmony may result.

Resolving Conflict: A Journey of the Heart

Table 1.2
Communication Skill Selection

Need	Skill area A Normal Communication Patterns	Skill area B Other has pressing need	Skill area C You have pressing need	Skill area D Both have conflicting pressing needs	Skill area E Discrepancy exists between current and desired state

	You Other	You Other	You Other	You Other	You Other
Skill area	Information sharing	Reflective listening	Assertion	Conflict management	Problem solving

Source: Neil H. Katz and John W. Lawyer, <u>Communication and Conflict Resolution Skills</u>.[1]

Effective conflict management is directly related to good reflective listening and assertion skills. Without these, neither party in a conflict can truly hear the other's concerns, or clearly express his or her own needs. Both communication skills, however, can become rather gimmicky if one focuses solely on technique rather than the real intent, in which case they could actually interfere with genuine communication. In some cases they may actually escalate the conflict by being perceived as insincere and manipulative. Therefore, it is important to look closely at these two important and powerful skills.

1. Dubuque: Kendall/Hunt, 1985 pg. 17. Reprinted with the permission of Kendall/Hunt Publishing Company.

Mediating Interpersonal Conflicts: A Pathway to Peace

Conflict often ensues from a breakdown in communication between the involved parties. Words, actions, and expressions are often misinterpreted during the process of decoding a message received. When one person sends a message, it is encoded in his or her own life culture, context and meanings. The recepient attempts to decode it in his or her life culture, context, and meanings. The intent of a message sent does not necessarily match its effect. If a message results in hurt feelings, some assume that was the intent of the sender. Such is rarely the case. Unless the receiver listens attentively to the message and thereby correctly infers intent, misleading assumptions can often lead to escalating conflict and the demonizing of the sender. In communicating with others, we need to express our intentions clearly. We also need to verify our assumptions about what the other person has said, particularly when it is the source of irritation.

The essence of good reflective listening is empathy, caring, and respect shown through keeping the focus on the other person. Paraphrasing and summarizing can be important in reflective listening, but by themselves these techniques may strike the other person as routine and manipulative. In fact, the more the other person in the conflict is knowledgeable about paraphrasing and other communication techniques, the more likely frequent use of these skills can get in the way.

Reflective listening involves three clusters of skills: attending skills, following skills, and responding skills. Attending skills require being fully present and aware of posture, eye contact, distance, touch, gestures, environment, and interested silence. Following skills focus on continuing the flow of the interaction through the use of door-opener-type statements, acknowledgment responses, and open-ended questions. Responding skills check out the meaning of the message that has been received through reflecting content, reflecting feeling, reflecting meaning, and summarizing. Reflecting content, feeling, or meaning is accomplished through paraphrasing, restating in one's own words the content and feeling of the other party.

Conflict Management Through Negotiation

Negotiation is the art of getting from no to yes without destroying a relationship. It involves face-to-face communication between the parties in conflict, without the assistance of a third party. Negotiation requires ongoing back-and-forth use of reflective listening and assertion skills by one or both parties. Management of conflict through effective negotiation requires listening to the other party; indicating that you understand his or her concerns; expressing your feelings; stating your points in a firm but friendly manner; linking your points to points expressed by the other party; and working toward a joint resolution that builds on the ideas of both parties and addresses all concerns.

In their classic <u>Getting to Yes,</u> Fisher and Ury (1991) describe five key points of effective negotiation:

1. Don't bargain over positions
2. Separate the people from the problem
3. Focus on interests, not positions
4. Invent options for mutual gain

5. Insist on objective criteria

It is particularly important to understand the difference between positions and interests. A position represents a fixed demand, such as either you change your behavior or I'm leaving. Positional statements in managing conflict tend to escalate tension, because these win/lose messages usually trigger defensiveness in the other person. Interests relate to a person's underlying values and priorities. A focus on interests leads to the question, What is the most important concern the other party has in trying to resolve this dispute. Interests that frequently appear in interpersonal disputes include approval, recognition, inclusion, identity, security, justice, and power. Rather than quickly making a judgment about what the other person is saying, we need patiently to ascertain the interests and needs underlying his or her statements. By doing this, we are more likely to identify a common ground upon which some resolution of the conflict may be possible.

A six-step model of negotiation can help manage and resolve conflict between two or more parties.[1]

Step I. Preparation
(Reflect on the situation, plan your approach, and express your commitment for a positive outcome.)

Step II. Setup
(Find a safe neutral place, schedule a time convenient to both, establish a comfortable and nonconfrontational environment, describe the process and secure agreements

1. Mediation Services 1993.

to proceed.)

Step III. The Conversation
(Ask the parties to describe the situation from their perspectives and how they felt, paraphrase for clarification, express your perspective and feelings.)

Step IV. Summarize The Issues
(Prepare a verbal or written list of the key issues that must be addressed.)

Step V. Discussion
(Review and discuss each issue, one at a time, brainstorm a list of possible solutions for each issue.)

Step VI. Agreement
(Select a mutually acceptable solution, express the agreement in clear and specific terms.)

The preferred technique for managing conflict is talking and negotiating with each other directly, without the assistance of a mediator who is not always available. Good negotiators always separate the people from the problem by paying attention to the relationship; putting oneself in their shoes; recognizing emotions; allowing emotional steam to be released; actively listening; discussing perceptions; speaking in the first person; and face saving of all parties.[1] Effective negotiation can strengthen relationships while achieving your goals. On the other hand, direct negotiation is not always effective. Numerous problems in communication may emerge, including statements that make a personal judgment, sending solutions, or ignoring the other's concerns. There may even be a lack of commitment to the process itself and a desire by the other party for a clear win/lose solution. When the negotiation process stalls or reaches what seems to be a major barrier, an impartial third party is required to help the disputants to continue to negotiate, most commonly through the process of mediation.

SUMMARY

The resolution of interpersonal conflict in important relationships requires far more than the use of a set of communication techniques and skills. Effective conflict resolution is a journey of the heart, as well as the head. It involves openness and transformation through a process of dialogue and mutual aid.

A two dimensional model for understanding how people deal with conflict consists of assertiveness on one end of the spectrum and cooperativeness on the other. This model identifies five styles of responding to conflict— competing, avoiding, accommodating, compromising, and collaboration-based upon the level of assertiveness and cooperation.

Communication skills, such as information sharing, reflective listening, assertion, conflict management and problem solving, are essential in mediation, and influence

1. Fisher and Ury, 1991.

how we deal with conflict. Without a basic understanding of these skills and an ability to use them, conflict is often dealt with indirectly, leading to a destructive experience that avoids the true causes of the conflict and often evolves into personal attacks. Utilizing good communication skills will encourage a direct approach to the conflict and its causes, and supports the mediation paradigm of being hard on the problem or behavior, but soft on the person.

Negotiation skills allow the parties in conflict to speak directly with each other and resolve the issues. There are five key aspects of negotiation: don't bargain over position, separate people from the problem, focus on interests, invent options for mutual gain, and insist on objective criteria. For many disputes, however, the direct negotiation process encounters too many obstacles. A neutral third party then becomes necessary to assist with further discussion and negotiation. The mediation process can be applied in multiple settings.

The essence of good communication skills in resolving conflict is to be found in the presence of integrity—a consistency between that which we are thinking, are saying verbally, our bodies are communicating, how we are feeling, and the deeper values within our heart.

2
THE MEDIATION MODEL

The mediator's role is: (1) to encourage the empowerment of the parties-i.e., the exercise of their autonomy and self-determination in deciding whether and how to resolve their dispute; and (2) to promote the parties' mutual recognition of each other as human beings despite their adverse positions. . . . It is not the mediator's job to guarantee a fair agreement, or any agreement at all: it is the mediator's job to guarantee the parties the fullest opportunity for self-determination and mutual acknowledgement.[1]

Mediation is a time limited problem solving intervention that is proving to be effective in a wide range of interpersonal disputes and conflicts. It does not focus primarily on past behavior and specific weaknesses or emotional problems of individuals. Instead, mediation is future oriented and builds upon the strengths of the people in mediation to work with each other in resolving the conflict. The field of mediation has truly become an international movement, during the past two decades, with many thousands of mediators and programs throughout the world.

Mediation can occur when there is a conflict

1. Bush, 1989.

between individuals or between groups or organizations. This book will focus on the application of mediation in interpersonal conflict within the context of many areas of life, including neighborhoods, families, communities, schools, criminal justice systems, and workplace settings. Within each of these areas, variations of the generic mediation model in this chapter will be highlighted, information about what we have learned from research will be presented and critical issues identified. A list of resource organizations for training and written/video materials, as well as, specific role play scenarios of each area of conflict mediation is presented in Appendix 6 for those interested in learning more about mediation.

Mediation is one approach to conflict resolution, but not the only one. Other methods range from the informal and *ad hoc* to the formal and legalistic. They include such well-established methods as negotiation, conciliation, ombudsman, arbitration, and adjudication. Mediation fits somewhere in the middle of this continuum.

Direct negotiation is the most basic method for resolving conflict. The two or more parties in conflict speak directly with each other about their differences. No third party is required to intervene. They attempt to identify underlying joint interests and develop a plan for resolving the conflict. Negotiation is typically based on the principle of compromise and is often, but not always, informal in nature.

If parties in direct negotiation get stuck, they may opt for the informal and unstructured method of conciliation. Conciliation, which uses a third party who has no coercive powers, facilitates additional discussions

Table 2.1
Alternative-Dispute-Resolution-Continuum

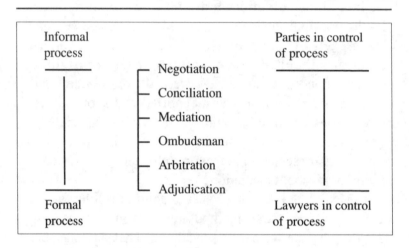

between the parties. This may involve face-to-face meetings at a neutral place provided by the conciliator or simply indirect communication with the conciliator serving as a go-between. Conciliation is often associated with its shuttle-diplomacy function of indirect communication. When the parties' issues are addressed through a process of conciliation, it represents a process of indirect mediation. In some cultures, such indirect mediation or conciliation is far more common than direct face-to-face mediation. For some practitioners, the terms conciliation and mediation are interchangeable.

The involvement of an ombudsman-a neutral, independent fact finder-moves beyond the informality of negotiation and conciliation. Rather than the parties in conflict attempting resolution, an ombudsman investigates what happened. Very little direct communication between the parties in conflict occurs, other than phone calls and letters. The ombudsman does not usually possess the power to compel adherence to his or her findings, which are presented as a nonbinding opinion, although often considerable persuasive power is inherent in the position.

In arbitration, a formal hearing is conducted by one or more arbitrators. Each side states its position and furnishes related evidence to the arbitrator in a procedure that often mirrors the formality of the court. The parties in conflict are not facing each other and there is no direct communication or negotiation between them. Instead, they stand or sit side by side, facing the arbitrator. Arbitration can be binding (the decision must be followed), or nonbinding (the decision is a recommendation). In either case, the arbitrator makes the final determination of how the dispute is to be resolved. Going to arbitration is usually indicative of disputants' voluntary participation.

Adjudication and litigation of a dispute in a formal and binding court hearing is for many the most familiar conflict resolution method. A judge conducts the hearing in a court of law and within the context of the highly coercive, formal powers of the state. Lawyers, representing the disputants, present very narrowly focused arguments in a highly formalized and structured process. The judge makes the final decision based on the formal presentations and it is binding on the involved parties.

Definition Of Mediation
Mediation lies approximately midpoint in the

continuum of conflict resolution methods. It is neither as informal and unstructured as direct negotiation nor as formal and coercive as court adjudication. A generic definition of mediation is:

> Mediation is an informal, but structured, process in which one or more impartial third parties assist disputants in talking about the conflict and in negotiating a resolution to it that addresses the needs and interests of the parties. Mediators do not impose a settlement and participation in the process is usually voluntary.

The word "voluntary" is noteworthy. Mediation does not involve the coercive power to compel agreement to specific terms. However, getting the parties to the table may involve less than the truly voluntary participation noted in the definition. For example, in family mediation, (either divorce or parent child,) the court frequently requires that mediation be attempted. People are strongly encouraged to try mediation as a way to resolve a dispute before other methods are offered.

For an understanding of the mediation process, it is important that several terms related to mediation be explained. Most often, the parties in conflict are referred to either as (1) disputants, when referring to both parties, or as (2) the complainant, the person initiating the grievance, and the accused, the person whom the grievance is directed toward. The mediator's taking a break in the joint mediation session and meeting with the disputants separately is referred to as caucusing. Conducting a caucus during the mediation process is frequently used to explore issues, to check out information, or to reduce tension through taking a break. Many programs routinely use co-mediators. One of the co-mediators often takes the lead role and the other a supportive secondary role. Mediation is a process of dialogue and negotiation with the assistance of a third party. Mediation is often not required unless the disputants have first attempted and failed to negotiate a resolution of the conflict directly with each other.

Phases of the Mediation Process

There are a number of different approaches to the mediation process. For example, the process used by the Children's Hearings Project in Cambridge, Massachusetts, has eight stages, which include joint and private sessions, referred to as caucuses, with the parties. Most victim-offender mediation programs have four phases, which include separate meetings with the parties prior to scheduling the joint session. This four-phase model only occasionally employs caucusing and separate meetings during the mediation session. One of the most extensive descriptions of the various strategies involved in the mediation process is seen in the twelve-stage model[1] (see Table 2.2).

Generic Mediation Model

All of these various descriptions of mediation, including those highlighted later in this book, involve four essential phases: case referral and intake, preparation for mediation, conducting the mediation session, and case

1. Moore 1986.

Table 2.2
Twelve-Stage Mediation Model

1. Initial contacts with the disputing parties
2. Selecting a strategy to guide mediation
3. Collecting and analyzing background information
4. Designing a detailed plan for mediation
5. Building trust and cooperation
6. Beginning the mediation session
7. Defining issues and setting an agenda
8. Uncovering hidden interests of the disputing parties
9. Generating options for settlement
10. Assessing options for settlement
11. Final bargaining
12. Achieving formal settlement

follow-up. The case referral and intake phase begins when cases are logged into the program and preliminary information about the conflict is obtained. The preparation for mediation phase involves the development of strategies for proceeding with the case and collection of additional information, through separate meetings with the disputants, phone conversations or letters. This phase varies considerably among different programs and types of mediation. The third phase, conducting the mediation session, usually involves six tasks consisting of:

1. Introductory or opening statement by mediator(s)
2. Storytelling by each disputant
3. Identification of issues and interests

4. Exploring options and problem solving
5. Reaching agreement
6. Closing statement by mediator(s)

In the first task, an introductory statement by the mediator(s) covers the role of mediation, communication ground rules, confidentiality matters, and the agenda for the session. The second task, storytelling, gives each party uninterrupted time to share his or her perspective on the conflict, often face-to-face with the other party; frequently, they are given a choice as to who begins. The third task involves identification of the most important issues and the underlying interests of the parties. During the fourth task a variety of options for resolving the conflict are identified and reviewed. The disputants conclude the problem-solving process by selecting one of the options during the fifth task. The terms of the agreement are constructed by the disputants and the mediator writes an agreement that will be signed by them. The final task of the session involves a brief closing statement by the mediator(s) explaining how the agreement will be handled by the referral source and thanking the disputants for their participation.

The fourth and final phase of the generic model of mediation is follow-up. Questions about the resolution are asked: Has the agreement been adhered to? Do any of the disputants need further assistance or referral to other services? Were the parties satisfied with the mediation process and outcome?

More detailed descriptions of how various mediation processes are conducted in specific areas of conflict are provided in chapters 3 through 8. Each of these applications is examined in the context of its similarity to the basic phases and tasks portrayed in the generic mediation model (see Table 2.3).

Table 2.3
Generic Mediation Model

Phase	Tasks
I. Case referral and intake	•Log in referral •Obtain preliminary information
II. Preparation for mediation	•Obtain additional information about case through personal contact with disputants •Explain mediation process to disputants •Secure agreement to mediate •Schedule mediation session •Prepare strategy
III. Conducting the mediation	•Introductory statement by mediator •Storytelling by each disputant •Identification of issues and interests •Exploring options and problem solving •Reaching agreement •Closing statement by mediator
IV. Case follow-up	•Monitor compliance to agreement •Make appropriate referrals, if needed •Conduct follow-up meeting, if needed

Styles of Mediation

Mediation involves a variety of styles. Just as there is no single best style of psychotherapy or teaching for all situations, the mediation experience can be quite different, depending on the mediator's perspective, as well as the disputants' needs. Specifically, the relational skills of the mediator have a significant impact on the style of mediation practiced. It is helpful to view mediation along a continuum, ranging from highly directive (with the mediator doing most of the talking) to highly nondirective (with the disputants talking to each other most of the time).

Often the nature of the conflict dictates the style of mediation. For example, a highly emotional and volatile conflict between spouses or partners usually requires a more directive style of mediation. Rather than facing each other and talking directly, the disputants are often directed to address their initial comments to the mediator. The mediator tightly controls the flow of comments in order to de-escalate the conflict. It is important to understand the dynamics of power in the process of mediation (see Appendix 1).

For many mediators, however, the style of mediation has less to do with the nature of the conflict than with the relational skills and values of the mediator. Mediators with a more directive and bargaining style typically embrace a confrontational perspective: conflict is viewed as a power struggle between individuals with conflicting interests. This view focuses on cutting losses. Mediators practicing a more nondirective and therapeutic style of mediation typically embrace a consensual perspective: conflict is viewed as a temporary disruption of social harmony and shared interests. Rather than a systemic view of conflict grounded in a perception of endless power struggles, the consensual perspective represents a relational view of conflict. Repairing relationships and restoring social harmony is strongly emphasized.

Two distinct styles of mediation have been

identified: an empowering style, which is nondirective, and a controlling style, which is highly directive.[1] These styles have also been referred to as therapeutic and bargaining.[2]

An empowering style of mediation focuses on three main tasks of the mediator: getting the parties to the table; starting the meeting; and getting out of the way. The ability of the mediator to get out of the way through use of a nondirective style of mediation is directly related to the quality of the pre-mediation work conducted. Through establishing rapport, listening to their stories, collecting information, and building trust with the parties in separate pre-mediation sessions, the mediator is more likely to be able to use a nondirective style in which the involved parties do most of the talking. Instead of a mediator dominated conversation during the joint session, the parties can engage in a process of mediator assisted dialogue and mutual aid.

Getting the parties to the table through development of trust and rapport with the disputants is the foundation upon which the entire process is built. Their willingness to try the mediation process often has far more to do with their trust of the program staff and mediator than it does with their philosophical commitment to the value of mediation. The task of starting the mediation session sets the tone for instilling ownership of the process among the disputants. It is important for the mediator to make the parties as comfortable as possible so they feel safe in openly discussing the conflict and expressing their feelings.

In the opening statement, the mediator needs to lay out the role of the mediator, the purpose of the session, how the mediation will proceed, and ground rules for

1. Umbreit 1988.
2 . Sibley and Merry 1986.

communication. Then the storytelling phase is initiated. The empowering style of mediation emphasizes the importance of the disputants' communicating their perspective of the conflict face-to-face, assuming they feel comfortable doing so within the context of their culture and traditions. For many within certain cultures, such as Hispanic or Native Americans, direct eye contact between disputants is neither likely or even desirable.

Getting out of the way is often the most difficult task of the mediator, and can be crucial within the context of an empowering style. When the parties are speaking directly to each other about the conflict and engaging in problem solving, the mediator should intervene only to clarify issues, assist with transitions, respond to questions, or prevent verbal abuse. When a moment of silence occurs and the mediator has an urge to comment or offer some assistance, he or she should first mentally count to ten. This allows more time for the disputants to reflect and can encourage further conversation.

A nondirective style of trying to get out of the way should not be confused with passivity or lack of leadership by the mediator. Control of the process, not the outcome, must always remain with the mediator. The mediator needs to be monitoring the disputants interaction to detect any abuse or intimidation, although a good deal of latitude in the expression of anger is usually allowed. While a mediator remains in control of the process, even with a very nondirective style, such control does not mean verbally dominating the session or intimidating the disputants. This control should be understood more as facilitation rather than as domination.

When practicing an empowering style of mediation, the mediator is most verbal during the beginning, when he or she is describing the process, instilling a sense of ownership, and initiating the disputants face-to-face telling of their stories. The mediator is also quite verbal toward the end of the session, when offering assistance in structuring an agreement, presenting options, restating the terms of the agreement, securing signatures, and closing the session.

Face-to-face communication between the disputants is highly valued. When such communication occurs, interruptions by the mediator are discouraged. The mediator allows, and even encourages, discussion of the larger context of the conflict, rather than just focusing on narrow issues. The expression of intense feelings often occurs, as does the sharing of appropriate personal information. A content analysis of a mediation session involving an empowering style is likely to reveal that the mediator was talking roughly 20% of the time, while the disputants were engaged in conversation 80% of the time. The mediator fades into the background once direct communication between the disputants has been initiated. Disputants are far more likely to "buy in" or take ownership of the process through an empowering style of mediation. For these reasons, it is our belief that a nondirective and empowering style of mediation is the preferred method. We do recognize, however, that certain conflicts and disputants require a more directive style of mediation than our preference might suggest.

The first two mediator tasks of getting the parties to the table and starting the mediation are also required within a controlling style of mediation. A more aggressive and manipulative strategy, however, is often used. For example, rather than patiently encouraging ownership in the process and voluntary participation, the mediator may be quick to persuade the disputants that they should participate. An efficiency conception of mediation simply precludes devoting significant amounts of time to such pursuits.

In starting the mediation session, the mediator practicing the controlling style would communicate a sense of authority, perhaps even stressing her or his credentials. The mediator might require that the parties speak to and through the mediator, rather than directly to each other. They would not be seated across from each other, allowing for face-to-face communication, but seated side by side, and their comments would be directed to the mediator. Instilling active ownership of the process and promoting uninterrupted face-to-face communication between the disputants are not highly valued. Questions are likely to be posed by the mediator rather than by one party or the other.

A controlling style of mediation narrows and focuses the range of issues to be discussed. The larger context of the dispute or the feelings experienced by the disputants are of little relevance. A bottom line orientation, with a focus on reaching an agreement, dominates this style. Mutual recognition of the parties common humanity and facilitation of their experience of dialogue and empowerment are of less concern.

A rather judgmental tone is often expressed by mediators who practice a controlling style. The mediator may impose what she or he thinks would be a fair settlement. This could even result in the mediator constructing the agreement and submitting it to the disputants for their approval. A controlling style of mediation is likely to result in the mediator doing most of the talking, perhaps even 80% of the time, with the disputants often responding briefly to a series of questions from the mediator. Controlling mediators are much less likely to fade into the background. They remain actively involved, in a rather domineering way, throughout the entire session. They often perceive themselves as the experts and don't want to lose control or even give the appearance of losing control. Table 2.4 highlights the differences between these two styles of mediation.

Table 2.4
Empowering and Controlling Styles of Mediation

Mediation Elements	Empowering	Controlling
Direct communication between disputants	Maximum	Minimal
Disputants facing each other	Always	Sometimes
Range of discussion	Broad	Narrow
Importance of context and feelings	Very	Minimal
Presentation of choices by mediator	Frequent	Infrequent
Judgmental tone and statements by mediator	Infrequent	Frequent

An empowering style of mediation is more likely to humanize the conflict and actively involve both parties in a process of dialogue and mutual aid. This style, however, is not always appropriate. In some cases, one or both of the disputants may be inarticulate or uncomfortable with talking face-to-face. In other cases, one of the parties may be so intimidating and aggressive that the weaker party could be abused. In both of these situations, the controlling (directive) style of mediation would ensure a fairer and safer process of resolving the conflict.

The two styles-empowerment (nondirective) and controlling (directive)-represent extremes along a continuum of mediation styles. In actual mediation practice, elements of both of these styles are often used, depending on the nature of the conflict and the characteristics of the disputants.

Is Mediation Therapy?

Mediators do not conduct therapy sessions. Emotional benefits may often be experienced by people in mediation, but the mediator has a role distinct from that of a therapist. The mediator facilitates a process of talking about and resolving a specific conflict, with equal attention to the needs of both parties. The mediator does not take sides with either party, and emotions related to the conflict are allowed to emerge but are not explored in great depth. While strong and painful feelings can be acknowledged in mediation, it requires a therapist to further explore and work on those feelings.

In contrast, the psychotherapist's role is to develop insight and to bring about personal and behavioral change. The primary focus is on the person and relationships rather than a specific conflict or issue. Expression of emotions is encouraged and feelings are explored, often extensively. Background information about the client's life is far more available to the therapist and the relationship entailed is usually longer term than in mediation. And the distinction between mediation and therapy can be more complex than many would suggest, depending on the styles of mediation and therapy used (see Appendix 2). In most situations, mediation and therapy share a set of core skills related to good communication and problem solving but require far more specialized knowledge in their respective areas.

Cultural Implications of Mediation

The way in which mediation is used is affected by culture and ethnicity. In fact, all of what has been presented in this chapter must be put through cultural filters related to the individuals involved in specific conflicts. Failure to understand the behavior of disputants in the context of their culture often leads to the mediator misinterpreting their verbal and nonverbal communication. For example, direct communication and eye contact between parties in conflict is usually viewed as a desired outcome of mediation. If one or both parties avoid direct conversation or eye contact it could be interpreted by the mediator as lack of interest in the process, bad-faith bargaining, or even arrogance. Such an assessment could be terribly inaccurate from a Hispanic or Native American perspective. Lack of direct eye contact and direct verbal communication between parties in conflict is common in these cultures. If the disputants have little direct eye contact with the mediator, this could be because of culturally induced deference to authority.

For a mediator to facilitate meaningful conflict resolution, it is vital that he or she recognize the impact of culture and ethnicity upon the intervention at many different levels. Awareness of one's own cultural values-ethnic, economic, organizational, or professional-is crucial to enabling the mediator to consider and understand the cultural dynamics which might affect a mediation. The mediator needs to also recognize and understand the cultural contrasts which may exist between his or her culture and that of the parties. In addition, one needs to be aware of any cultural contrasts which may exist between the parties themselves. For example, a model of mediation that is culturally sensitive to Native Americans and aboriginal people in Canada would be quite different from the dominant Western models (see Appendix 4). Such a model is likely to include consensus decision making; preference for co-mediation; separate premediation sessions with each person; involvement of elders in the mediation; presence of chosen family members; circular seating; silence as comfortable; interruptions as inappropriate; nonlinear agenda; and the use of cultural metaphors and symbols.[1] From this cultural perspective, mediation occurs within a larger spiritual context:

> Mediation is seen as a growth and a healing process. Honoring the spiritual allows people to participate in emotionally charged discussions and resolve differences with integrity. Native communal ties are vital to the individual, so mediation can enhance an individual's sense of belonging and identity, strengthening community relationships, as well as relationships between conflicting parties.[2]

1. Huber 1991.
2. ibid.

Similar changes in the dominant Western model of mediation would be required in responding to disputants from other cultural backgrounds. In fact, the Western model may simply not be appropriate, even with changes, for some cultures. A wide variety of ethnic perspectives related to communication and conflict management exist (see Table 2.5). These perspectives are meant to be suggestive of patterns that are often found in different ethnic traditions. It is important for mediators to understand these varied perspectives in order to adapt the mediation process to different cultures. It is also extremely important that, in our concern to be culturally sensitive, we do not create new stereotypes. While Table 2.5 clearly indicates some frequent ethnic perspectives, one must realize that there exists a great deal of diversity within each ethnic tradition as well.

Summary

Mediation is defined as an informal but structured process in which one or more impartial third parties assist parties in talking about a conflict and in negotiating a resolution to it that addresses the needs and interests of the parties. Mediators do not impose a settlement, and participation in the process is usually voluntary.

A generic model of mediation consists of four phases: case referral and intake, preparation for mediation, conducting the mediation, and case follow-up. Six important tasks are addressed during the mediation session: introductory statement by the mediator, storytelling by each disputant, identification of issues and interests, exploring options and problem solving, reaching agreement, and a closing statement by the mediator.

Styles of mediation range from very directive and controlling at one extreme to very nondirective and empowering at the other. Often mediators mix elements of both styles depending on the nature of the conflict and the characteristics of the parties. The amount and quality of premediation contact with the parties contributes greatly to the effectiveness of the style used by the mediator. A nondirective and empowering style of mediation requires separate meetings with the involved parties before the joint mediation session.

In the final analysis, good mediation has less to do with strategic techniques and moves than it does with connecting with the parties at a human level, communicating a sense of warmth and trust, offering a comfortable structured space in which the parties can feel safe to talk openly with each other about their conflict, and cultural sensitivity. The mediation intervention is not benign. Just as with psychotherapy, mediation can be quite manipulative. For mediation to have its full impact in offering an experience of empowerment and mutual recognition for the parties in conflict, it is important for the mediator to be grounded in a sense of integrity: a consistency between what is being said, what is being done, and the inner values of the mediator. When mistakes are made in the practice of mediation, it is usually better to err in formal technique rather than the relational skills of empathy, warmth, and genuineness. It also is often important to say less rather than more, and to use interested silence as a tool for empowering the parties to work the conflict out and experience the benefits of dialogue and mutual aid, the journey of the heart.

Table 2.5
Cross-Comparison of Ethnic Perspectives for Mediators

Reaction	American Indian / Alaskan Native	Black Afro-American	Mexican	Puerto Rican/Cuban	Asian	Franco-American/ French Canadian	British	Irish	German	Greek	Italian	Jewish	Polish	Norwegian	Vietnamese	Iranian
Reaction to need for outside help from professionals																
Feels shame, sense of failure, personal weakness		•			•	•	•	•	•	•		•	•		•	•
Distrusts agencies and helping systems in general	•	•		•												•
Feels a threat to personal authority/family hierarchy	•		•		•	•			•		•		•		•	•
Turns first to members of our community			•		•	•			•	•	•		•			•
Distrustful of many related questions		•			•	•	•		•	•				•		•
Reaction to interpersonal conflict																
Denies the conflict until manifest conflict behavior is intolerable	•	•	•	•	•	•	•	•	•	•	•	•	•	•	•	•
Accepts the conflict but feels helpless to act				•		•	•		•		•	•	•			
Represses anger and other negative feelings				•							•	•				
Uses explosive verbal/nonverbal communication, then begins problem solving												•				
Reaction to time and schedules																
Future orientation												•				
Present orientation	•	•	•			•	•				•		•		•	

The Mediation Model

Past orientation

Punctual, expects to start and end on time

Clocktime less important; "forgets" to cancel or reschedule

Works wells with crisis/marathon style done at home

Needs many appointments to avoid rushing awareness/information release

Reaction to mediator's credentials

Questions education and experience to determine quality

Relies on others within the subgroup for referral

Accepts the mediator as an expert

Mediator must prove ability, trustworthiness

Reaction to mediator's role, techniques

Unused to intrafamilial equality in decision making

Gives complete information, helps professional

Asks mediator for advice as higher authority

Complies in sessions but may undermine decisions later

Prefers more affective than contractual tone

Needs action-oriented pace

Reaction to fees

Unwilling to pay before services are given or approved as "right"

Pays grudgingly due to ambivalence

Pays regularly

Does not accept "charity"; if can't pay in full, will find another service

Fees are understood, acceptable, but prefers third-party reimbursement

Source: Jay Folberg and Alison Taylor, pp. 322-323. Mediation: A Comprehensive Guide to Resolving Conflicts Without Litigation (San Francisco: Jossey-Bass, 1984). Reprinted with the permission of Jossey-Bass Publishers.

NOTES

3
COMMUNITY MEDIATION

Fred and Al lived in adjoining apartments. When Fred returned home from work at 6:00 P.M., he looked forward to peace and quiet. He often sat in his favorite chair and read the paper to wind down. Al returned home from his job at about 5:30 P.M. He was bored with his job; it was not very demanding. He looked forward to getting back to his apartment, turning on his new stereo, and making plans for partying that evening.

Ever since Al had moved in two months ago, Fred had been getting increasingly angry about Al's loud stereo. He had talked to Al about turning down the volume, and Al said he would, but never did it. After one very stressful day at work, Fred again heard the stereo, and he blew up. "I've had it. That S.O.B. has got to turn that damn thing down." He rushed over to Al's front door and pounded on it. When Al opened it, Fred unloaded his anger and told Al he had called the police.

After the police officer arrived and had listened to the complaint, he referred Fred and Al to mediation. Somewhat reluctantly, they both went to the community mediation program the following day. To their surprise, they found the mediator helpful in letting them talk about the dispute and work out the conflict. Their underlying interests were identified as well as their common desire to live peaceably in their apartments. An agreement was negotiated that seemed fair to both.

Mediating Interpersonal Conflicts: A Pathway to Peace

A wide range of interpersonal disputes between neighbors or among residents within a community are now being referred to hundreds of programs employing conciliation or mediation to resolve conflicts. Whether an organization calls itself a community dispute resolution center, neighborhood justice center, community mediation program, or community board, these programs all share a commitment to offering a community-based nonadjudicative forum, usually involving trained local volunteers as mediators, for resolving disputes between people in their community.

The contemporary origin of these community mediation programs dates back to the late-1960s War on Poverty era and the community activism which demanded more local power and control in many urban oppressed neighborhoods. It was being increasingly recognized that overcrowded courts were not well equipped to respond to many of the cases brought to their attention. It was believed that conflict among members of the community should be resolved at the community level, through the initiative and leadership of local residents. Many of the early advocates of community mediation believed that these conflicts should not be taken over by the system, resulting in further disempowerment of oppressed communities. During the early 1970s a handful of community mediation programs were initiated in various locations both by local community based organizations, such as the Center for Dispute Settlement in Rochester, New York, and by agencies of the formal justice system, such as the nationally recognized Night Prosecutors Program in Columbus, Ohio. The program in Columbus diverted a wide range of neighborhood disputes from the court system. The Center for Dispute Settlement in Rochester was developed in response to a number of community wide conflicts, including police brutality in the minority communities, gang violence and racial conflict. In 1978, the federal Department of Justice provided grants for the development of three experimental Neighborhood Justice Centers in Los Angeles, California (sponsored by the bar association), Kansas City, Missouri (sponsored by the city manager), and Atlanta, Georgia (sponsored by the courts). By the mid-1980s, many other cities throughout the country had community mediation centers initiated by local residents, often with the support of the local bar association.

In 1981, New York was the first to initiate a statewide policy, along with start-up and operational funds, to support the development of mediation centers to serve all counties in the state. Funding from the Community Dispute Resolution Centers Program of the Unified Court System of the State of New York would support up to half of the cost of operating the local program which was to be administered by a community-based nonprofit organization. Technical assistance and support would also be provided by the state office. Local funding and active involvement of local residents as staff and volunteers for these programs was critical to their eventual success. During a recent year, a total of 44,923 disputes were referred to the sixty-five community mediation programs in New York. Of these referred cases, 15,479 were involved in mediation, 6,713 in conciliation with no face-to-face contact, and 715 in arbitration.

Rationale For Community Mediation

The development of community mediation programs, in general, has been based on the belief that many civil and criminal complaints which flood the courts in nearly all jurisdictions could be more effectively resolved through mediation and at less cost. The resources of the court are both limited and costly. Moreover, a formal process of adjudication often heightens the conflict between the parties. For these reasons, mediation advocates argued that by diverting relatively minor disputes from the court to mediation, the conflict could be kept from escalating and resolved relatively quickly and at a reasonable cost. This was particularly the case when people knew each other and were likely to have to deal with each other in the future. Diverting relatively minor disputes would allow the court to focus on the more serious civil and criminal complaints, thereby giving these cases more attention and better service.

One of the earlier efforts in community mediation, the Community Dispute Settlement program of Friends Suburban Project near Philadelphia, Pennsylvania, based its pioneering work in the field of community mediation on the following beliefs:

- People are willing and able to change their behavior.
- People should be responsible for running their own lives.
- People prefer to be friendly, warm, honest, open, and cooperative.
- Conflict is made worse by poor communication and cannot be resolved without improving that communication.

- Understanding each other usually leads to better relations.
- Many people want, or at least learn, to live peaceably.
- Persistent conflict can be resolved by confronting, by talking things out.
- Disputants are the experts on their own problems. With help they can make better decisions for themselves than others can make for them.
- People are more willing to negotiate when they are treated with respect and when they do not lose face.
- When people work hard to reach agreement, they will be more committed to respect the contract.

The mission statements of various programs in community mediation reveal wide differences in goals and practices. Seven categories of goals were expressed by participants at a conference on community mediation:[1] (1) individual client satisfaction, (2) individual autonomy, (3) social control, (4) social justice, (5) social solidarity, (6) personal transformation, and (7) administrative economy.

The underlying reasons for community mediation can be more clearly understood in the context of the values upon which specific programs are based. Three specific categories of value systems in community mediation projects have been identified.[2] The first, delivery of dispute resolution services, concerns contrast with the courts. This category of programs stresses efficiency, relief of court congestion, and provision of a more appropriate forum for

1. Bush 1988
2. Harrington & Merry, 1988.

dispute resolution. The second category of programs focuses on the value of social transformation, which emphasizes the importance of restructuring society. They embrace the values of creating a new sense of community, community empowerment, decentralized judicial decision-making, and the use of community members in resolving local conflicts rather than professional dispute resolvers such as police and judges. The goals of reconciliation and reduction of interpersonal violence would also be included in the belief system of social transformation held by many community mediation programs. The third category of programs is those that adhere to the values of personal growth and development. They center on the importance of personal empowerment and the acquisition of new conflict-resolution skills. The process of mediating disputes within a community is likely to be far more humane and responsive to the parties than the courts.

A pioneer in the contemporary development of community dispute resolution, Ray Shonholtz (1984), speaks of the importance of building a neighborhood justice system through community boards composed of residents trained to facilitate resolution of the conflicts brought to their attention by other residents. Shonholtz favors a macro as well as micro approach, particularly through his advocacy of a new system of neighborhood justice. He identifies four important assumptions underlying this approach:

1. Conflict has positive value, which can lead to change and improvement of relationships.
2. Peaceful expression of conflict within the

community is healthy and can lead to greater mutual understanding and reduced tensions if handled appropriately.

3. Individuals and the neighborhood should exercise responsibility for conflict rather than promoting professional attention to conflict through the courts, which further disempowers the community.

4. Voluntary resolutions of conflict between disputants are far superior to coerced resolutions.

Shonholtz holds that a community-based conflict-resolution system provides a forum for the clarification of values and norms, a justice forum that teaches individual and collective responsibility. It builds skills, gives a feeling of accomplishment to individuals, and provides opportunities for a diverse set of people to work together on concrete problems. Individual grievances can be transformed into collective problems.

Community Mediation Process

Just as there are several overall purposes of community mediation, there are different program designs and procedures for engaging the process. Some of the programs are sponsored and administered by a justice system agency, such as the Los Angeles City Attorney, with more than 28,000 cases a year referred to mediation, or the 17th District Judicial Court in Broward County (Fort Lauderdale), with more than 3,000 cases referred to mediation.[1]

1. McGillis, 1986.

Many other programs are sponsored by private community-based organizations, such as the Neighborhood Justice Center in Hawaii, which mediated 1,488 cases with 200 volunteer mediators during a recent year. Another example is the Dispute Resolution Center in St. Paul, Minnesota, whose pool of 40 trained volunteer mediators handles more than 500 cases a year.

As the field of community mediation has grown over the years, most programs fall within one of three categories: justice system-based, community-based, or a composite of both, which the statewide initiative in New York exemplifies. As Table 3.1 indicates, there exist considerable differences between these categories of mediation programs.

Two early models of community mediation that are particularly well grounded in values of community empowerment, and social justice are discussed below. The Community Dispute Settlement program of the Friends Suburban Project near Philadelphia grew out of the social activism of local community residents who had a strong commitment to nonviolence, peacemaking, and the empowerment of communities and individuals. And, the Community Board Program in San Francisco, which represents a community-organizing model of dispute resolution based on the work of Ray Shonholtz. This program is grounded in the values of affirming diversity, the empowerment of communities and individuals, and the importance of local residents' owning and resolving their conflicts rather than giving them over to the state. Both programs have had a major impact on the development of community mediation over the past decade. They are not, of course, representative of all community   mediation

Table 3.1
Typical Features of the Major Types of
Community Dispute-Resolution Programs

	Justice System-Based	Community-Based	Composite
Sponsorship	Justice system agency	Nonprofit agency	Government or nonprofit
Area served	Entire city	Either entire or part of a city or county	Mixed approach
Major referral source	Justice system agency	Sources outside justice system	Justice system and outside sources
Intake coercion	Typically high	Typically low	Intermediate
Hearing length	Typically brief	Typically long	Intermediate
Hearing settings	Typically formal	Typically informal	Intermediate
Caseload size	Typically large	Typically small	Intermediate
Budget size	Typically large	Typically small	Intermediate

Source: Daniel McGillis, *Community Dispute Resolution Programs and Public Policy* (Washington, D.C.: National Institute of Justice, 1986), p. 21.

programs. For example, programs operated by courts are likely to be more formal and more concerned about efficiency and economy than community or individual empowerment.

As the field of community mediation becomes more professional, formalized, and closely aligned with the justice system, some of its earliest advocates fear a possible loss of focus on social justice.[1] The Community Dispute Settlement and Community Board Program represent initiatives that continue to embrace the community-empowerment ideology that was the driving force behind the community dispute-resolution movement.

Community Dispute-Settlement Model

The Friends Suburban Project in Delaware County, southwest of Philadelphia, had initiated many programs addressing issues of peace and justice in their community. After many years of such activism, this Quaker group decided to launch a new project in 1976 called Community Dispute Settlement. It was established to provide an alternative step between resolving conflicts in the community either through solely private means or through engaging public forums, such as the courts. As noted above, Community Dispute Settlement was grounded in a clear value base which affirmed the importance of openly confronting conflict through empowering disputants to be actively involved in its resolution. The most common cases referred to the program are neighborhood disputes involving barking dogs, common driveways, harassment, property lines, and noisy or rebellious children.

From its inception, Community Dispute Settlement has used pairs of trained volunteer mediators. Initial case development is handled by a staff person, who usually briefs the pair just prior to the mediation session. The mediators have no prior contact with the disputants. A typical mediation, which usually lasts about two hours,

1. Wahrhaftig, 1981.

involves six tasks that closely parallel those of the
mediation phase in the generic mediation model presented
in Chapter 2:

1. Opening statement by mediator(s)
2. Uninterrupted time for disputants to tell their
   stories
3. The exchange of information and feelings
   between the disputants
4. Building an agreement through exploring mutual
   interests and needs
5. Writing the agreement that has been constructed
   by the disputants
6. Closing statement by the mediator(s)

The style of mediation used is nondirective, an
approach to mediating conflict that has been called
therapeutic or empowering. It is in stark contrast to the
bargaining or controlling style, which assumes most
disputes result from conflict over resources and power
within society and the best that mediation can do is to cut
losses through negotiation and compromise, with the
relational element of the dispute being irrelevant.

Although clearly not psychotherapy, the
nondirective style of mediation used by Community Dispute
Settlement defines success by degree of reconciliation, not
by speed of reaching agreement. The expressions of feelings
by disputants are highly valued. Providing an opportunity
for people to work at healing individual disputes is viewed
as an important contribution toward the resolution of larger
social conflicts.

The six tasks of this approach to conducting a mediation session all support providing a safe structure for the open expression of the emotions that drive interpersonal conflict. Giving each disputant uninterrupted time to tell his or her story is designed to help each better understand the other. The exchange of information and feelings is meant to allow for the venting of strong emotions. Mediators in Community Dispute Settlement, unlike mediators in many other programs, give disputants much leeway in terms of outbursts, crying, and shouting, in the belief that such airings are critical to eventual healing or reconciliation. During the problem-solving task of building an agreement, the mediators continually emphasize the importance of the disputants ability to determine the outcome.

Community Dispute Settlement also has a distinct style that fosters connecting with the disputants at a friendly level rather than an impersonal professional and technical level. Mediators dress in street clothes and sessions are held at neutral facilities in the community, such as a church, synagogue, or library, rather than in the offices of the program or in the court building. Disputants are given choices as to meeting places. Although mediators facilitate the process, they do not verbally dominate it or establish a very controlling tone during their opening statement of the mediation session.

Contrary to many court-related community mediation programs, mediators in the Community Dispute Settlement program discourage use of court terms like hearing, caucus, complainant, and respondent. Instead, they encourage everyday language that feels normal to everyone present. No release forms are required beforehand, even though this is a routine procedure in many other similar programs with more formal procedures.

The entire process of mediation employed at Community Dispute Settlement is meant to provide a safe, nonthreatening, and neighborly setting in which conflict can be understood and responded to in the most effective way possible for the disputants themselves. The mediators are not present as expert professionals who can solve the problems but, rather, are on hand to facilitate and manage a process that allows the disputants to be fully and actively empowered to work with each other in dealing with the conflict through mutual aid. Through a laid-back style of case management, the mediators in Community Dispute Settlement strive to establish an atmosphere of warmth, empathy, and genuineness, all of which are fundamental skills of connecting with others in any area of social work practice or human services.

Community Board Model

The Community Board Program began in San Francisco in 1977, the first neighborhood-based justice system in the United States. It identifies conflicts in the neighborhood, expresses the conflict in a community forum, resolves the conflict in the forum, and builds the community's capacity to resolve future conflicts. Instead of receiving referrals primarily from the formal agencies of the justice system, such as the police or prosecuting attorney's office, the Community Board Program receives about fifty percent of its referrals from neighborhood residents. Referrals are also encouraged from neighborhood organizations, block clubs, schools, churches, synagogues, and other community groups. A good deal of outreach is required in the Community Board's approach to dispute resolution, and some observers have noted the similarity of its methods to those used in community organizing.

The mediation process is initiated when someone calls Community Board with a dispute. A volunteer case developer talks with the people involved, explains how the program operates, and encourages both parties to attend a hearing. Participation in the Community Board Program is entirely voluntary. At the hearing three to five volunteer conciliators help the disputants to gain a better understanding of what happened and to work at development of a possible agreement for resolution of the conflict. Panelists do not make any judgments of guilt or innocence. A written agreement is usually worked out and case follow-up monitors compliance with the agreement to resolve the conflict. Community Board clearly identifies panel members as conciliators, but their actual function is mediation.

Three specific roles for community volunteers are central to the Community Board model.[1] A small paid staff provides administrative support to the 300 volunteers who serve as outreach workers, panelists, and trainers. Outreach workers continually meet with people and give presentations to promote the Community Board Program as a viable way to resolve conflicts in the neighborhood. Panelists provide a safe, impartial, and structured process for openly dealing with the conflict. A team of three to five conciliators is used at each panel hearing. Trainers are involved in training new volunteers in the Community

1. Community Board, 1984.

Board Program. Prepanel briefings and postpanel reviews are also conducted by trainers.

The Community Board panel process consists of six tasks: (1) opening statement by panel of mediators, (2) defining the problem, (3) working toward mutual understanding of the conflict, (4) acknowledgment of new understandings, (5) development of an agreement, and (6) a closing statement by the panel.

The opening of the panel session consists of welcoming the parties, introducing everyone, and a few opening remarks by one of the panelists. Panelists read the case report. During the opening of the panel session, and through the next task, the disputants are sitting in such a way that they face the panelists rather than each other.

The second task of the panel session is to help the parties define the problem. The first party is asked to describe the dispute to the panelists briefly and how he or she feels about it. The second party is then asked to do the same. The panelists ask questions of both parties to help clarify the specific nature of the conflict and the feelings of the parties.

During the third task of the session, the parties are asked to speak to each other about their interests and needs. Sometimes this involves moving their chairs so that they now face each other. The objective is to help each party understand how the other experiences the conflict. The panelists select one main issue and encourage the disputants to talk directly with each other about it. The panelists facilitate the conversation and acknowledge points of mutual understanding that emerge and progress that is being made.

Task four of the session helps the disputants acknowledge their new understanding of what occurred and encourages further work on resolving the conflict. The panelists ask each disputant questions, such as What new understanding do you have about this conflict? If this situation arises again, how would you handle it? The disputants are then queried regarding their willingness to go further in trying to develop a resolution to the conflict.

The panelists actively help the parties work out an agreement during the fifth task. Each party is asked to describe what he or she thinks would be a fair solution. Specific terms of an agreement are identified. The panelists summarize the agreement and make sure that the parties agree. The agreement is then written up.

Finally, the closing task consists of reading the written agreement to the parties for their confirmation. Any additional clauses that might be requested and agreed upon are appended. The parties sign the agreement, along with the chairperson of the panel. The disputants are congratulated for their work, and after they leave, a trainer reviews the hearing.

As with the Community Dispute Settlement program; the six tasks of the Community Board panel's mediation phase of the process closely resemble the six tasks of the mediation phase in the generic mediation model presented in Chapter 2.

What We Have Learned From Research

The majority of community mediation programs are currently affiliated with the courts, even though they may not be directly administered by a justice system agency.[1] In 1984 only one-third of community mediation programs were court-affiliated. Clients involved in community mediation programs tend to be from the poor or lower-middle class; many are from various minority groups.[2] During the period 1989 to 1990, more than half of all parties initiating a complaint to the sixty-five community mediation programs in New York had annual incomes under $16,000.[3]

One of the most interesting findings is that parties who attempt to resolve conflict through a community mediation program are very likely to reach an acceptable agreement. An agreement rate of 75 per cent is reported by some programs.[4] In Massachusetts and New York, states with many programs, an agreement rate of 85 per cent has been reported.[5] A recent evaluation of three programs in North Carolina found an agreement rate of 92 per cent.[6]

Community residents who participate in a mediation session tend to be very satisfied with the program. In New York, with its sixty-five community mediation programs throughout the state, 90 per cent of disputants reported they were satisfied with the process.[7] High levels of client satisfaction have also been found in a number of related studies.[8]

When agreements are successfully negotiated in community mediation programs, the compliance rate is

1. Singer, 1990.
2. ibid.
3. Crosson, 1990.
4. Kolb & Rubin, 1989.
5. Crosson, 1990.
6. Clark, Valente, & Mace, 1992.
7. Crosson, 1990.
8. Cook, Roehl, & Sheppard, 1980; Davis, Tichane, & Graysonn, 1980; MeEwen & Maiman, 1981; Clark et al. 1992.

quite high. Of those programs listed in a recent American Bar Association directory,[1] compliance rates in excess of 80 per cent were frequently reported. The sixty-five community mediation programs in New York reported a compliance rate of 80 per cent.[2] A study of mediation in small claims courts in Maine found a compliance rate of 70.6 per cent for mediated settlements; versus 33.8 per cent for adjudicated settlements.[3] However, the caseloads of many community mediation programs are small when compared to the caseloads of the related court systems. For example, in the Dorchester Urban Court the mediation program conducted 438 sessions during its first two years of operation, compared to about 12,000 non-motor-vehicle cases in the lower court during the same period.[4] Similarly, the Dispute Resolution Center in St. Paul receives 500 referrals a year, a small fraction of the total number of related cases in the court system of St. Paul and Ramsey County in Minnesota. Because of the relatively small caseloads, it is still unclear if community mediation programs are having any significant impact on reducing the caseloads of the overcrowded courts.[5]

There has been little research to determine if cases referred to community mediation from justice system agencies would have been prosecuted in the first place, as opposed to dumping these minor cases as referrals to the mediation alternative. "Widening the net of social control" has been suggested by three evaluations, which found that mediated cases would most likely have not been prosecuted

1. ABA, 1990.
2. Crosson, 1990.
3. McEwen & Maiman, 1981.
4. Felstiner & Williams, 1978.
5. Merry, 1982.

had they not been referred to mediation.[1] Others argue that net widening is not a major concern in community mediation because the focus is on de-escalating conflict that could lead to criminal acts.

Unresolved Issues in Community Mediation

Many issues continue to be unresolved even as the field of community mediation continues to expand throughout North America. Three particularly important issues are (1) program sponsorship and referrals, (2) serving the courts while emphasizing local community empowerment, and (3) quality of justice.

Program Sponsorship and Referrals

One cannot help but wonder if the community mediation movement will ever divert a large number of conflicts from the formal justice system, or, if it will remain important but essentially marginal. Currently, apart from a relatively few programs operated by justice system agencies in urban areas that have huge caseloads, many programs continue to have a rather modest number of cases referred to them. On the one hand, a truly community-based mediation program need not rely entirely on the justice system for referrals. Many voluntary referrals directly from the community could figure in their caseloads, but many of the programs that are the purest in design have the fewest referrals. On the other hand, programs that have linked themselves closely to courts often become highly formalized, viewing their primary mission as helping to reduce the caseload of the justice system.

1. Moriarty, Norris, & Salas, 1977; Evaluation Group, 1980; Davis et al., 1980.

Perhaps the best answer to the dilemma is to be found in the New York model of statewide implementation of community mediation: an integrated approach to the advocacy and development of dispute resolution, initiated by the justice system, state funded, broad access to cases, and a community-based structure of service delivery through private nonprofit community agencies.

Serving the Courts and Local Community Empowerment

A second issue of concern is directly related to the growing linkage of community mediation programs with the courts. As the programs become preoccupied with gaining more cases and meeting the needs of the courts they serve-that is, a reduction of court caseloads and dealing with problematic cases-they may begin to mirror the same routine and impersonal, if not dehumanizing, manner in which large courts deal with people. Then the initial vision of empowering local community residents through a reasonably comfortable, informal, and understandable process will be lost. In fact, some mediation programs may be experienced by clients as just one more bureaucracy. This is especially so if mediation becomes highly impersonal and insensitive to the issues involved in their cases. Fortunately, there is no evidence of widespread dissatisfaction with community mediation; to the contrary, very high levels of consumer satisfaction have been consistently found. Well- developed mediation programs, however, remain ever- vigilant about monitoring the quality of the process and outcomes.

Quality of Justice

Is community mediation a second-class form of justice reserved for the poor and working class, as argued by some? As noted earlier, the vast majority of consumers of community mediation are the poor and lower-middle class. Is this justice reform effort simply leading to a two-tier system of resolving disputes, with the courts and lawyers reserved for the more well to do? Critics argue that the focus of mediation on individual problem solving for the poor and working class short-circuits the development of collective solutions to problems in the community.

For mediation to stand in the way of larger issues of social justice would be contrary to the values of ethical social work practice. A leading practitioner in community mediation and an advocate of social change states, "Careful analysis will reveal that although there is danger of dispute resolution programs being used as an opiate, they can be conceived of, and in some cases are operating, as vehicles of social change."[1]

Summary

Originating in the community activism and War on Poverty initiatives in the 1960s, many hundreds of programs now mediate interpersonal disputes between neighbors or between members of a community. Motivating the development of community mediation was the belief that "the system" would take over community conflict and lead to further disempowerment of communities. The hope was that community mediation would effectively resolve conflicts, develop local supports to de-escalate or more

1. Wahrhaftig, 1981.

quickly resolve future conflicts, and enhance the strengths of communities.

Community mediation programs vary according to value systems, sponsorship, and design. Three distinct purposes define a program's focus: (1) to contrast with the processes of the court system, (2) to seek social transformation by restructuring society, and (3) to enhance personal growth and development through empowerment and conflict-resolution skills. Community mediation programs may have public or private sponsorship or funding, but most are affiliated with the courts. The design of a community mediation program may be justice system-based, community-based, or a combination, such as the statewide initiative in New York.

The results of community mediation programs have been very good in reaching agreement, compliance with agreement, and client satisfaction. On the down side, the caseloads of many community mediation programs tend to be small compared to those of the courts. Furthermore, the cases referred to mediation are often minor and in any event may not have been prosecuted if mediation services had not been available. Three important unresolved issues regarding community mediation programs are (1) sponsorship and referrals to the program, (2) serving the courts and local community empowerment, and (3) the quality of services, in that the majority of clients are poor and lower middle class.

4
SCHOOL MEDIATION

Five students from an inner-city school were in continuous conflict and were frequently brought to the principal. The four girls were Eritrean and the one boy was Ethiopian. The age-old conflict between their respective African nations seemed to play itself out in their contacts at school. They argued and called one another names in two different African languages. The principal and other staff were not able to deal satisfactorily with the behavior, and the situation came to a head when a multicultural festival was being planned. The five students absolutely refused to work together and share a booth, and in consequence were referred to a new peer mediation program. The mediators began with a statement of their role and ground rules, but the five quickly got into a shouting match of insults. The mediators tried to regain control and get them to speak one at a time, in English. After a long period of venting, they all settled down a bit. By the end of the mediation session, ninety minutes later, an agreement had been made to work together at the festival. Despite the mediators' frustration and uncertainty about the outcome, the agreement was abided by. School officials are amazed that the five students have since not been involved in any major disputes.

Although this case is certainly not typical, it does illustrate that mediation in a school setting can help resolve a very hostile, multicultural conflict. Mediation programs in which students from fourth grade through high school are trained to mediate their own conflicts began in the early-1980s. For example, in 1982, the Community Board School Initiatives (CBSI) Program in San Francisco, having already pioneered neighborhood-based mediation as noted in chapter three, became one of the first programs in the United States to experiment with training student conflict managers in elementary schools. Students in the fourth and fifth grades received fifteen hours of training in conflict resolution and mediation skills, after which they would then receive orange T-shirts emblazoned with "Conflict Manager" in big letters. During recess and lunch periods they would assist other students in resolving disputes.

The CBSI program later expanded to intermediate and secondary schools. In 1984 it was commended by the California legislature, which requested the State Board of Education to explore the feasibility of including conflict-resolution training in a core curriculum kindergarten through twelfth grade.

Around the same time, in New York City, the School Mediators' Alternative Resolution Team (SMART) program was being initiated by the Victim Service Agency at a high school in Queens, which had a large, ethnically diverse student body. The program had four essential components. First, classroom seminars were designed to gain broad support for mediation, to recruit mediators, and to secure referrals of conflicts. Second, students, teachers, other school staff, and parents who volunteered to be mediators were given twenty hours of training. Third, those who completed the training conducted actual mediation sessions involving intrastudent, intrafamily, and student-teacher conflicts. Fourth, follow-up was provided on all mediated cases to determine compliance with the negotiated agreements and to offer additional service if needed.

The National Association for Mediation in Education was established in 1984 in response to the steady growth of school mediation programs in North America. Currently, there are more than 2,000 school-based peer mediation programs. School social workers have often played several important roles in school mediation development, serving as program initiators, consultants, planning committee members, trainers, and organizers.

A number of organizations provide extensive training and technical assistance in this area of mediation practice. Among them are the Community Board Program in San Francisco, the New Mexico Center for Dispute Resolution in Albuquerque, and the Grace Contrino Abrams Peace Education Foundation in Miami, Florida. They offer model curriculums, training videos, and other materials to schools interested in starting a mediation program. Periodically, they also offer training institutes at various locations throughout the country for school mediation organizers. The addresses of these organizations appear in Appendix 6.

Rationale for School Mediation

Just as conflict is a normal part of child and adolescent development, so it is a frequent reality in nearly all school settings. School officials and parents seek to replace the use of guns and other forms of violence with nonviolent forms of conflict resolution, including mediation. Schools are uniquely situated to influence the creation of new ways to resolve school conflict and to model techniques that may be effective in other settings.

No other social institution is responsible for the care and supervision of children and youth for such an extended period of time. Precisely because schools have kids for a large portion of each day, against the preferred wishes of many students, frequent conflicts are inevitable. These conflicts involve student to student disputes, as well as student to teacher disputes. While conflicts among students can lead to violent, if not lethal, confrontations, the more typical disputes between students center around rumors, miscommunication, and misinterpretation of verbal and nonverbal messages, such as dirty looks. Student conflicts that eventually end up in a mediation session are often referred to as "he said she said" type of disputes. For elementary schools, much of this conflict emerges during recess on the playground. In secondary schools, these student to student disputes are more likely to be seen throughout the entire school day, within classes, over lunch, or in the halls between classes. Increasing demands are placed upon school administrators to do more with less. It is an inefficient use of limited resources to have teachers, assistant principals and others, including school social workers, continually dealing with students' minor fights, arguments and the resulting behavioral problems. The time and energy required to fulfill the primary task of providing a good education to their students is diminished by this. It is precisely because of this that a growing number of school districts throughout North America are enthusiastically embracing the concept of school-based peer mediation.

The underlying rationale for promoting school mediation has been most clearly stated in the following objectives.[1]

1. To promote a more healthy understanding of conflict as a positive force that can lead to personal growth and institutional change.

2. To help students, school personnel and community members to gain a deeper understanding of themselves and others through improved communication. This can lead to a more inclusive climate within the school and community while preparing students to live in a multicultural world.

3. To increase appreciation for the ability of conflict resolution training to enhance academic and lifetime skills considered basic to all learning, such as listening, critical thinking and problem solving.

4. To encourage a greater sense of citizenship by increasing students' knowledge of nonadversarial conflict resolution, its relationship to the United States legal system, and the role it can play in promoting world peace.

1. Davis & Porter, 1985.

5. To recognize the unique competence of young people to participate in the resolution of their own disputes, while allowing teachers and administrators to concentrate more on teaching and less on discipline.

6. To offer a more effective and appropriate school based method for resolving disputes than expulsion, suspension, detention or court intervention, thereby reducing violence, vandalism and chronic school absences.

Secondary School Mediation Process

The New Mexico Center for Dispute Resolution in Albuquerque operates the largest secondary school mediation program in the United States, involving more than 160 schools throughout the state. Like San Francisco's Community Board School Initiatives program, it has developed extensive training materials and model curricula, and provides in-depth training at locations throughout North America and abroad. At the core is a seven-step process of implementing mediation in secondary schools;[1] each will be discussed separately.

1. Creation of an implementation team and selection of program coordinators
2. Program planning
3. Faculty and staff orientation and training
4. Student orientation
5. Selection of mediators

1. Smith & Sidwell, 1990.

6. Providing mediation training information
7. Program implementation

Implementation Team and Program Coordinators

The development of a mediation program within a school requires a broad base of support and participation. Although an individual teacher, administrator, or counselor may take the lead in advocating such a new effort, the formation of an implementation team is crucial. The team should minimally include a school administrator, counselor, special-education person, and a teacher with disciplinary responsibilities. School social workers could also play a key advocacy role in both promoting the concept of mediation and in linking the school with available mediation training and technical assistance.

The New Mexico Center for Dispute Resolution suggests that the implementation team focus on five tasks:

- Establishing a plan for program implementation;
- Establishing policies and procedures for the program;
- Determining how mediation will be integrated into the existing disciplinary policies of the school;
- Promoting the program among staff and students; and
- Identifying program coordinators for the student program.

The center recommends designating at least two program coordinators early in the stage of the program planning who will meet regularly to handle all the details related to program development and implementation. It is important that the coordinators have credibility with other staff members and with students because they will be responsible for conducting the ongoing training of mediators, promoting the program, and monitoring its quality.

Program Planning

Planning for the school mediation program requires completion of a number of key tasks:

- Gaining support from staff and administrators;
- Developing a climate within the school that is complementary to mediation;
- Integrating mediation program into the disciplinary policy of the school;
- Identifying a referral process of channeling disputes into mediation;
- Developing intake procedures;
- Identifying a time and place for the scheduling of mediations;
- Developing weekly schedules for available mediators;
- Establishing a plan for following up on mediation sessions; and
- Developing a plan for record keeping and data collection.

A referral process consisting of more than one or two sources is integral to an accessible and effective program. Student conflicts could be referred to the program by teachers, administrators, other staff, and disputants themselves or their friends. The New Mexico Center for Dispute Resolution program has found that the use of mediation tends to be better internalized by students when they themselves seek a form of conflict resolution alternative to the usual arguing and fighting.

Orientation and Training of Faculty and Staff

The New Mexico experience suggests that all teachers and staff at the school should participate in a training session relative to the new mediation initiative. This orientation furnishes an overview of conflict resolution, mediation, and how the program could operate. Specific program components such as curriculum, training, and implementation procedures are highlighted. Without an understanding and acceptance of the mediation process, it is likely that teachers and administrators may fall back upon old patterns that would subvert the students' mediation efforts. Options are presented to demonstrate how staff can participate in the mediation program; the various roles include program support, referral source, participation in mediation as a disputant, participation in conflict resolution training, participation as a staff mediator, membership on the implementation team, and designation as a program coordinator.

Orientation of Students

All students participate in an orientation session about the mediation program to learn about how the process works. They are invited to participate, either as mediators or consumers. Recruiting and training students to serve as mediators is a primary task in developing and maintaining a mediation program. Promoting the availability of peer mediation among the wider student body is of equal importance. This can be done through posters throughout the school, periodic announcements about peer mediation in school publications or on a school radio or television station, and, most important, through students talking about mediation with other students.

It is essential to promote the availability of peer mediation in order to develop a sufficient referral base. Training an enthusiastic group of students to serve as mediators, but then to have insufficient referrals could quickly lead to disillusionment and marginal impact.

Selection of Mediators

The selection criteria for student and staff mediators help clarify a mediator's expectations. For example, in the New Mexico model, student mediators are expected to have the following qualifications: leadership ability, whether it has lead to negative or positive behavior; respect and trust of peers; good verbal skills; and a commitment to serve for the entire school year. School staff who serve as mediators in student-staff disputes are expected to commit fully to the program and have the necessary communication skills. Respect of colleagues and students is also highly desirable.

Mediation Training Information

After support has been developed within the school for initiating a peer mediation program, mediation training must follow. It is most effective when all staff and students are trained in basic conflict management skills, and the more involved staff and students receive further training as mediators. Although such comprehensiveness provides the most useful foundation for starting a mediation program within a school, it is rarely achieved without a significant amount of forethought. School mediation consultants emphasize that planning ensures that training in conflict management can be integrated into the curriculum on a annual basis. Fortunately, there are some excellent model curricula and teaching aids available to facilitate this, as noted in Appendix 6.

Program Implementation

According to the New Mexico Center for Dispute Resolution, there are five essential tasks in moving from planning to full implementation of a mediation program. First, the initial referral system is reviewed to insure that it is clearly understood and in place. Second, periodic meetings for the mediators are regularly scheduled as a forum for learning new skills and providing support. Third, plans are made for maintaining mediator discipline because student mediators are role models. Fourth, ongoing promotion of the program is set up. Fifth, mediator training is provided at least twice during the school year.

The training for student and staff mediators offered by the New Mexico center consists of ten hours spread over four days. Topics covered include understanding conflict, listening skills, role of the mediator, and demonstration and practice of all tasks of the mediation process. The mediation process consists of the following tasks, which are similar to those in the generic mediation model presented in Chapter 2.

- Opening (roles and rules): explain how mediation works and provide the ground rules.

- Defining the problem: allow parties to describe their views of the situation and to express their feelings.

- Sharing feelings: help parties understand each other's point of view.

- Finding a solution: brainstorm ideas and decide on a solution agreeable to both parties.

- Closing (writing the agreement): write down the points of the agreement and have the parties sign.

Mediator Tasks

After a case is referred to mediation, the session should be scheduled as soon as possible. Using co-mediators is often quite helpful in offering greater gender and racial diversity and in providing peer support. Many programs have an adult, the supervisor of the program, close by in case problems arise; however, it is not always desirable that an adult be present in a mediation session because peer mediation programs are committed to empowering students, as they resolve their conflicts. Nevertheless, having a team of co-mediators consisting of one adult and one student is frequently of assistance in a student-teacher conflict.

After determining that the disputing parties agree to

have the conflict mediated, the student mediators or student and adult team generally do several things. They explain that their purpose is not to make judgments about who is right or wrong but, rather, to help both parties talk about the conflict and explore resolution possibilities. Then they present ground rules for the session, which include telling the truth, trying to solve the problem, no interrupting, no fighting, no name calling, and no gossiping.

After their opening comments, one of the co-mediators may ask which disputant would like to begin. Each has a chance to explain the conflict from his or her perspective. After telling their stories, they may ask each other questions to help clarify what was said. The mediators will also encourage them to brainstorm about possible solutions to the conflict that both might be able to live with.

The mediators help the students identify a preferred solution. They then consider if the solution is realistic or simply sets them up for future conflicts. Once a solution has been agreed upon by both disputants its terms are written in an agreement that is signed by all present, including the mediators. The written agreement is kept in the files of the peer mediation program to monitor compliance; to maintain confidentiality, the agreement is not sent elsewhere.

Mediation in secondary schools has been highlighted in this section, but a similar process can be applied at the primary-school level. (More extensive material on the development of school mediation at any level, can be obtained from the organizations listed in Appendix 6.) For example, the Community Board School Initiatives program in San Francisco uses conflict managers in fourth and fifth grades, who put into practice the following script:

- If you see a conflict brewing during recess or at lunch, introduce yourself and ask both parties if they want to solve their problem.

- If they do, go to the area designated for solving problems. Explain and get agreement to the four basic rules: (1) agree to solve the problem, (2) don't call each other names, (3) do not interrupt, and (4) tell the truth.

- Decide who will talk first. Ask that person what happened and how he or she feels, repeating back what is said, using active listening skills. Do the same with the other person.

- Ask the first party and then the second party for alternative solutions.

- Work with the students to get a solution that they both think is good.

- After the agreement is reached, congratulate the parties and fill out a Conflict Manager Report Form.

What We Have Learned from Research

A small but growing number of studies have found that establishment of a mediation program within a school setting is likely to generate numerous positive benefits. The first empirical study of school mediation examined a program at the middle-school level in New York State.[1] The school had a disproportionate number of students participating in a compensatory remedial program, the majority of whom had minority backgrounds and were from low-income families. Three primary areas of mediation impact were examined: on school-discipline climate, on student mediators, and on student disputants, including any impact on disciplinary problems. During the period of this study, eighty-one cases were mediated by students; about half involved harassment or actual physical fights, and the other half were of the "he said, she said" nature. Seventy-five per cent of the disputants reported that they would have had a fight over the conflict if they had not participated in mediation.

The study data, which included pre- and postintervention measurements, indicated that implementation of a student peer mediation program in this middle school had a positive impact on the overall school climate. For example, there was a reduction in school disciplinary problems; a decrease of 16.7 per cent was found in reported fighting incidents when compared to the year prior to implementation of the mediation program.[2] One of the most interesting findings was that mediation improved the self-image of the student mediators, as it did student attitudes toward school involvement, school discipline, and school problem solving.

Research on the mediation programs simultaneously implemented in three (elementary, intermediate, and high) Honolulu schools[3] targeted five questions: (1) To what extent can mediation programs be implemented in a school?

1. Stern, Van Slyck & Valvo, 1986.
2. ibid.
3. Araki, 1990.

(2) Can mediation as a technique to manage disputes be used by students? (3) What are the attributes of an effective and successful mediator? (4) What are the attributes of disputants? (5) What is the nature of conflicts or disputes in the school utilizing mediation?

Effective implementation of a mediation program in the three school settings was directly related to the effectiveness of the start-up phase. During this critical four month period, a wide range of training and orientation activities were conducted prior to starting the mediation program or hiring a coordinator. Small and large groups of teachers and counselors were invited to provide input on the best ways to implement mediation in their schools. A twenty-hour conflict management and mediation training was provided to students and adults, simultaneously.

A full-time district coordinator of mediation was then hired because three schools were involved. This person played a key role in organizing the effort at each school, seeing that appropriate orientation and training occurred, and establishing and monitoring referral of conflicts to the new mediation programs. Araki found that frequent communication between the coordinator and staff and parents was vital for program success and that ongoing, intensive mediation training was important.

A total of 127 student-to-student disputes (331 disputants-most of whom were in the seventh, eighth, and ninth grades--of whom 66 per cent were female) had been mediated during a two-year period; 92 per cent resulted in a completed agreement. Staff at the schools, as well as mediators and disputants, consistently indicated that mediation was an effective way of managing many types of such disputes. Particularly successful student mediators were confident; understood the mediation process; had the ability to write clear agreements; possessed leadership qualities; were directive, responsible, caring; listened well; and asked questions to good purpose. The ethnic groups with the highest percentage in mediation were, in descending order, Japanese, Caucasian, part Hawaiian, and Chinese. Araki found eight major clusters of student-to-student conflict: gossip or rumors (27 per cent); arguments (20 per cent), dirty looks, classroom behavior, harassment (27 per cent), jealousy, fight or pending fight, and invasion of privacy.

A review of the Student Mediators' Alternative Resolution Team (SMART) program in New York[1] found that during the initial five years more than 22,600 high school students participated in the classroom seminars on mediation and nonviolent problem solving. The twenty-hour mediation training course was completed by 551 students and 114 adults. Mediators handled 2,137 disputes (5,223 students) ranging from communication problems (student-teacher or student-parent) to fistfights involving multiple students.

Suspensions of students for fighting was reported to have dropped significantly at each high school where the SMART program had been in place for two or more semesters. At William Cullen Bryant High School, where SMART began, suspensions lessened by 46 per cent during its first year of operation. Even larger decreases were experienced at most of the other schools: Taft High School, 45 per cent; Eastern District High School, 70 per cent;

1. Moore & Whipple, 1988.

Prospect Heights High School, 60 per cent; Far Rockaway High School, 65 per cent, and Brandeis High School, 58 per cent. The standard procedure at these schools now for dealing with all student disputes not involving weapons, drugs, or injuries is to refer them to mediation. During the study, more than eighty students involved in a mediated dispute became mediators themselves. The vast majority of disputants were satisfied with the mediation process and found it to be helpful. Mediation agreements were adhered to in more than 90 per cent of the cases.

Unresolved Issues

School mediation clearly has many benefits for the specific disputants and the larger school environment. More and more school districts are beginning to develop mediation programs because of their demonstrated value in addressing a multitude of disciplinary problems. However, school mediation is not easy to implement nor is it without its own yet-to-be-resolved issues. These issues include resistance by adults, staff belief in and use of mediation, confidentiality of mediation, and building ongoing support.

Resistance by Adults

Development of a student mediation program that focuses on student-student and student-teacher conflicts creates a fundamental shift in power dynamics within the school culture. Teachers and other staff are no longer able simply to rely on adult dominance and on rigid disciplinary codes that punish misbehavior.

With the onset of mediation, the playing field is leveled, as students become empowered to confront adults with whom they have disputes and are in positions to try to negotiate resolutions. The lack of power most students experience in relationships with adults is offset by the presence of a mediator; rather than focusing on the deficits of students, mediation builds upon and strengthens their competencies. It is this new equation that many teachers and staff view as extremely threatening. Mediation requires a significant change in the role of teachers and staff, from a typical authoritarian communication style to a far more respectful, collaborative style. In short, the development of school mediation programs require significant changes in individuals and the organizational culture, both of which are likely to be resisted by many.

Staff Belief in and Use of Mediation

Whereas the more developed school mediation programs resolve conflicts among and between students and adults, many schools are choosing to have the programs apply only to student conflicts. Advocates of this limited application seem to believe that although mediation is clearly beneficial for students, it is inappropriate for student-adult conflicts because it weakens the authority of teachers and other staff. There appears to be little recognition that student respect for adults in the school may well increase through the use of negotiation and mediation because of their respectful, collaborative nature.

Not allowing student-adult conflict within the school environment to enter mediation is setting a very tight boundary, which may work against the long-term impact of the program. Adults are modeling a mixed message to young people: mediation is okay to resolve disputes between and among students but not between students and adults, which requires more traditional use of authority and power. It is a policy that results in a double standard of conflict resolution within the school community. For this reason, advocates of school mediation emphasize that all teachers and staff in the school need to be trained in conflict-resolution skills so that they can model those skills for students and it is hoped, over a period of time participate in student-adult mediations.

Confidentiality of Mediation

Many of the student conflicts that lead to mediation are based on rumors or misperceptions. If the confidentiality of the mediation session is not strictly maintained, and student mediators tell other students about the details of what happened between the two disputants, even more conflict could be generated. It would not take very long for students to lose their confidence in the desirability of mediation. Similarly, if statements made by students during the mediation session are obtained by adults and used to discipline the students, the entire credibility of the mediation process is jeopardized. The only exception is information about clearly illegal behavior and suspected abuse (the reporting of the latter to the authorities is legally mandated) that emerge during the mediation session. A clear policy in this regard must be in place so that all students, mediators, and disputants understand the necessity to report these activities to the responsible officials.

Building Ongoing Support for School Mediation
As with many new programs, it is often not difficult

to obtain seed money or other resources to initiate a mediation program within a school. The trick is to secure ongoing funding for its operation and expansion. Unless a good deal of thought is given to moving from soft money, often foundation grants or special project funds within the school district, to hard money, the regular operating budget of the school, the school mediation program may end abruptly. With the shrinking of many school budgets, this is a major issue for the school mediation movement. It appears, however, that a good number of school districts are still willing to make a long-term investment in school mediation. In fact, some may view it as essential, given the reduction in fiscal resources.

Summary

School-based peer mediation provides opportunities to improve the quality of student and teacher experiences at school. At a very basic level, it prompts a healthy understanding of conflict as a normal part of child and adolescent development by recognizing that conflict is inevitable and that there are appropriate ways to deal with it. It also empowers students through peer-based mediation and recognizes students as a resource for resolving student conflicts, which typically revolve around rumors, miscommunication, and misinterpretation. As a result, teachers can spend more time on teaching and less on resolving student conflicts. School mediation also offers an effective alternative to violence, expulsion, suspension, detention, and court intervention.

Research is just beginning on school-based peer mediation. So far the overall findings show benefits for students, teachers, and schools among them less student fighting and improved school climate. Concerns about school-based peer mediation include resistance by adults because mediation creates a fundamental shift in power dynamics within the school culture; staff belief in and use of mediation, where mediation includes student conflicts but excludes student to adult conflicts; confidentiality of mediation; and building ongoing financial support.

5

DIVORCE AND CHILD-CUSTODY MEDIATION

Jim, age 41, had his own electrical contracting business and his world was falling apart. He and his wife, Kay, age 40, had been married for twenty-one years. Kay had worked as office manager and bookkeeper in the business until the birth of their first child, Jamie, age 17. Kathryn was born three years later, followed by Thomas in two years. They used to have a lot of fun in the early years until Jim's drinking became problematic, resulting in his inpatient treatment for alcoholism in 1984. By 1988, things had seemed to return to the old patterns only without the alcohol. In 1992 the couple found themselves in a mediation office settling their divorce. It was the first time they had ever sat together with another person and analyzed their finances, marital net worth, and their children's needs, all without blame and fault. They were determined to divorce. The mediator directed them through a structured process that controlled their communication and behaviors while educating them about the issues of a divorce settlement, particularly as it affected the children. They discussed ways to divide their property fairly

Note: This chapter was written by Marilyn McKnight, director of Family Mediation Services in Minneapolis, Minnesota, and past chairperson of the Academy of Family Mediators.

and how they could best finance the living costs of all of them. Kay attended a career-counseling program and found her interests and skills to be in financial planning. They worked out a property settlement that gave Kay the home, which she wanted, in exchange for Jim's having full ownership of his business, yet the ultimate winners were the children. Jim and Kay developed a plan whereby they would both be active parents, following exchange schedules that balanced work and school time with the children's needs. They strove to keep the pain at a minimum by mediating their divorce with a well-trained, competent mediator, and hiring collaborative lawyers to prepare the legal documents necessary for an uncontested divorce.

Divorce mediation is a cooperative process for couples whose marriages have foundered to create their own divorce settlements. Its goal is to meet the needs of the husband, wife, and children in a private, confidential setting.

Beginning in the late 1950s, family courts, divorce lawyers, and divorcing families around the country began more openly to recognize the complexity of the divorcing process and the weakness of the adversarial legal system for resolving issues regarding child custody and visitation. County-run "domestic relations" departments were created to provide counseling for couples experiencing divorce in order to facilitate their coming to agreement on child custody and visitation. For example, Hennepin County (the

Minneapolis, Minnesota, area) established its Domestic Relations Department in 1957 by an act of the state legislature. Many other publicly funded programs were established about then, especially in California.

Although not formally called mediators until the 1970s, family court counselors functioned in what would now be called a social work "therapeutic mediation model." This model emphasizes "a discussion of the marriage, the reasons for the divorce, and exploration of the potential for reconciliation, and a focus on the future relationship between the couple."[1]

During the 1970s, attorney O. James Coogler (1978) developed the "structured model" for divorce mediation, which focuses solely on the legal issues of custody, visitation, property, and finances. It is an approach mainly used by attorneys and does not deal with the unresolved emotional issues that might serve as obstacles to reaching agreement. Coogler and his associates, jointly with family therapist Virginia Satir, Hennepin County Domestic Relations Department, and others, sponsored the first national conference on divorce mediation in 1976 in Atlanta. Participants attended mediation training and were said to have gotten into heated discussions about whether their work with clients should be called mediation or a form of family therapy.[2]

In 1974, Coogler and therapists Judith Wood and Will Neville began the first practice of divorce mediation in Atlanta, collaborating on a new process of marriage dissolution for divorcing couples. Shortly thereafter, Virginia Stafford, a colleague, opened the second mediation

1. Milne, 1983.
2. P. Casperson, personal communication, March 17, 1994.

practice, in Winston-Salem, North Carolina. In 1977, Family Mediation Services was established in Minneapolis by Marilyn McKnight, Steve Erickson, and five others. These pathbreakers offered mediation services through private practices. At about this same time, some of the conciliation and family courts began to refer divorcing couples to court-administered domestic-relations mediation counseling services for child custody disputes, often provided initially by former probation officers.

Money Magazine published the first article on divorce mediation in 1980, which occasioned calls to Coogler from lawyers and therapists from across the United States and Canada asking where they could be trained. Coogler, Wood, Stafford and Erickson consequently set out to offer divorce mediation training. The first sessions, totaling forty hours in all, were held in August 1980. Forty hours has since become the normal length of such initial training in divorce mediation and is one of the few formal requirements laid down by many courts for eligibility for referral clients.

The divorce mediation field has grown into a legitimate, full-scale profession. In the late 1970s, Coogler founded the Family Mediation Association, the first national professional organization of divorce mediators. The Academy of Family Mediators was formed by Erickson, John Haynes, and Sam Margolis as a Minnesota nonprofit corporation in 1981, and today it is the largest such organization in the world. In the first years of these organizations, they concentrated on training mediators as a way to organize and influence the field and to finance start-up expenses. Members and other training organizations soon charged that the academy's training was self-serving. By 1984, training was being offered by private groups, many of whom submitted their programs to the academy for approval. The academy continues to be the only organization that approves the forty-hour divorce mediation training programs. In 1983 the academy participated with other North American organizations and groups in developing Standards of Practice for Family Mediators.

Academy membership was exclusive in the early years-only trained mediators with either law degrees or a master's degrees in one of the mental health fields-but educational requirements for membership other than the forty-hour training program were abandoned in 1988. It has established the category Practicing Mediator Member, and recommended to the state courts that they refer only to mediators who have sixty hours of training, mediation of at least ten cases, ten hours of supervision, and one hundred hours of mediation experience. To date these are the only qualifications recommended by any major organization for the referral of family mediation cases.

The number of family mediation practitioners continues to grow. Most of the 2,400 members of the academy practice privately and receive some court referrals. Most mediators have educational backgrounds in law or one of the mental health professions, such as social work or psychology, although these are no longer required.

Rationale for Divorce and Child-Custody Mediation

Many mediators strongly believe that divorce should be treated as a family problem, not a legal problem. Divorce, they argue, has the characteristics of a temporary mental illness, because people in the midst of divorce often suffer bouts of depression, irrational behavior, insomnia, hysterics, loss of memory, paranoia, low work performance, rage, and even suicidal tendencies.[1] While experiencing perhaps the worst trauma of their lives, they are expected to compete with each other in an adversarial system to settle the divorce, using lawyers who are untrained in assessing and treating the emotionally distraught. At a time when divorcing couples desperately need understanding and compassion, they must appear in court; then each side must listen to the other speak disparagingly of it in trying to convince the court of unfitness to parent the children, or of their deceitful, dishonest, and despicable ways.

Divorcing couples can often benefit from an impartial third-party mediator who can constructively assist them with the divorce process rather than undergo a legal, adversarial process which may encourage dysfunctional behavior. The mediator encourages positive behavior by managing the process and improving their communication and listening skills. Mediation approaches divorce as a problem to be solved rather than a contest to be won. It can empower participants to make decisions through identifying issues, needs, and interests; gathering all of the necessary information; creating various options about settlement; and leading them in their final settlement discussions toward a workable solution. A primary goal of the process is to empower those who created the problems to take responsibility for the solutions, to develop their own law or standard of fairness.

Divorce mediation aids in the divorcing persons'

1. Kaslow & Schwartz, 1987.

healing process by offering an opportunity for the couple to get their affairs in order privately rather than a publicly. "This process by which parties to a marriage are empowered to create their own enforceable legal commitments is a form of private ordering".[1] Through mediation, they create order out of the chaos and dysfunction of divorce. They begin to take charge of their lives, and plan separate futures by designing a detailed, well-planned map for the settlement. This map is based upon their own standard of fairness, as explored in the mediation process.

Mediation can offer a superior process of divorce settlement, one that finds answers by concentrating on the future rather than the past. It encourages letting go of the hurt and pain of the past, which is often played out in bitterness and revenge toward the other party. This highly intense, detailed, honest, thorough, practical process serves their needs and assists in their recovery. Advocates of divorce mediation believe that it is therapeutically valuable and one of the best ways to dissolve a marriage.

The Mediation Option for Divorcing Families

Divorce causes a major disruption in family functioning and relationships, affecting the couple and their children. The couple's parents and extended families may also experience pain and suffering. The mediation process presents a way for families to reduce the amount and duration of pain. "Basic principles of mediation, such as empowerment, consideration of the best interests of all involved family members, cooperative problem solving, and

1. Mnookin & Maccoby, 1992.

equitable distribution of assets are consonant with the theory and practice of marital and family systems therapy".[1] The mediator constantly encourages couples to negotiate, by modeling and teaching positive, constructive negotiation skills, and stresses no fault or blame. In fact, the mediator propels them into listening to and communicating with each other in a structured and safe way.

Children never totally escape the hurt of divorce, and may carry the hurt for many years. They feel their world crashing down upon them when their parents tell them of an impending divorce. Children react variously to the separation of parents, depending upon their age and many other factors. They are often distraught and in denial from when they first learn of the divorce. Their adjustment to the separation is directly related to the length and duration of the parental conflict.[2]

Mediation educates parents about what happens to children in the midst of divorce; the adversarial process encourages each parent to keep records of the children's behavior upon returning from the other parent's home in order to prove the unfitness of the other parent, and thereby tries to ascertain the better parent. In mediation the question is what parenting arrangements can be agreed to that best serve the children and allow each parent to have the best parenting relationship in the future. When one parent is having problems or the children are agitated, the mediation process refers them to neutral psychologists and social workers who specialize in working with divorcing families. In contrast, the adversarial process would have each parent hire an expert, who would be encouraged to

1. Kaslow, 1988.
2. Wallerstein & Kelly, 1980.

build a case for that parent and against the other. Such divisiveness is severely destructive and counter to all that is known about a child's needs and adjustments to divorce. The adversarial process exacerbates the conflict; the mediation process encourages cooperation and honesty as keys to the future parenting of the children.

Mediators believe that when those who created a problem-in this instance, divorce-are responsible for its solution, compliance with the outcome is greater. In addition, they have built a safety net into mediation agreements that addresses how the parents will settle any future disputes. Lawyers welcome these clauses, which are often worded as follows:

> The parties agree that should they have any disagreements in the future regarding their parenting arrangements and/or support, they will first try to settle such disagreements on their own. If they are unable to settle, they will next seek settlement in a mediation process before either will refer it to a court process.

Courts usually respect these clauses and will not hear such a case until mediation has been sought and is unsuccessful. So if compliance becomes an issue in the future, the positive process of mediation and self-determination is mandated in the divorce decree. In practice, this technique has proved very successful. For example, the author of this chapter has mediated several such returns to mediation well after the decree; all were settled, and none proceeded to court for a ruling.

Divorce Mediation: A Multidimensional Process

There are two distinct aspects of divorce: legal and emotional. In the adversarial process for divorce legal issues are uppermost and emotional issues tend to be neglected. In divorce mediation both take center stage and the divorcing couple report a greater degree of satisfaction with the process. A recent study found that "divorce mediation was a successful means of reaching full resolution of divorce issues for the majority of those who entered the process, and was seen by its participants as significantly more satisfactory along multiple dimensions than respondents in the adversarial divorce process".[1]

The Legal Divorce

The process of mediating divorces occurs on several levels. The legal relates to the mediator's ensuring that all issues necessary for the court-ordered divorce decree are addressed in mediation. Divorce mediation occurs in the shadow of the court[2], and the conditions and circumstances that influence the decisionmaking may be legally defined, such as child support. It is important for the mediator to have a working knowledge of the law, and to refer the parties to their lawyers to have legal questions answered. Some divorce mediators believe that mediation operates only on the legal level, and that the primary task is to reach a settlement that closely approximates the probable case outcome if it were tried in a state court. Many other divorce mediators believe that this one-dimensional approach is inappropriate and does not address other matters that, if

1. Kelly, 1990.
2. Mnookin & Maccoby, 1992.

considered, produce a more thorough, well-rounded settlement based on the desires and needs of the parties and their children rather than just the law.

The Emotional Divorce

The emotional divorce is set forth in the Erickson Conceptual Framework of Divorce Mediation;[1] which describes the multidimensional system of problem solving used in the Erickson model of mediation. In this model, the mediator works to engage the parties' cooperation and influence attitudes as they mediate their divorce. To understand this, it is necessary to discuss the emotional divorce process itself.

Most divorcing couples do not understand what happens to them when they divorce. They are thrown into negative emotional states that create the immense conflict in divorce. Divorcing couples, especially those who are parents, need to know that there is an emotional process that is common and unique to the situation. Going through a divorce involves grieving, a life crisis, and an irreversible change in family structure and relationships, all occurring simultaneously. The process of divorce involves multiple stages.

Stage I. Considering and Deciding to Divorce

One spouse begins to consider the possibility of divorce. "As interpersonal conflict and personal dissatisfaction increase, at least one of the marital partners begins to recognize the source of these problems is the marital relationship itself."[2] When that spouse decides to

1. Erickson & McKnight Erickson, 1988.
2. Ahrons & Rodgers, 1987.

move in the direction of divorce and shares the decision with the other spouse, the conflict between them worsens. The intensification is occasioned by the attempts of the latter, in disbelief and denial that this is happening, to improve the relationship and bring about reconsideration. The children, who may know nothing of the discussions between their parents, nevertheless sense that things have gone awry and that family unity is threatened. They, like the parent not yet accepting of divorce, will often deny the possibility and look for clues to the contrary in family interactions.

The typical emotions and behaviors that begin with considering divorce are numerous. There is often guilt about causing a major change in the family structure, and fear of what will happen when the decision to divorce is shared, which may keep the person from disclosing the decision until some crisis-when it then comes out negatively and destructively. Anger, hurt, despair, and depression also frequently accompany this stage as a spouse reasons why to divorce, ponders lost dreams, and wonders if life is worth living. Thoughts of suicide are not unusual. Insomnia is not uncommon, nor is waking at about the same time each night and not being able to get back to sleep. Lack of sleep can lead to irritability and impatience, which are often portrayed or perceived as anger. Work performance often drops temporarily during this period, as well. Even so, when the person considering divorce finally makes the decision to divorce and shares it with the spouse, it is often a relief; emotions may settle down somewhat, or at least change. This is when the other spouse begins to experience the emotions the first person has been experiencing. It is often at this time that couples seek information about divorce and may inquire about how mediation works.

The question of appropriateness of mediation often surfaces with a couple at this stage because one spouse is ready to move forward and the other often is not. The mediator, instead of assessing appropriateness, leads them through the discussion of how no-fault divorce operates, that is, one spouse may accomplish a divorce without the cooperation or involvement of the other. The other spouse may feel coerced into divorcing by this information; however, that is not the same as being coerced to mediate. Because one party can move forward with a legal divorce process, the mediator needs to enlighten the couple as to how the mediation process may be of greater benefit to each.

Stage II. Separation

Separation is usually the most traumatic event in the divorce process, especially when there are children. Until one spouse moves out of the family residence, children, and maybe the other spouse, may remain in denial and avoid the reality of the impending divorce. The departure of a parent signals the turning point for a family from whole to divided. As Judith Wallerstein and Joan Kelly (1980) report in Surviving the Breakup, "For children and adolescents, the separation and its aftermath was the most stressful period in their lives." This is when parents need to be most available to their children, though in reality parents are emotionally so consumed with the separation and the issues of the divorce that they are less available.

Stage III. Adjusting to the Separation and Divorce

Most parents have ideas and hunches about what is happening to their children during their separation and divorce, and research confirms what the parents observe as significant negative changes in behavior and attitudes. Through the mediator's explanation of the normality of such reactions, the parents have more latitude in dealing with the changes and helping their children, rather than attaching blame to a spouse. If parents observe unusual behaviors, they are encouraged to talk to each other about how they can assist in the children's adjustment to the situation. A mediator knowledgeable about such matters initiates this topic when parenting problems arise, and gives parents information, resources, and perhaps even a referral to a professional children's counselor, and then helps with divising parenting arrangements.

Settling all or most of the issues related to the emotional divorce is critical to family members' adaptation to the new circumstances. The mediator may be the facilitator for the parents to engage other professionals for assistance during and after the divorce. This dimension of the mediation process of divorce is probably the most important to the future parenting of the children, the satisfaction of the parties, and the compliance and longevity of the settlement. It surpasses the legal issues and goes to the depth of the relationship itself. It is a learning experience for the spouses to hear each other's feelings and perspectives, and to step outside self-interests to empathize, let go, and perhaps even forgive each other,-or at least begin to understand the value of forgiveness and consider it.[1]

1. Bush, 1989.

For those who cannot move beyond the associated emotions, the mediator offers other strategies. A referral to a therapist who specializes in marriage closure therapy may be most helpful in ending the marriage and mediating the divorce with dignity. Mediation continues while they attend therapy; the commitment to therapy calms the emotions sufficiently so the couple may successfully mediate the divorce. Unfortunately, the adversarial divorce process has less ability to accomplish such referral and the couple is left to play out emotions through that process.

The Value Dimension of the Mediation Process

The divorce mediation process must also consider another dimension of the settlement: the value differences of the parties. The differences may originate in parenting philosophy, as culture, religion, or life experience. They are often the basis of the conflict that cause marriage breakdown and keeps it from settlement. In one divorce mediation, for example, one party insisted that marriage is a business relationship and that decisions are based upon profit and loss; the other party believed that marriage is a personal loving relationship in which children and family are the most important elements. Mediation brings the differences into the open, where they can be acknowledged and their impact on the divorce settlement understood, even though they may not be mediated to the full satisfaction of each party.

Needs and Interests in the Mediation Process

The needs and interests of a divorcing couple are treated dissimilarly in mediation and in the divorce court. A cornerstone of the mediation process is exploration of those needs and interests relative to various aspects of the settlement. Take child custody. The court asks, Who is the fitter parent? The question looks to the past and sets up a competition to prove parental fitness in order to win custody. In mediation the question is, What arrangements can the two of you agree to that will allow each to have the parenting relationship you want in the future? This invites the couple to create a parenting plan[1] and is followed by, What do your children need from you in a parenting relationship? It allows the possibility that the less-involved parent during the marriage may become a more active parent in the future. The need of each parent to have a good parenting relationship is discussed, and the responsibility for specific arrangements is theirs-with the assistance of the mediator.

The Phases and Tasks of Divorce Mediation

The divorce mediator manages a very structured process that weaves the more abstract dimensions mentioned above with the concrete issues that need resolution. The first phase is the initial consultation, an informational session that describes the entire process, answers questions, and prepares the divorcing couple for mediation. It is conducted by the person who will mediate their case if they choose mediation.

A screening of the couple is done with intake sheets that ask for facts about them, their children, their concerns, and the level of violence in their relationship. The mediator considers the date in deciding whether to see them

1. Erickson & McKnight Erickson, 1992.

separately first. If there has been violence, the mediator meets with them individually regarding the appropriateness of mediation, based upon the information elicited. If they proceed, they meet with the mediator and learn about the three areas of settlement: divorce and parenting arrangements, financial support, and property division. Additional issues include how the mediation process addresses these areas, what is done in mediation, how long it takes, and an explanation of forms and fees. The mediator often answers their questions by demonstrating how mediation would work with a particular concern of theirs, and points out areas of agreement to illustrate that they have already had a meeting of the minds on some things. The initial consultation is informal and practical, comparable to preparation for mediation phase of the generic mediation model in Chapter 2.

The mediation phase of the process usually requires three to five two-hour sessions over two to three months and completes eight tasks:

1. Introductory remarks by mediator
2. Mediator's collection of additional information
3. Clarification of information
4. Agreement on information by parties
5. Identification of needs and interests
6. Development of options for settlement
7. Construction of an agreement
8. Finalization of a memorandum of agreement

The pacing of meetings is set as the process goes along, based on availability of information and the needs of the parties. Information gathering is the very important and complex initial work of the early sessions. Questionnaires provide most of the data about assets, liabilities, income, and monthly budgets; however, the figures need to be verified, documented, and agreed upon. Agreement is an indispensable aspect and may take time. For example, to agree on a house's value, each party needs to understand appraisal and its variables. Deciding on parenting arrangements also requires discussion and possibly trying out tentative schedules.

Unlike other forms of mediation, divorce mediation does not usually begin with the parties telling their stories through opening statements; this would bog down the process or alienate the parties to the extent that they might subsequently be unable to work together in mediation. Further, opening statements of divorcing couples would usually offer premature solutions or a litany of reasons for the divorce. The parties would then proceed to defend the statements rather than analyze the issues together and consider options. Opening statements would limit creative possibilities and solutions, and are individuals' views of a settlement, not the product of a cooperative venture that takes into account the best interests of each party.

Once there is agreement and understanding about the data and issues, the mediator directs the parties into option development. One rule in divorce mediation property settlement is that you can give away anything you want as long as you know its value. So option development can begin only after all the relevent information is gathered, understood, verified, and discussed.

The divorcing couple next begins to choose what

will work best for each and consider consequences of particular settlements. Trade-offs occur as they fashion various agreed-upon elements into a settlement. The mediator assists by recording agreements and drafting the final settlement, the memorandum of understanding. This approved document is then taken to their attorneys for translation into the marital-termination agreement, which is submitted to the court for the divorce decree. All of this is accomplished without either party's ever stepping into a courtroom; matters are put to rest with the help of the mediator, thoroughly and respectfully.

Summing up, many argue that mediation should be the primary dispute-resolution process for divorcing couples and families. They stress its superiority over adversarial divorce by virtue of its many positive characteristics. Mediation promotes and influences cooperative behavior, in its pursuit of informed, joint decisionmaking. It's private nature allows those responsible for a problem to decide upon a solution. It also renders a public value by teaching the parties to consider their own and others' interests, thereby promoting self-determination and self-transcendence-universal values and a key form of moral education.[1] In addition, mediation is a future-oriented process that encourages a fluid settlement that can change as the children grow and the parents remarry or move. Mediators look beyond the settlement to assure parties that they have mediated for resolving future conflicts. (For a list of issues to consider in planning child care after divorce see Table 5.1.) Mediation is also practiced in concert with other professionals, who assist the family through and beyond the

1. Bush, 1989.

divorce so it can restructure and children can flourish.

Table 5.1
Issues to Consider in Planning Child Care after Divorce

1. Week-to-week time arrangements
   • Schedule and transportation
2. Time arrangements for holidays and special days
3. School vacations
   • Time arrangements
   • Parents' vacations with and without children
4. Health care decisions
   • Emergency medical treatments
   • Informing other parent
   •Well-child checkups (medical and dental)
   • Child's illness interrupting child-care plan
   • Parental access to medical records
   • Health insurance
5. Education decisions
   • Consultation between parents regarding any
     change in school, special educational needs,
     tutoring, and so on
   • Access to school records
   • Attendance at parent-teacher conferences and
     school events
6. Religion
   • Religious education and attendance at services
7. Grandparent or extended-family visitation and
   involvement with children
8. Communication between parents
9. Communication when child is with other parent
10. Independent or consultative decisionmaking
11. Changes in child-care schedule
    • If parent cannot care for a child when scheduled, should the
      other parent have right of first refusal
12. Support of children's respect and affection for other parent
13. Resolving disagreements and changes regarding parenting plan
    • Understanding how to resolve disagreements
    • Understanding how to modify arrangements should changes in
      parents' or children's lives require
14. Parenting plans should geographical relocation of a parent occur

From Helping Children Succeed After Divorce, A Handbook For Parents, Children's Hospital
Guidance Centers, Columbus, Ohio, 1993 pg. 28.

What We Have Learned from Research

Divorce and child-custody mediation research is limited to court-related studies and studies of suburban private programs, and is based upon mediations that occurred in the early and mid-1980s. None of the several projects and results reported on have specifically addressed programs for low-income clients or cases of spousal abuse. The court-related programs involved only custody mediation; the private programs mediated all aspects of a divorce. Research is also lacking in the equity and outcomes of mediated and adjudicated divorces, which would reveal how women and children actually fare. Another consideration regarding the findings is the location of the research groups: most of the research is from California, which has a long-standing preference for court referral to mediation. One study from South Carolina found striking differences due to the court's preference for mothers as custodial parents. Although questions remain, research has begun on compliance and client satisfaction, and differences between public and private mediation services. The following is an overview of some findings:

- The vast majority of participants in court and private mediation services were satisfied with the overall process.[1]
- In private and public mediation services, women were found to be generally satisfied with the process.[2]

1. Kelly, 1989; Kelly, 1990; Emery & Jackson, 1989; Depner, Cannata, & Simon, 1992; Duryee, 1992; Slater, Shaw, & Duquesnel, 1992.
2. Kelly, 1989; Kelly, 1990; Duryee, 1992.

- Parents generally reported very favorable results in the mediation process.[1]
- Mediation was clearly more satisfactory, even with issues that were perceived to be better settled in court.[2]
- Mediation was considered a fair forum for women regarding power and advantages vis-à-vis their husbands.[3]
- Men fared much better in mediation in court and private settings regarding parenting than did their counterparts in the adversarial process.[4]
- It is important for the mediation process to encourage, and teach if necessary, consideration for each spouse's feelings and point of view.[5]
- In court and private mediation processes there was higher compliance with settlements than with adversarial divorce settlements.[6]

Unresolved Issues

Mediation of Spousal Abuse Cases

The debate that has dominated the field of family mediation for the past ten years is the appropriateness of mediating cases in which spousal abuse has occurred during the marriage. The position of the Battered Women's Coalition has been that mediation is not appropriate for any woman who does not have power and bargaining skills that

1. Depner et al., 1992; Slater et al., 1992.
2. Emery & Jackson, 1989; Duryee, 1992; Kelly, 1989; Kelly, 1990.
3. Kelly, 1989; Kelly, 1990; Duryee, 1992.
4. Kelly, 1989; Kelly, 1990; Emery & Jackson, 1989; Depner et al., 1992.
5. Slaikeu, Pearson & Thoennes, 1988; Bush, 1989; Kaslow, 1987.
6. Kelly, 1990; Emery & Jackson, 1989.

equal her husband's. The most recent report on the subject is that of the Toronto Forum on Women Abuse and Mediation (June 1993), which addresses four major areas of concern and makes the following recommendations:

1. <u>Woman Abuse and the Education and Training of Family Mediators</u>. Family mediation organizations should establish (a) training standards that specifically address issues of woman and child abuse; (b) standards and qualifications for family mediation trainers; and (c) training models that enlist the participation of service providers for abused women and disadvantaged populations.

2. <u>Premediation Screening</u>. Because few cases of domestic abuse are suitable for mediation, (a) mediation clients should be interviewed separately in a safe environment to assess specific issues of domestic abuse; (b) screening instruments should be carefully designed, but they do not replace the need for high levels of investigative interviewing and assessment for cases that might proceed to specialized mediation; and (c) specific criteria should be set for exclusion of abuse cases or referral to a specialized mediation process.

3. <u>Safety and Specialized Mediation</u>. In regard to safety and specialized mediation, (a) risk should be minimized and safety maximized through the development of protocols, promotion of research, and support of services for abused persons;

(b) provisions for safety should be made, including policies to ward and protect abused persons and requirements to report abuse; (c) staff should be trained to address the safety needs of clients; (d) screening should be done for abuse, and safety provisions should be maintained throughout the mediation process; and (e) specialized mediation should be provided for domestic abuse cases to ensure safety before and after sessions, to compensate for power imbalances, and to terminate mediation without harm.

4. Alternatives to Mediation. Jurisdictions should (a) offer several marital-dissolution models; (b) provide education about the benefits and risks of alternatives, fund safe and timely access for abused persons to alternatives, and fund participation of advocates for abused persons in marital-dissolution alternatives; (c) furnish abused persons with affordable legal representation; (d) address the needs of children living with domestic abuse in custody cases; (e) allow the courts to exempt abused persons and parents of abused children from mediation; (f) enable courts to develop protocols to assure uniform, safe, and equitable resolution of family-law disputes; and (g) train and certify intake staff, mediators, arbitrators, lawyers, guardians ad litem, and court personnel to serve abused persons in the context of marriage dissolution.

The Toronto report summarizes the critical issues of mediating divorce and child custody when there has been spousal abuse. It is the first to go beyond whether to mediate cases of spousal abuse to specific recommendations concerning the issue. It must be noted that those who work with battered women still hold to a refutable presumption against the use of mediation in such cases, but even so, many participated in formulating the recommendations of the report. Of the above recommendations, the most important is to promote research that will begin to answer some of the major questions about safety and methods of best serving abused persons in the settlement of their divorce and child-custody matters.

Mediator Qualifications and Certification

Another critical issue in the field of family mediation is qualifications to mediate divorce and child-custody settlements. For the family and conciliation courts that offer mediation services, in-house, it is less pressing because they have job descriptions and requirements for employment in place. However, fiscal constraints are forcing many to close down their programs and refer to private family mediators. The minimum criterion of many court programs is completion of an approved forty-hour divorce-mediation training program. The number of private mediators has grown considerably since the early 1980s, and their concern is that anyone can advertise as a family mediator, and compete in the market, without having been trained at all.

Within the larger field of mediation, the Society of Professionals in Dispute Resolution in the mid-1980s assigned a commission on qualifications to define mediator qualifications. One of its major findings surprised the practitioners: there is no correlation between higher education and the ability to mediate. Even so, work has been done and continues to be done on a test to measure family-mediator competency.

Family mediation will be the first sector in the field of mediation to offer a valid and reliable measure of mediator competency. (This will have a great impact because as one sector of mediation moves in the direction of certification, others may be compelled to do so in the future to satisfy the public). It is the initial step in family mediation's self-regulation, though its purpose was to assure quality and serve mediators and the public. Moreover, because family mediation is closely tied to justice systems, it is important that the action was self-imposed rather than imposed by the courts or other entities.

SUMMARY

Divorce mediation began in the early 1970s and allowed couples to create their divorce settlements through a cooperative, confidential, and private process that focuses on the current and future needs of the husband, wife, and children. The rationale for divorce and child-custody mediation is that divorce is a family problem, not a legal problem. It approaches divorce as a problem to be solved, and empowers those who created the problem to take responsibility for its solution. Mediation also addresses the multidimensional aspects of divorce, which include the legal divorce, the emotional divorce, personal values, and personal needs and interests. In contrast, the adversarial legal approach views divorce as a contest to be won, and focuses on the legal issues.

Divorce mediation begins with an initial consultation, in which the mediator explains the mediation process and the couple fills out intake sheets about themselves. If they decide to mediate the divorce, the process usually requires three to five two-hour sessions over two to three months. In divorce mediation, there is usually no opening statement by the parties, as in many other mediation applications. Instead, after data and issues are gathered, understood, verified, discussed, and valued, the mediator directs the parties into option development.

Research has been limited to court-related studies and suburban private programs studies; however, the findings have generally been positive in regard to satisfaction with the process and the results. There is higher compliance with mediation divorce settlements than adversarial divorce settlements. Issues of major concern about mediating divorce include how to handle cases that include spousal abuse, and how to regulate the quality and certification of divorce mediators.

6
PARENT-CHILD MEDIATION

By the time Kevin turned 16, constant conflict between him and his mom or stepdad seemed to overshadow all other aspects of the family relationship. It seemed to him that they wanted to control his every movement, so the more they set rules and curfews, the more he openly defied them. Kevin started to cut classes, without his parents' being aware of it. After the twelfth occurrence the principal referred his case to the juvenile court for truancy. Kevin had no prior record and in lieu of proceeding with the normal court process, the judge referred Kevin's case to a local mediation program. During the mediation, Kevin and his parents were able to talk openly about what was going on without outbursts from either side. His mom and stepdad learned that Kevin was having a very rough time with growing up and dealing with authority, and that his girlfriend had dropped him. Kevin felt he had no one to talk to. He learned that his parents really loved him but they, too, were having a rough time with this phase of Kevin's life. They were worried about his education. Together, with the aid of the mediator, they negotiated an agreement by which Kevin would not cut school, his parents would ease up on some of the rules, and they would meet periodically with the mediator to check out how things were going.

A small but growing number of programs are developing throughout North America to provide mediation between parents and their children who are referred to juvenile court. The concept of parent-child mediation was pioneered in the early 1980s, by the Children's Aid Society's Persons in Need of Supervision (PINS) Mediation Project in New York City and by the Children's Hearings Project (CHP) in Cambridge, Massachusetts. Two other early programs were the Exeter Mediation Program in Exeter, New Hampshire, and the Parent Child Mediation Program of the Connecticut Superior Court's Family Division. All of these initial programs focused on diverting status offenders from the juvenile justice system through participation in mediation with their parents.

Parent-child mediation programs are often conducted under the auspices of private nonprofit community agencies. Some are operated by public agencies, such as probation units. Influenced heavily by the Scottish Children's Hearing System, the CHP was endorsed by the Massachusetts Department of Social Services and replicated in numerous other jurisdictions. Most programs, private or public, make use of trained volunteers as mediators. The explicit goal of parent-child mediation is "to obtain a balanced and specific agreement that the family believes will meet its needs and that family members will be able to adhere to."[1] The technique employed is mediation, not therapy, even though a strong social service component is often present. Family therapists often refer their clients to mediation, and, following mediation, the family goes to the therapist. Advocates of parent-child mediation stress that

1. Phear, 1985.

mediation and therapy usually do not occur simultaneously.

Rationale for Parent-Child Mediation

The structure of American families has dramatically changed over the past few decades. The majority of children now grow up in single-parent families and blended families involving stepparents, not in the traditional two-parent family. At the same time, the level of poverty and violence within society is placing increased stress and economic hardships on families. Even in two-parent blended families, economic need often requires that both parents work outside the home. There is often little interaction between parents and children, regardless of socioeconomic status. The increase in divorce rates and the reality of single parenting have made rearing children very difficult and stressful. There is a tremendous need for teaching parenting skills and offering the mutual aid of support groups to parents and children.

Even under the best of circumstances, some conflict between adolescents and parents is a normal part of youth development. For some, this shared journey is a temporary inconvenience and irritant that does not threaten the core of the parent-child relationship. It is a matter of hanging in there and getting through it for both parties. For others, adolescence represents a painful, exhausting, grief-ridden, and, at times, life-threatening journey that cuts into the bond between parent and child .

What seem to be relatively minor conflicts over a dirty room, coming home too late, not doing chores, or having the wrong type of friends frequently escalate into major blowups in which relationships are destroyed or deeply wounded. Often, the more parents attempt to impose their will upon the rebelling adolescent, the more they push their son or daughter in the very direction they detest. A continuously escalating and dysfunctional cycle of conflict-- the child acting out, the parent overreacting, the child acting out again--can be triggered. Parents may be too authoritarian, which leads to greater adolescent rebellion, or too lenient, which results in not enough structure being provided.

Some adolescents turn inward and become depressed and inactive. Others act out their anger through experimenting with drugs or alcohol, cutting school, running away, or breaking the law. Still others respond favorably to parental guidance, no matter how strict or confining it might be. There seems to be no standard technique of parenting that all or even most kids respond to in a favorable manner. Two adolescents within the same family can have radically different personalities and needs relative to parental guidance and support.

The relationships of families caught in an escalating dysfunctional cycle of conflict are disrupted, a circumstance that may lead to a daughter or son's being referred to juvenile court for behavior such as truancy, running away, or being beyond parental control. Mediation may offer a way for families to de-escalate the conflict. It is appropriate for social workers and others to promote the mediation option because turning family conflict over to the more impersonal court system often results in a superficial decision that deals only partially with the conflict. The adversarial court process pits child and parent against each other, while focusing exclusively upon the juvenile for problems that are often related to the family as a system. In contrast, mediation examines the conflict in context of the family and empowers the parent and child to own the conflict and solution. The agreement reached fits the circumstances of the people involved, and mediation models a technique of negotiation that the family members can use in the future.

Parent-Child Mediation Process

Two conditions are essential for nearly all forms of parent-child mediation. First, the participants must express a desire to preserve an existing relationship through resolution of the conflict. Second, they must be relatively equal participants. The process of mediating conflict between parents and children is examined in the context of these conditions because several important issues are raised by them.

The first condition that participants must desire to resolve the conflict and preserve the relationship, is often strongly felt when a family enters the parent-child mediation process. Often other attempts to deal with the tension, frustration, and strain on their relationship have failed. In court-related parent-child mediation, the child's experience of the conflict has been heightened to the point of being brought to the attention of the juvenile justice system. This usually means multiple incidents; for example, in many schools it is only after the twelfth or fourteenth truancy that a case is filed in juvenile court.

All family systems comprise a complex and reciprocal set of intense and intimate relationships. A good deal of work by the mediator is required in order to enter a family system effectively. It is particularly important that the mediator remain impartial and not allow feelings about his or her own family life to enter the process.

Whether positive or negative, parents and children maintain a lifelong relationship. The Children's Hearings Project states, "This parent child bond is one fact that makes mediation 'inside the family' special." However, it is not always successful. When it is, an enhancement of the family's commitment to positive change may be the result. When it is not, an increased disappointment in a relationship that doesn't work may eventuate. It is the job of the mediator to help family members focus on their common interests so that each can receive what he or she needs and the overall relationship can be improved.[1]

The second condition that participants must have relative equivalence, is particularly important in parent-child mediation. Childhood is by definition a subordinate status: children do not have the rights and responsibilities that adults have. That is precisely why there exists a separate juvenile justice system. Therefore, parent-child mediators clearly do not assume that children have equal decision making power with their parents. Parents should and do have more power than their children. However, in parent-child mediation the reason to pursue relatively equal participation is that it aids the process of clarifying the issues and potential solutions by having all participants express their views. There is a significant difference between being able to participate versus being able to decide.

In fact, the issues that cause a family to be referred

1. Zetzel & Wixted, 1984.

to parent-child mediation almost always involve power struggles. Often, it is the child who is increasingly challenging the authority of the parent(s). The parent(s) may be feeling increasingly powerless and frightened by changing relationships. The purpose of mediation is not to try to restructure the family system by taking authority away from the parent(s); more appropriately, it is to try to clarify expectations, which may lead to a redefinition of some of the rules and responsibilities. It allows for all views to be expressed by family members and for the negotiation of an agreement on resolving specific disputes. Mediation allows parents to reestablish power and authority through the setting of realistic limits that are respected because they are jointly arrived at with the child. The Children's Hearings Project notes:

> Making constructive use of the power struggle defuses it. Moreover the mediation process, by its nature, helps to offset the seeming inequality between parent and child. The youth is treated as an equal. As mediator, you accord each participant the same kind of respect, listen with the same seriousness to their concerns, pay equal attention to their expressed needs and hopes. The youth is made an active partner in solving the family's conflict.[1]

Roughly similar steps are followed by most parent-child mediation programs. Following an intake and orientation session that prepares the family, a mediation is

1. ibid. pg. 119.

scheduled. There are usually several distinct stages in a mediation session. First, the entire family is together, then a series of separate meetings between individual family members and the mediators follow. Finally, the family meets as a unit to finalize the agreement. Most programs follow up the mediation by making referrals to appropriate family service agencies and subsequently check on how the agreement is going.

The parent-child mediation process involves five phases: setting the stage, defining the issues, processing the issues, resolving the issues, and making the agreement. These five phases are similar to the phases in the generic mediation model noted in Chapter 2. Table 6.1 presents the relationship between these phases and various stages in the mediation process.

Table 6.1
Parent Child Mediation Phases and Stages

Phases	Stages
Setting the Stage	I. Preparations
	II. Initial Joint Session a. Opening remarks by mediators
Defining the Issues	b. Storytelling by family members
	III. Mediator Recess IV. Initial Private Sessions
Processing the Issues	V. Later Private Sessions and Mediator Recesses
Resolving the Issues	VI. Final Private Sessions and Mediatior Recesses
Making the Agreement	VII. Concluding Joint Session
	VIII. Post-Hearing

Source: Zetzel and Wixted, 1984.

In many programs, mediators spend two or more hours working with the family prior to the mediation session. Some programs have only one planned mediation session, usually a long one; other programs may have two to five mediation sessions per case. The average length of a mediation session can range from two to three and a half hours. Many programs routinely use a pair of co-mediators; some use a single mediator. The Children's Hearings Project (CHP) model is presented here because of its influence upon the development of the field of parent-child mediation. The CHP shares a growing belief with many juvenile justice and child welfare advocates that family conflict can be handled more appropriately outside a formal court. Mediation has become an effective alternative in cases involving children in need of services (CHINS), such as truancy, running away from home, or behavior considered beyond the parents' control, cases that otherwise would have appeared before the juvenile court. Cases are usually referred by the court or the social service system. Schools may also refer cases to parent-child mediation in an attempt to intervene before the case even enters the juvenile justice system.

Community volunteers are trained as mediators to serve in pairs. One mediation session, lasting approximately four hours, is usually planned. Sessions are held at a convenient site in the community, in the evenings, to make them more accessible. In addition to the child and the parent(s), other parties such as a social worker or school official are at times also present.

Throughout the mediation process, the child and parent(s) are given an equal voice in expressing their concerns and interests while working toward resolution of the conflict. The adversarial atmosphere of the court is totally absent; the parties are encouraged to express their feelings and needs openly in the less formal, more relaxed setting.

A case coordinator, who is a professional staff person, is responsible for initial case development, which includes the intake and orientation of family members. The case is then assigned to a pair of mediators. There are eight distinct stages in the mediation process used by the Children's Hearings Project.

Stage I. Preparations

The primary tasks of the mediators during this stage are scheduling and taking care of some preliminaries before mediation. The mediators give the staff a schedule of available days and times for mediation. The case coordinator then talks with the family about a suitable date. A week may go by between the time the volunteers are asked to do the mediation and when the date is set. Mediators are informed of the name of the family, the time and place of the mediation, and the name of the case coordinator. If the volunteer mediators know the family, they disqualify themselves for the mediation.

The mediators arrive on-site thirty minutes before the mediation to get acquainted with each other, review the general circumstances of the case, and check over the room and arrange seating. If they have not handled a case together before, they decide on how to divide up responsibilities during the mediation session.

Stage II. Initial Joint Session

Opening remarks by the mediator set the tone for the meeting, clarify the roles and expectations of all present, and outline the process. They first describe how mediation works by emphasizing how it differs from juvenile court or public social services. It is a voluntary alternative to the court, and family members have agreed to develop their own solution to the problem they face. The role of the mediators, trained volunteers from the community is then reviewed. It is emphasized that, as mediators, they are not going to be making any decisions for the family nor making judgments about who is right or wrong. Rather, they will assist the family members in constructing an agreement that all parties believe is fair and workable. After pointing out that everything said in the meeting is confidential and that notes will be immediately destroyed, the mediators describe the mediation process.

In the second part of Stage II, the family members present their versions of what is happening. This stage focuses upon the tasks of fact-finding, trust building, and observing how family members communicate with one another. A mediator asks each person to describe the situation to the mediators from his or her perspective, without interruption. The parties are directed to tell the mediator, rather than to speak directly to the other family members. This technique of controlling communication by preventing the parties initially from speaking directly to one another is not embraced by all mediators and programs but is used routinely in the Children's Hearing Project and related programs. During this sharing of stories, the mediators are trying to create an atmosphere of respect and openness, in which the parties begin to identify what they would like to see happen.

The joint session ends when the mediators have obtained a basic understanding of the conflict, based on the statements by all parties. It may also be ended if one party is clearly dominating the conversation. Prior to closure, the mediators inform the family members that they, the mediators, need now to take a break to review some of what they have learned. While the parties wait for private sessions with the mediators, they are to continue thinking about specific things that could change in order to manage the conflict more effectively.

Stage III. Mediator Recess

During the recess stage, the mediators review the notes taken during the joint session to ascertain just what they had learned about the family and their perspectives on the dispute. Any factual discrepancies in the parties' accounts are discussed and potential areas of common interest are identified. They will develop a working strategy that may include identifying the issues that seem most likely to be resolved through mediation. The mediators decide the order in which to meet individual family members and which mediator should take the lead, decisions that can change, depending on topics or family member.

Stage IV. Initial Private Sessions

During the private sessions with each family member, the mediators point out that everything that is said is held in confidence. By asking open-ended questions in a nonjudgmental manner, they probe to identify the most important concerns and underlying interests of each party, while avoiding counseling or advice giving. The family member is encouraged to continue thinking about the issues, needs, and interests that are important to him or her, and to identify potential changes that could help resolve the conflict. The mediators try to show optimism about the progress being made. They check to see if any of the information can be shared with the other parties.

Prior to meeting individually with the other family members, the mediators take a break among themselves to further review and discuss the case, and make any necessary changes in strategy.

Stage V. Later Private Sessions and Mediator Recesses

This stage allows for additional private sessions during which further information can be gathered, expressed concerns can be clarified, negotiable issues emerge, and movement can be made toward eventual resolution. During these sessions, allowable information can be transmitted between the parties. This type of shuttle diplomacy by the mediators is an integral part of the Children's Hearings Project mediation model. Reality testing of the various positions held by family members may occur. Issues to be negotiated for resolution are narrowed and often reframed in a manner that addresses the interests of all parties.

For some cases, Stage V might mean only one additional private session with each party; in other cases, multiple additional private sessions. After all of the issues and concerns have been clarified and a potential agreement constructed, a final joint session with the parent(s) and child is conducted.

Stage VI. Final Private Sessions and Mediator Recesses

Working out the details of the agreement is the focus of this stage, assuming one has been reached. Through additional individual sessions, the mediators actively work with the parties in constructing the final terms of the agreement. When necessary, the mediators will recess to review the case further with each other, without the parties being present.

Phase VII. Concluding Joint Session

To conclude the mediation process, the mediators bring the child and parent(s) together in a joint session. The agreement developed with the parties during individual sessions is read in the presence of all the family members. It is then signed and a copy is given to each person. The parent-child mediation session ends with the mediators thanking the parties for the work they have done in resolving their conflict.

Phase VIII. Post-Hearing

After the family members leave, the mediators review the process and its outcome. Particular attention is given to what seemed to be the most critical point in the mediation and how it may have contributed to the final outcome. The debriefing of the mediators is conducted by the staff member who served as the case coordinator.

What We Have Learned from Research

In an evaluation of the Children's Aid Society's PINS Mediation Project in New York City[1] the investigators

1. Morris, 1983.

found that the vast majority of children and parents were very satisfied with the process and outcome. Written agreements were reached in 73 percent of the cases, and 77 percent of the families reported either moderate or high success had been achieved. They cited such factors as the child now was more manageable, the presenting problem was resolved, or the child had not returned to juvenile court within eight months following mediation. However, data were not available to compare the results of mediation to some other form of intervention, or to no intervention.

In an evaluation of the Children's Hearings Project,[1] it was found that the most common issues addressed in parent-child mediation process revolved around truancy, chores, curfews, and the child's social life. About 66 percent of the families in this parent-child mediation program were single-parent households from working-class neighborhoods. Nearly 60 percent of the adolescent participants were girls, with a mean age of 14. A profile of a typical family would be a woman in her thirties, with a clerical job, who is a single parent and had her middle or younger child living with her.

The average meeting length was three hours and twenty minutes, with only thirty-five minutes of this being in a joint session with all family members present. A single mediation session was the most common, although 26 percent of the cases had two sessions. Of the cases referred to mediation, 48 percent were actually mediated; others chose not to participate, despite referral by the court. Eighty-four percent of the families in mediation reached an agreement.

1. Merry & Rocheleau 1985.

Nearly two-thirds of family members in mediation indicated that the mediated agreement helped with overall management of the conflict and that it was being abided by, in full or part. A high level (83 percent) of satisfaction with their experience was declared by participants. Nine in ten respondents indicated that the mediation process was a good or partly good idea. Nearly half of the family members in mediation said it was easier to talk with one another after the session; 41 percent indicated they learned something new about the others' feelings; and 59 percent stated that they had a better understanding of the others' point of view.[1]

The Center for Dispute Settlement (CDS) at the District of Columbia's Mediation Service of the Citizen's Complaint Center wanted to ascertain whether mediation could have an impact on the prevention of child maltreatment. The CDS is a citywide service that has its office in the Superior Court building. The parent-child mediation program it chose to study serves primarily African American adolescent girls (mean age of 15) and their single mothers. This exploratory study (N=fifty client families), found a high degree of client satisfaction and self-reports of fewer family conflicts.[2] The average length of mediation sessions, including joint and separate sessions, was about two and one-half hours. The parents and children were interviewed at one week and again at two months after the mediation. Of the families in mediation, 87 percent reached an agreement, and 39 percent were referred to other social service agencies for additional assistance. The mediators indicated that 91 percent of the adolescents and all of the parents actively participated in the various phases

1. ibid. pg. 128.
2. Stahler et al., 1990.

of the mediation process. Satisfaction with the mediator's performance was indicated by 98 percent of the adolescents and 93 percent of the parents.

The process of mediating conflict between these parents and children appeared to reduce further family conflicts. One week after the mediation, the original problem was reported to have been solved by 62 percent of the parents and 68 percent of the adolescents, and at least partially solved by an additional 27 percent of the parents and 29 percent of the adolescents. Little change was reported when family members were interviewed two months later.

Mediation was perceived as either completely successful (78 percent of parents, 74 percent of adolescents) or partially successful (16 percent of parents, 21 percent of adolescents). Nine out of ten of all the family members would recommend mediation to a friend whose family was having similar problems.

Unresolved Issues

Several unresolved issues exist in the field of parent-child mediation, such as the targeting of appropriate families, power imbalance, emphasis on separate sessions, and specific versus underlying problem focus. As more parent-child mediation programs are developed in communities throughout North America and Europe, these and other emerging issues will need study.

Targeting of Appropriate Families

The process of mediating conflict between parents and their children is not appropriate for all families. For families with multiple problems, including physical abuse, the process may even be harmful by masking the need for different and more intense interventions. Participating in parent-child mediation and reaching an agreement could give the appearance of peace, but because of the nature of the family system, the reality of conflict and violence would continue.

It is unknown to what extent parent-child mediation is appropriate in the context of different ethnic cultures. Mediation may be a direct threat to the traditional cultural values of many immigrants, such as those from Asian or Islamic traditions.

Power Imbalance

The major imbalance of power that is present in the relationship between all parents and children is likely to continue to be difficult to address. The role of parenting requires such an imbalance. When conflict emerges between parents and children, parents will most often rely upon the position of power that is intrinsic to their role. As conflicts escalate and become increasingly dysfunctional, attempting to resolve them through the exercise of parental power becomes less and less effective.

For a parent-child mediation session to succeed, equal participation in the mediation process is critical. The mediator must help the child trust the process so that he or she will be straightforward in expressing needs. If the mediator fails to address the power imbalance, the child could feel further disempowered, and the process might break down.

Emphasis on Separate Sessions

The process of mediation used by most programs focusing on parent-child conflict consists of joint and separate meetings. However, in practice, the mediator spends far more time in separate meetings than in joint sessions. A relatively brief joint session is held in the beginning to start the process and at the end to formalize and sign the agreement that was negotiated indirectly through separate meetings. The rationale for this focus is that there is often such intense hostility between parents and children that separate sessions with a shuttle-diplomacy style of relaying messages is required.

The shuttle-diplomacy style mediation, which places the mediator in a very active, if not controlling, position, raises a serious question about what is being modeled to the family members. Family members are not coached or encouraged to speak for themselves in negotiating directly with one another. The opportunity to model and use a valuable conflict-resolution process is lost, and there may be less likelihood that such communications will take place when no mediator is present. The process models family reliance on external expertise rather than empowering family members to negotiate directly.

Specific versus Underlying Problems Focus

Many parent-child mediators have a tendency to focus solely on the immediate issue that led to the conflict, such as the child's being truant or hanging around with the wrong kind of friends. By concentrating on specific behaviors rather than on the underlying interests and needs of all the family members, the mediator may miss a wonderful opportunity to assist the parties in developing a broader understanding of one another. For example, the underlying interest of parents in conflict with their children often is their love reflected in a concern for the children's safety and development. Sometimes children are unaware of the love and of its expression in concern. Negotiating an agreement to prevent further truancy may resolve an immediate problem but does little to ensure that the child will come to understand parental motivation. Similarly, the underlying interest of rebelling adolescents is usually related to their need for space, for independence. It would probably be good for parents to hear this need expressed. They might be able to adjust their parenting style to respond to it, even though in the current conflict their focus may be on establishing clear boundaries.

As the practice of parent-child mediation has developed over recent years, some observers argue that it should be more closely linked with other institutions, such as schools and neighborhood agencies. Currently, it is tied to only the formal juvenile justice system, and by the time cases have been referred to mediation by the courts, family conflict has already escalated considerably. In contrast, if services could be delivered upon receiving referrals from schools and community-based agencies, mediation might have a greater impact on preventing escalation of family conflict. Many advocates of parent-child mediation also suggest that services need to be more aligned with diverse communities and neighborhoods. They believe that trained volunteer mediators from those communities must be used; mediation should not become a process of pushing white middle-class values upon families from minority cultures.

SUMMARY

Parent-child mediation was pioneered in the early 1980s with the intention of diverting status offenders from the juvenile justice system by having them participate in mediation with their parents. Mediation offers an earlier option, before juvenile court intervention is required, to de-escalate the cycle of dysfunctional conflicts between parent and child that may lead to negative relationships and delinquent behaviors. There are two conditions necessary for successful parent-child mediation: (1) a desire to resolve the conflict and preserve the relationship, and (2) the relatively equal participation of family members in the process.

The parent-child mediation process involves five phases: (1) setting the stage, (2) defining the issues, (3) processing the issues, (4) resolving the issues, and (5) making the agreement. Family members meet separately with the mediators except during the first and last phases.

Research on parent-child mediation has been limited, but findings appear to be positive: most participants are satisfied with the process and results of the mediation, and parents and children report a better understanding of the others' points of view. Major issues of concern include the targeting of appropriate families; power imbalance between parent and child; emphasis on separate sessions for much of the mediation process; and specific versus underlying problem focus.

7
VICTIM-OFFENDER MEDIATION

Linda and Bob Jackson's house was broken into while they were visiting friends in another city. Their frustration, anger, and growing sense of vulnerability far exceeded the loss of their television set and stereo. Allan, the young burglar, was caught and entered a plea of guilty. When the Jacksons were invited to participate in a program that allowed them to meet their offender, they were eager to ask him questions, such as Why us? and Were you watching our movements? The mediation session provided some answers, gave Allan a sense of how violated the Jacksons felt, and allowed negotiation of a plan for Allan to pay them back. Nervous at first, Allan soon relaxed. Everyone treated him with respect, even though he had committed a crime, and he was able to make amends. The Jacksons felt less vulnerable and were able to sleep soundly. All parties were able to put the event behind them.

The concept of a crime victim sitting face-to-face with the perpetrator is difficult for many public officials and citizens to grasp. People who are unfamiliar with the actual process of victim-offender mediation frequently ask questions. Why would any victim want to meet the criminal? What's in it for the victim? Why would an offender be willing to meet his or her victim? What is there to mediate or negotiate anyway?

Despite these concerns, in a growing number of communities throughout North America and Europe, many hundreds of crime victims are meeting their offenders in the presence of trained mediators to tell them how the crimes affected the victims personally. They can get answers to lingering questions, such as Why me? and Were you watching my movements? Those who have committed certain types of criminal offenses are able to tell their stories, portray a more human dimension of their characters, own up to their behavior, and make amends. Together, both parties have the opportunity to negotiate a mutually agreeable restitution plan.

Only a handful of programs provided victim-offender mediation and reconciliation services in the late 1970s, nearly exclusively in the United States and Canada. Today there are approximately 125 such programs in the United States and nearly 30 in Canada.[1] Most are operated by private nonprofit correctional agencies working closely with the local courts. Some are sponsored directly by probation departments or state departments of corrections, as in Oklahoma. Nearly all work with nonviolent property offenses and minor assaults, with some programs processing a small number of more violent offenses.

An even larger number of programs operate in Europe, where the field began developing in the mid-1980s, largely based upon the Victim Offender Reconciliation Program (VORP) model in Canada and the United States, and is now growing more rapidly than in North America.

1. Fagan & Gehm, 1993; Hughes & Schneider, 1989.

England has established 18 programs; Germany, 25; France, 40; Belgium, 8; Norway, 54; and Finland, 20. Austria recently adopted a policy to promote the use of victim-offender mediation for young offenders nationally. Victim-offender mediation is no longer simply an experiment. Rather, it is an emerging field of alternative dispute resolution that continues to grow yet is little understood by many.

The victim-offender mediation movement has devloped in the United States out of at least two distinct traditions. Particularly during the mid to late 1970s, experimenters in each group appeared to have little awareness of the other and little information sharing went on.

The field of victim offender mediation in the United States is most often associated with the development in 1978 of the first Victim Offender Reconciliation Program (VORP), in Elkhart, Indiana.[1] This joint effort of the Mennonite Central Committee and the Prisoner and Community Together (PACT) organization was modeled after the initial VORP, in Kitchener, Ontario, that began in 1974. The VORP tradition remains the most clearly articulated and documented expression of victim-offender mediation and has greatly influenced the larger field, particularly private community-based agencies, including some church-related organizations.

Another tradition actually predates the VORPs. The initial attempts to bring crime victims and their young offenders face-to-face can be traced to the mid-1960s, when a small number of probation departments began to see the

1. Umbreit, 1985; Zehr, 1980.

value of such a confrontation. A total of thirty-four programs involving victim-offender mediation-in public criminal justice agencies, primarily probation departments-began between 1965 and 1979.[1] The language of mediation is largely absent from these programs because they began before other efforts in the field took shape. However, the actual process employed in these early years, although certainly not fitting a more technical definition of mediation, clearly approximates what we now understand to be victim-offender mediation.

Another early example is the Minnesota Restitution Center established in 1970 in Minneapolis by the Minnesota Department of Corrections.[2] The program diverted adult property offenders from prison and placed them in a residential center where they met with their victims to fashion restitution plans. Although this nationally recognized program did not frame what it was doing as mediation, the actual process was quite similar in many respects to what we now call victim-offender mediation.

Rationale for Victim-Offender Mediation

The criminal justice system focuses almost entirely upon the offender. It is dominated by a "trail 'em, nail 'em, and jail 'em" philosophy that often does little to meet the emotional and material needs of the actual victim. Crime victims are nearly always placed in a totally passive position by the criminal justice system, and have minimal direct participation in or influence upon the process of holding the offenders accountable. Oftentimes they don't receive even basic assistance or information about the cases.

1. Hughes & Schneider, 1989.
2. Hudson & Galaway, 1974.

Most victims feel powerless and vulnerable; some feel twice victimized, first by the offender and then by an uncaring criminal justice system that does not have time for them. Offenders rarely comprehend, much less confront the human dimension of their criminal behavior. They often fail to recognize that victims are real people, not just objects to be abused. Also, offenders have many rationalizations for their behaviors. It is not unusual for anger, frustration, and conflict to increase as the victim and offender move through the justice process.

Instead of continuing the frequent depersonalization of victims and offenders in the criminal and juvenile justice systems, the victim-offender mediation process draws upon restorative justice principles that recognize that crime is fundamentally against people, and not just against the state. Victim-offender mediation facilitates a very active and personal process to work at conflict resolution by emphasizing the importance of restoring emotional and material losses. The people most affected by the crime are allowed the opportunity to become actively involved in resolving the conflict, in the belief that holding offenders personally accountable for their behavior and achieving some closure for the victim is far more important than focusing on past criminal behavior through ever-increasing levels of costly punishment.[1] In contrast, the court system marginalizes the victim by relegating him or her to a passive role and requires of the offender little or no direct accountability to the person wronged. Further, the system reinforces an adversarial dynamic, and offers little emotional closure for the victim or offender. By far the

1. Umbreit, 1991a; Wright, 1991; Zehr, 1980.

most clear distinction between the old paradigm of retributive justice and the new paradigm of restorative justice has been developed by Howard Zehr (1990) (see Table 7.1).

Victim-Offender Mediation Process

As the most visible expression of restorative justice, the victim-offender mediation process can vary a great deal between programs in regard to referral source, diversion versus postadjudication referral, use of volunteer mediators, and so on. Still a basic case-management process tends to be present in most of the programs in the United States and Canada.[1] It comprises the four phases of mediation identified in the generic mediation model in Chapter 2: case referral and intake, preparation for mediation, conducting the mediation session, and follow-up.

Nearly all victim-offender mediation and reconciliation programs strive to provide a conflict-resolution process that is perceived as fair by the victim and the offender. The mediator(s) facilitates this process, by first allowing time to address informational and emotional needs, followed by a discussion of losses and the possibility of developing a mutually agreeable restitution obligation. Examples include payment for loss or damages, work done by the offender for the victim, or the victim's choice of a charity.

The process of mediating a victim-offender conflict begins when the offender, often convicted of such crimes as theft and burglary, is referred by the court. Most programs accept referrals after a formal admission of guilt has been

1. Umbreit, 1988.

Table 7.1
Old and New Paradigms of Justice

Old Paradigm	New Paradigm
1. Crime defined as violation of the state.	1. Crime defined as violation of one person by another.
2. Focus on establishing blame, on guilt, on past (did he/she do it?).	2. Focus on problem solving, on liabilities/obligations, on future (what should be done?).
3. Adversarial relationship and process are normative.	3. Dialogue and negotiation are normative.
4. Imposition of pain to punish and deter/prevent future crime.	4. Restitution as means of restoring both parties; goal of reconciliation/restoration.
5. Justice defined by intent and process: right rules.	5. Justice defined as right relationships; judged by outcome.
6. Interpersonal, conflictual nature of crime obscured, repressed; conflict seen as individual versus the state.	6. Crime recognized as interpersonal conflict; value of conflict is recognized.
7. One social injury replaced by another.	7. Focus on repair of social injury.
8. Community on sidelines, represented abstractly by state.	8. Community as facilitator in restorative process.
9. Encouragement of competitive, individualistic values.	9. Encouragement of mutuality.
10. Action directed from state to offender • victim ignored • offender passive	10. Victim and offender's roles recognized in problem/solution: • victim rights/needs recognized • offender encouraged to take responsibility
11. Offender accountability defined as taking punishment.	11. Offender accountability defined as understanding impact of action, and helping to decide how to make things right.
12. Offense defined in purely legal terms, devoid of moral, social, economic, political dimensions.	12. Offense understood in whole context--moral, social, economic, political.
13. "Debt" owed to state and society in the abstract.	13. Debt/liability to victim recognized.
14. Response focused on offender's past behavior.	14. Response focused on harmful consequences of offender's behavior.
15. Stigma of crime unremovable.	15. Stigma of crime removable through restorative action.
16. No encouragement for repentance and forgiveness.	16. Possibilities for repentance and forgiveness.
17. Dependence upon proxy professionals.	17. Direct involvement by participants.

Source: Howard Zehr, <u>Retributive Justice, Restorative Justice</u> (1985). Reprinted with the permission of the Mennonite Central Committee, Akron, PA.

entered with the court. Some programs accept cases that are referred prior to formal admission of guilt, as part of a deferred prosecution effort. Each case is assigned to either a staff or volunteer mediator. During the second phase, preparation for mediation, the mediator(s) meets with the offender and victim separately before the mediation session is scheduled. During these individual sessions, the mediator(s) listen to the story of each party, explain the program, and encourage participation. Usually mediator(s) meet first with the offender, and if he or she is willing to proceed with mediation, then with the victim.

Program advocates emphasize that the victim should not be victimized again by the mediation program, even unintentionally, stressing that he or she should never be coerced into participating; however; mediators do encourage the victim to consider participation. Many programs have found that it is the presentation of choices, including the choice of participation, that leads to a sense of empowerment among victims and offenders.

The preliminary separate meetings with the victim and offender require effective listening and communication skills. Victim participation can be lost at the first phone call. Experienced mediators have found that initially building rapport and trust with the victim and offender, and gaining valuable information through the separate meetings, are essential to the quality of the later joint meeting with both individuals.

Much of the literature in the field implies that offenders voluntarily participate in the mediation process; in practice this is not always the case. When offenders are ordered by the court through probation, or are diverted from prosecution if they complete the program, a rather significant amount of state coercion is exercised. In such circumstances, research indicates that offenders may not perceive the process as voluntary. To deal with this perception, many programs seek referrals in the least coercive manner and allow offenders strongly opposed to mediation, or who are deemed inappropriate for mediation by the program staff, to opt "out" of the program.

If both parties during the initial separate meetings agree to mediation, the mediator(s) arrange a face-to-face meeting. The mediation session between the involved parties is conducted during the third phase. This phase requires the completion of six tasks, slight variations of the six tasks of the mediation phase in the generic model presented in Chapter 2:

1. Introductory opening statement by mediator
2. Storytelling by victim and offender
3. Clarification of facts and sharing of feelings
4. Reviewing victim losses and options for compensation
5. Developing a written restitution agreement
6. Closing statement by mediator

The mediator's opening remarks at the mediation session typically include the following:

- Introductions and seating arrangements.
- Explanation of mediator's role: "To help both of you to talk about what happened and to work out a restitution agreement, if possible. I am not a

court official and will not be requiring you to agree to anything, nor will I be taking sides with either of you."

- Explanation of ground rules: "No interrupting of each other."
- Identification of the agenda: (1) review facts and feelings related to the crime, (2) discuss losses and negotiate restitution.
- Emphasis on sense of equity: "Any restitution agreement that is reached must feel fair to both of you."
- Initiation of direct communication between victim and offender, who are facing each other:
  "_____[victim], could you tell _____[offender] what happened from your perspective and how you felt about the burglary."

After the opening statement by the mediator(s), each party has uninterrupted time to tell his or her story. Usually the victim precedes the offender.

The first part of the session constitutes a discussion of the facts and feelings related to the crime. The victim is given the rare opportunity to express his or her feelings directly to the offender and to receive answers to many lingering questions, such as Why me? How did you get into my house? Were you stalking me and planning on coming back? It is often a relief finally to see the offender, who usually bears little resemblance to the frightening character who may have been conjured up.

The offender is in the very uncomfortable position of having to face the person violated. He or she is given the equally rare opportunity to display a more human dimension and even to express remorse in a very personal fashion. Through open discussion of feelings, victim and offender can deal with each other as people, oftentimes from the same neighborhood, rather than as stereotypes and objects.

The second part of the session focuses on discussion of losses and negotiation of a mutually acceptable restitution agreement as a tangible symbol of conflict resolution and a focal point for accountability. If victim and offender are unable to come to terms on the amount or form of restitution, the case is sent back to the referral source, usually the sentencing judge or prosecutor, with a good likelihood that the offender will be placed in a different program. Mediators do not impose a restitution settlement. In many programs, however, about 95 percent of all mediations end with a written restitution agreement negotiated and signed by the victim, offender, and mediator. Joint victim-offender meetings usually last about one hour, with some in the two-hour range.

The application of mediation techniques to victim-offender conflict involving property crimes and minor assaults is both similar to and different from more traditional mediation programs. It is clearly a rather unusual application. Even so, it is not contrary to the basic definition and criteria related to mediation. Nearly all other applications of mediation are among individuals with some type of prior situational or interpersonal relationship (landlord and tenant, spouses, employer and employee, farmer and creditor, and the like). In the context of victim-offender conflict most, but not all, participants in mediation are strangers. The issues related to the conflict are clearer.

There is an obvious victim and a perpetrator who has admitted guilt. Determination of guilt is not the purpose of the mediation process, which is a time-limited problem-solving intervention. It promotes a more restorative sense of justice through dialogue and mutual aid, including negotiation of restitution by the victim and offender themselves.

The inequality in power is a major concern to most mediators. Precisely because there is a delineated victim and offender, an enormous situational imbalance of power tends to exist. It would be inappropriate to assume that both parties are contributing to the conflict, which would impose the need for more neutral terminology, such as "disputants." One of the individuals has been violated, and hence special attention must be directed toward the victim to ensure that he or she is not revictimized by the mediation process. The sensitivity to the victim does not have to come at the cost of being insensitive to the offender or violating the very process of mediation through an impartial third party. It does, however, mean that the victim must have absolute voluntary choice about participation in the program. The time and location of the mediation session must not violate his or her sense of what is safe, appropriate, and convenient.

Applying the mediation process with strangers may be considered by some to be quite difficult. Experience in the field of victim-offender mediation suggests the contrary. Far less emotional and historical baggage is present. During the mediation process, the prominent dynamic is one of breaking down stereotypes and related fears rather than having to address issues of betrayal and mistrust that are rooted in highly charged emotions and/or lengthy relationships.

In mediating victim-offender conflict, there is usually a generational imbalance of power. The offender is frequently a juvenile or young adult and the victim is an adult. When the offender is inarticulate, it is important to prepare, even coach, the offender during the prior individual meeting. This type of coaching is more like informal role playing than directing the individual on what to say in response to specific questions the victim might ask.

The opportunity to think through some of the possible questions and express their thoughts in a less threatening situation is important for many offenders. They are then likely to be more prepared to interact fruitfully with the victim during the mediation session. This represents one strategy for attempting to even out power in the presence of age and communication differences. Sometimes this same dynamic is present when the victim is also a young person.

Victim-offender mediation differs from more traditional applications of mediation in terms of political ideology as well. Americans have strong feelings about crime and punishment, often resulting from media coverage of the most atrocious, and least representative, crimes and from politicians' rhetoric. We are an exceptionally punitive society, having recently surpassed even the former Soviet Union and South Africa in per capita rate of incarceration.

Alternative dispute resolution within the context of civil court conflict may still be controversial to some. It does not, however, confront major ideological barriers related to crime-control policy in American society. The moment mediation enters the criminal justice process, it has stepped over a powerful ideological threshold.

There is growing evidence among criminal justice officials and participants in victim-offender mediation that it can be quite consistent with the community's sense of justice and fairness. Yet, there is likely to remain strong resistance by some officials and citizens to the very notion of the restorative type of justice embodied in the victim-offender mediation process. The more dominant retributive sense of justice with its emphasis on the severity of punishment, on behalf of state interests, even at the cost of addressing the direct interests of the person violated by the offense, is deeply rooted in contemporary American culture. It is unlikely to be dramatically changed in the near future.

Working with Crimes of Severe Violence

Early one morning in August 1983, Stephen Molhan was driving home after a date with his girlfriend. At a stoplight in downtown Providence, Rhode Island, he was approached by a man who had already assaulted two other men in the area. Stephen was shot in the head, robbed, and left to die. Shortly after Stephen's death, his mother, Suzanne Molhan, founded Family and Friends of Murdered Victims in order to offer support to persons like her in Rhode Island. Nearly nine years later, she confronted her son's killer in a high-security prison, after ten months of preparation by an experienced mediator. Molhan found the victim-offender mediation process to be a pivotal moment in her long journey of grieving and her search for closure. Although recognizing that

such a meeting is not for all victims, she needed to
let the man who killed her son know the devastating
effect the crime had on her life, and to get answers
to many questions.

Suzanne Molhan is but one of a small but growing number of victims of extremely violent crime who, in the journey of grieving, have found direct confrontation with the person who hurt them to be an important step in their own healing. Another example is Gary Smith, a schoolteacher in New York City, who was brutally beaten with a baseball bat by a youth and not expected to live. He did live and decided to meet his attacker. Gary, who lost sight in one eye because of the attack, needed answers to many questions and wanted to let the youth know about how the brutal assault had affected him.

The need for closure through direct contact with the offender is also seen in a case involving a woman who was raped seven years ago in Wisconsin and who decided to meet face-to-face, in prison, with the man who assaulted her. She asserted that the experience of directly confronting the source of terror in her life and letting him know how deeply he had hurt her was helpful. She felt less fearful and more able to let go of the terror she had undergone.

Although not usually a replacement for some form of incarceration in severely violent crimes, victim-offender mediation appears to be effective for some, but clearly not all, victims of violence. These face-to-face meetings, in the presence of a highly trained mediator, are one more option that is available to some victims, along with many other important services. Mediators who work with severely violent cases emphasize that choice, rather than coercion, is the key principle, along with providing a safe setting and a highly competent and sensitive mediator. Experience with these cases has shown that understanding the grieving process, being comfortable with his or her own issues of death and dying, and being knowledgeable about post-traumatic stress are qualities as important for the mediator as the ability to apply the technical skills of mediation.

Bringing the victim of violent crime together with the perpetrator and a mediator is done in only a relatively small number of cases and usually at the request of the victim or a surviving family member. It requires a lengthy period of preparation for both parties and coordination of the mediation with other counseling services that are likely to be involved. In the case of Suzanne Molhan, the mediator did not proceed with the full preparation process until first being assured by her therapist that mediation would in no way interfere with the longer-term therapeutic process. In fact, it was the therapist who quickly recognized the important role that the mediation session could play in moving her to a greater sense of closure and facilitating her work in therapy.

During the actual mediation session, which lasted approximately two and one-half hours, including a break period, Suzanne's therapist was present in a passive support role, and a chaplain who had been working with the offender was also present in a passive support role. Neither spoke during the mediation session, yet their presence was important in the overall process of mediation.

Characteristics of Cases

Mediation in cases of murder and other severely violent offenses has a number of distinguishing characteristics. These include

- Emotional intensity;
- Extreme need for nonjudgmental attitude;
- Longer case preparation by mediator (six to eighteen months);
- Multiple separate meetings prior to joint session;
- Multiple phone conversations;
- Negotiation with correctional officials to secure access to inmate and to conduct mediation in prison;
- Coaching of participants in the communication of intense feelings; and
- Boundary clarification (mediation versus therapy).

Implications for Advanced Training

The field is only beginning to come to grips with how the basic mediation model must be adapted to serve the more intense needs of parties involved in serious and violent criminal conflict. Far more extensive training of mediators is required, as is an entire new generation of written and audio-visual training resources. For example, mediators will need special knowledge and skills related to working with severely violent crimes, in addition to the normal mediation skills. Advanced training would focus less on the mechanics of negotiation and mediation and more on an experiential understanding of the painful journey of the participants. Such training would deal with the process of facilitating a direct and frank dialogue between the parties related, for example, to a murder that occurred, the journey of grief being experienced by surviving family members, and the possibilities for closure and healing through a process of mutual aid.

Special Knowledge Required

From a victim perspective, it is important for the mediator to have the following:

- Understanding of the victimization experience and phases
- Dealing with grief and loss (our own and others)
- Understanding post-traumatic stress and its impact
- Ability to collaborate with psychotherapists

From an offender perspective, mediators need the following:

- Understanding of the criminal-justice and corrections system
- Understanding of the offender and prisoner experience
- Ability to relate to offenders convicted of heinous crimes in a nonjudgmental manner
- Ability to negotiate with high-level correctional officials to gain access to the offender

Mediator-Assisted Dialogue and Mutual Aid

The process of mediation in cases involving survivors of murdered victims and the offender, as well as other severely violent crimes, should be reconceptualized. It is less mediation in the traditional sense of negotiating a settlement between disputants and more a process of facilitating a dialogue between a person who has been traumatized and the person responsible for that pain. Far more than the mechanics of mediation is required.

Mediation in cases involving the most traumatic experiences one can imagine is ultimately a spiritual journey, an opening of the heart, a process in which the involved parties help each other heal. Perhaps the most appropriate reframing of the mediation intervention in such cases is that of "mediator-assisted dialogue and mutual aid." Through extensive preparation and coaching of the parties prior to the mediation session, the mediator can tap into the reservoir of strengths in the victim and offender, despite their pain; employ a very nondirective style of mediation that emphasizes direct dialogue between the parties; and facilitate a healing process grounded in the parties' helping each other through responding to important emotional and informational needs.

The Paradox of Forgiveness

It is particularly important to understand the paradox of forgiveness in severly violent, as well as many other criminal offenses. The more the concepts of forgiveness and reconciliation are mentioned to the parties prior to mediation, or in promoting the program, the more likely that fewer victims will participate in the process. For individual victims, the use of terms like <u>forgiveness</u> and <u>reconciliation</u> is highly judgmental and preachy, suggesting a devaluing of the legitimate anger and rage the victims may be feeling at that point. For victim advocates, the use of these terms often triggers a great deal of resistance and anger. On the other hand, if more safe and less judgmental language is used while encouraging victims to participate and if appropriate premediation casework is completed, it is very likely that elements of forgiveness and even reconciliation will emerge spontaneously, with no need for manipulation by the mediator, such as directing the parties to shake hands after the mediation.

Although forgiveness and reconciliation represent a powerful potential outcome of the process of mediator-assisted dialogue and mutual aid between crime victims and offenders, they must emerge in a natural and genuine manner that has meaning to the involved parties. Therein lies the paradox: the more one talks about forgiveness and reconciliation while encouraging parties to participate, the less likely it is that victims will participate and have the opportunity to experience elements of forgiveness and reconciliation.

For some victims of severe violence, offering forgiveness to the offender is an important and powerful act of inner spiritual strength, of letting go, regardless of the impact on the offender. For other victims, offering forgiveness is neither important nor even possible. In all cases, there should be no pressure by the mediator, however subtle and well intended, to elicit forgiveness. The power of remorse and forgiveness as the ultimate expression of mutual aid and closure must be allowed to emerge spontaneously. In addition, for all involved it may be helpful to understand forgiveness as a journey involving numerous elements and steps, rather than a onetime "all-or-nothing" event.

Cultural Traditions

The application of mediation in murder cases and other severely violent cases is contrary to the dominant definition of mediation in Western societies with their settlement-driven fixation. For mediation to be effective in such cases, we need to draw upon the richness and wisdom of other cultural traditions that more naturally embrace the principles of restorative justice. The Native model of mediation developed by tribal leaders in British Columbia (Appendix 4) is particularly helpful. It represents a nonlinear model of mediation based upon spirituality, connectedness between all participants, the importance of premediation sessions, frequent use of silence, and an opening of the heart. The model is not settlement driven; rather, it is driven by a search for social harmony through the encouragement of spirituality, self-esteem, and collective identity.

What We Have Learned from Research

A small but growing amount of research in the field of victim-offender mediation provides increasing insight into how the process works and the impact it is having on its participants and the larger justice system.[1] The most essential findings that have emerged from a variety of studies, primarily in the United States but also in Canada and Europe, are summarized in the following points:

1. Victims of property crime are quite willing to participate in a mediation session with their

---

1. Coates & Gehm, 1989; Dignan, 1990; Galaway, 1988, 1989; Gustafson & Smidstra, 1989; Marshall & Merry, 1990; Umbreit, 1986a, 1988, 1989a, 1991b, 1993a, 1993b, 1994; Umbreit & Coates, 1992, 1993; Wright & Galaway, 1989.

offenders when given the opportunity.[1]

2. Mediation is perceived to be voluntary by the vast majority of victims and juvenile offenders who have participated in it.[2]

3. Victim-offender mediation yields very high levels of satisfaction with the mediation process and perceptions of its fairness for both victims and offenders.[3]

4. Although the possibility of receiving restitution appears to motivate victims to enter the mediation process, following their participation they indicate that meeting the offenders and being able to talk about what happened was more satisfying than receiving restitution.[4]

5. Offenders involved in mediation programs in four states indicated that although anxious about a confrontation with the victim, meeting the victim and being able to talk about what happened was the most satisfying aspect of the program.[5]

6. The victim-offender mediation process has a strong effect in humanizing the justice system's response to crime for both victims and juvenile offenders.[6]

7. Victim-offender mediation makes a significant contribution to reducing fear and anxiety among victims of juvenile crime.[7]

1. Coates & Gehm, 1989; Gehm, 1991; Galaway, 1988; Marshall & Merry, 1990; Umbreit, 1991c, 1994.
2. Umbreit, 1994.
3. Coates & Gehm, 1989; Dignan, 1990; Marshall & Merry, 1990; Umbreit, 1988, 1991b, 1993b.
4. Coates & Gehm, 1989; Umbreit, 1988, 1991b, Umbreit & Coates, 1992.
5. Umbreit, 1994.
6. Coates & Gehm, 1989; Marshall & Merry, 1990; Umbreit & Coates, 1993.
7. Umbreit & Coates, 1993.

8. Victims of crime who participate in mediation are far more likely to experience the justice system as fair than similar victims who do not participate in mediation.[1]

9. Juvenile offenders seem not to perceive victim offender mediation to be a significantly less demanding response to their criminal behavior than other options available to the court. The use of mediation is consistent with the concern to hold young offenders accountable for their criminal behavior.[2]

10. About 40--60 percent of cases referred to programs end up in a face-to-face mediation session.[3]

11. Restitution agreements that are perceived as fair to both parties are negotiated in nine out of ten cases that enter mediation in many programs.[4]

12. A number of programs reported successful completion of restitution agreements in the range of 79--98 percent.[5]

13. Considerably fewer and less-serious additional crimes were committed within a one-year period by juvenile offenders in victim-offender mediation programs in three states of the United States, when compared to similar offenders who did not participate in mediation.[6] Consistent

1. Umbreit, 1994.
2. ibid.
3. Coates & Gehm, 1989; Galaway, 1988, 1989; Gehm, 1991; Marshall & Merry, 1990; Umbreit, 1988, 1991b, 1993b, 1994.
4. Umbreit, 1994.
5. Coates & Gehm, 1989; Galaway, 1988, 1989; Gehm, 1990; Umbreit, 1986a, 1988, 1991b, 1994, Umbreit & Coates, 1992.
6. Umbreit, 1994; Umbreit & Coates, 1993.

with two recent English studies[1], this important finding, however, is not statistically significant because of the size of program samples.

14. Victim-offender mediation had a significant impact on the likelihood of offenders' successfully completing restitution obligations when compared to similar offenders who completed restitution in a court administered program without mediation.[2]

15. There is some evidence that a larger portion of victims of violent crime than initially believed would be interested in confronting their offenders in a mediation process.[3]

UNRESOLVED ISSUES

As the field of victim-offender mediation continues to develop in North America and Europe, it faces four major dangers: (1) loss of vision and values, (2) elimination of premediation sessions, (3) failure to use mediation programs, and (4) increasing social controls.

Loss of Vision and Values

The possible loss of the underlying vision of restorative justice is perhaps the greatest danger facing this relatively young justice-reform movement. Similar to other reform efforts, victim-offender mediation programs inevitably become preoccupied with securing more stable funding sources and developing more routine day-to-day operating procedures. As these programs become more

1. Marshall & Merry, 1990; Dignan, 1990.
2. Umbreit & Coates, 1993; Umbreit, 1994.
3. Gustafson & Smidstra, 1989; Umbreit, 1986b, 1989b.

established and bureaucratic, it becomes increasingly easy to lose sight of the underlying values and principles that motivated their founders and that serve as the basis of their existence. Providing opportunities for addressing the emotional issues surrounding crime and victimization, including the possibility of forgiveness and reconciliation, is a foundational principle of the field. To suggest that forgiveness and reconciliation may emerge spontaneously in some mediations is not to suggest that these principles be pushed upon the parties during their journey through the mediation process. Rather, if forgiveness and reconciliation occur, they must be genuine and expressed by the victim and offender without manipulation by the mediator. Losing sight of the restorative-justice vision could easily result in a utilitarian and exclusive focus on simply determining restitution and payment, allowing little time for the sharing of information and feelings related to the crime, which can lead to a greater sense of closure for both parties. Rather than a journey of the heart by means of mediator-assisted dialogue and mutual aid, the process could become driven by the need to reach a settlement in the most quick and "efficient" manner.

Elimination of Premediation Sessions

Experience with thousands of cases over the past decade has consistently indicated that one of the most important effects of the victim-offender mediation process is that of humanizing the justice system for victim and offender. Victims are able to receive help in dealing with their emotional, informational, and material needs while playing an active role in the process. Offenders learn of the real human impact of their actions and are given an opportunity to make things right with their victims.

The process of the mediator's contacting the victim and offender separately before the mediation session, through phone calls and usually a meeting, has proven to be essential to connecting, building trust and rapport with both parties and encouraging their involvement in the most nonintimidating and understandable way. In the haste to become more "efficient" and to process more cases, the field could succumb to the temptation to eliminate the important work that is required during the preparation for mediation phase. A number of programs have already moved in this direction; after all, "Why bother with talking and meeting with them before mediation. The case will require a rather simple settlement. It's much more efficient to schedule a night when they can come to our office for the mediation."

There certainly are some cases involving very minor offenses that may well not require separate meetings before mediation. On the other hand, by eliminating the separate meetings and contacts with the parties on a more routine basis, the program begins to take on the characteristics of the normal court system, which has little time to listen to victims and offenders or to respond to their needs. A focus on restitution agreements alone ignores the importance of the emotional and informational needs left in the wake of crime, which are central to a restorative justice perspective.

Failure to Use Mediation Programs
As programs continue to be preoccupied with becoming acceptable or institutionalized, there can be a

tremendous tendency to take fewer risks, particularly related to the type of cases referred to the program. Young programs typically want successful cases because they are attempting to build a broader base of public support for their work. In a program's eagerness to negotiate new referral arrangements and get enough cases to justify itself, it may be too quick to accept "garbage cases"--cases in which the prosecutor's office lacked sufficient evidence or would prefer to drop.

If victim-offender mediation becomes identified with primarily easy cases--those that the system would have done little with and that may have involved offenders who were unlikely ever to commit another crime--the field will not be taken seriously. It will remain on the margins of how justice is done within communities.

Increasing Social Control

Restorative justice and the victim-offender mediation field are deeply rooted in the idea of the mediation process as an alternative to the criminal justice system whenever possible. The VORP model of victim-offender mediation, the most well-developed and documented model, was initially linked to the "alternative-to-incarceration" movement during the late 1970s and early 1980s[1], although this has not been emphasized as much during recent years. Taking the easy cases, many of which would not even enter the formal criminal justice system, may push the field into the ranks of many other so-called alternatives that research has demonstrated have led to wider and stronger nets of social

1. Zehr & Umbreit, 1982.

control.[1] Despite intentions to the contrary, programs will increase rather than limit state intervention into the lives of individuals who violate the law, many of whom the system would not otherwise respond to because of the very minor nature of the offense. Instead of being an alternative to the system, these programs could result in additional sanctions for more offenders, with increasing overall cost to the justice system. It is important to avoid unnecessary and costly "net widening" for relatively minor offenses. It is equally important to realize that for many more serious offenses the mediation process is valid simply because it increases the quality of justice for the victim and offender, even if a term of incarceration is a part of the sentence for more serious, particularly violent, offenses.

SUMMARY

Victim-offender mediation has two distinct traditions. One, from the mid-1960s, began when a small number of probation departments saw value in a young offender's meeting face-to-face with his or her victim. The other, from the mid to late 1970s, began with the Victim Offender Reconciliation Program (VORP). The goal of victim-offender mediation is to draw upon restorative-justice principles that recognize that crime is fundamentally against people, and not just against the state. It works to allow the people most affected by the crime to be actively involved in resolving the conflict.

The victim-offender mediation process has four phases: (1) case referral and intake, (2) preparation for mediation, (3) the mediation session, and (4) follow-up. A

1. Austin & Krisberg, 1982; Dittenhoffer & Erickson, 1983.

major effort is made to provide a conflict-resolution process that is perceived as fair by the victim and the offender. Furthermore, efforts are also made to deal with the power imbalance because both parties are not contributing to the conflict, and therefore special care is given to address the victim's needs. Victim-offender mediation is also beginning to be used in a small but growing number of cases of extremely violent crimes, usually at the request of the victim(s) or a surviving family member.

Although research is still limited, several findings have emerged: victims and offenders feel the process is voluntary, fair, and more humanizing; victims may go to mediation for restitution, but find talking with the offender about what happened is more important; and completion of restitution agreements is reported in the range of 79--98 percent. Major issues of concern include (1) loss of vision and values, (2) elimination of premediation sessions, (3) failure to use mediation programs, and (4) increasing social controls rather than serving as an alternative.

8
INFORMAL MEDIATION OF STAFF CONFLICT IN HUMAN SERVICES

When Emily was hired, her new co-worker Rachel had asked her not to smoke in their shared office, and Emily was happy to comply. However, after a few weeks, Emily started smoking in the office whenever Rachel was out. This bothered Rachel, and she confronted Emily. Emily responded that she had forgotten and would try to do better, but kept on smoking when Rachel was out. Allergic to smoke, Rachel began having headaches and red irritated eyes, and hence complained to the supervisor, who also smoked. The supervisor suggested a meeting to set a smoking policy; however, this approach had been tried before without success and most of the agency workers smoked. Rachel was contemplating quitting, when a co-worker suggested she try mediation to resolve the problem. The co-worker had a friend who worked as a community mediator and would mediate the conflict. Rachel had her doubts but agreed to give mediation a try. Emily was also willing to try mediation, and so they met at the community mediation center. Listening to each other's concerns, with an impartial third party present, Rachel and Emily were able to work out a solution that was acceptable to both.

People who have chosen a career of service to others appear to be well prepared to confront conflict constructively and openly. Their choice indicates a commitment to the importance of understanding and enhancing human relationships. Most are trained in the basic skills of helping, such as building a sense of trust, empathy and warmth with their clients. Many have also received some level of training in communication skills and problem solving. With such commitment and training in human relationships, teachers, social workers, counselors, nurses, and other human services professions supposedly are considerably advanced and skillful in managing conflict that occurs among their co-workers. Reality is quite otherwise. Staff in human services agencies are often poorly equipped to deal with workplace conflict in a healthy manner. They are also likely to engage in highly dysfunctional organizational conflict that tends to overpersonalize disputes. The situation stands in marked contrast to the values of the human services professions, which emphasize clear communication, relationship building, and problem solving.

Informal mediation of staff conflict in human service organizations is a relatively recent development, and there is little academic or empirical research to draw upon. The considerable literature dealing with formal mediation processes, such as labor negotiations or civil lawsuits, is not applicable to the informal mediation process. Accordingly this chapter draws largely from the author's own mediation experiences.

Rationale for Workplace Mediation

The difficulty that many human services professionals face in applying conflict-resolution skills in a workplace setting is related to at least two factors. First, a heightened sensitivity to human relationships can often lead to a strong desire to accommodate others. The frequent use of accommodation as a conflict-management approach, however, is not conducive to healthy conflict resolution. Second, many human services professionals are attracted to their fields because of a desire to attend to their own emotional needs. Through gaining a better understanding of human relationships and psychosocial development, individuals may gain an important sense of self, power, and control. In helping others, they are contributing to their own growth. This is not problematic in many situations, but the presence of strong unmet personal needs among staff in an agency can trigger powerful dynamics. Precisely because of this emotional baggage, these workers may be gifted in helping others but inadequate in dealing with their problems and issues. When other personal agendas are being played out in the midst of staff conflict, effective conflict management is difficult to achieve.

The dominant response to conflict among staff within an agency is often passive-aggressive behavior. For example, rather than going directly to the person at whom he or she is angry a worker will complain to co-workers about the behavior and the person. The person, not the behavior, may then become the problem.

The use of mediation in labor negotiations, including a growing number of human services agencies, is well established and draws upon the rich heritage of the labor movement. It has also been periodically used in other macro applications, such as interdepartmental conflict or interagency conflict. However, mediation as a technique for responding to interpersonal conflict in the workplace is not a well-developed practice. To apply mediation in interpersonal conflict in the workplace, adjustments of the basic model are required. When addressing conflict with co-workers, a mediator type of function can often be quite useful, even though a true impartial neutral mediator is not available or involved.

Workplace Mediation Process

The four phases of the generic mediation model described in Chapter 2 apply to mediating co-worker conflict. A conflict would be referred to a mediator. The mediator would prepare for the face-to-face mediation session by collecting information from the disputants prior to conducting the session. Some type of follow-up to the mediation would occur.

The specific tasks of the mediation phase in the generic model are followed, and consist of

1. Introductory statement by mediator;
2. Storytelling by each disputant;
3. Identification of issues and interests;
4. Exploring options and problem solving;
5. Reaching agreement; and
6. Closing statement by mediator.

Several applications of the mediation concept within the context of conflict in human services agencies will be described to illustrate the potential of the intervention. These examples are based on actual conflicts that have occurred in agencies.

Impartial Staff Person as Mediator

Carol and Steve were both hired as teachers in a high school during the past year. Carol had previously worked at a middle school for five years. Prior to this job, Steve had worked for two years as a teacher's assistant. Steve had a playful personality and liked Carol. He would frequently tease her and refer to her as Barbie, as in Barbie doll, because she was cute and petite. At first, this did not bother Carol; she thought it was simply Steve's way of being nice to a co-worker.

After several months and many references to her as Barbie, Carol began feeling increasingly uncomfortable with Steve. She actually confronted him on several occasions and stated that she would prefer not to be called Barbie-her name was Carol. Steve's behavior did not stop. Her discomfort was leading to frustration and anger; no matter how many times she confronted Steve, his behavior simply did not change. He just didn't get it. It was almost as though the confrontations triggered what he apparently deemed a playful response, repeated references to her as Barbie.

Feeling increasingly victimized and harassed by Steve's behavior, Carol went to the principal and expressed her concerns. The principal suggested she talk to Steve about her concerns with the assistance of a mediator, mentioning a trained mediator who taught social studies and also performed volunteer community mediation services.

Maybe he would be willing to mediate the conflict. Carol thought that this sounded like a good way of dealing with the situation.

The teacher, Bill, said he would serve as a mediator and decided to meet with Carol and Steve individually before bringing them together-this was his preferred style. Through separate talks he could learn more about what happened and he would have an opportunity to build rapport and trust with both. Bill felt far more prepared for a mediation session when he had had some prior contact with the involved parties. He also thought it was more comfortable for the disputants.

Bill chose to meet first with Steve to ascertain if he felt okay about talking about the conflict in a mediation session. Steve wanted additional information about what mediation involved. He was particularly concerned about the likelihood of an imposed settlement. After learning that the mediator simply assisted the two parties in talking about what happened and in trying to negotiate a resolution, that the mediator had no decisionmaking power, Steve agreed to participate in a mediation session. He was confused, though, about why this had become such a major issue to Carol. From his perspective, he had been very friendly with Carol and liked her; he teased only women he liked; he certainly had no intention of harassing her or causing her emotional distress.

The mediation was scheduled several days later at a time that was convenient for Carol and Steve, in a classroom after school hours. They sat across from each other and Bill sat at the end of the table. Bill began by explaining his role as mediator, stating several ground rules and saying that both parties would be able to give their accounts of what had occurred, without interruptions. Afterward, they could ask each other questions or express any concerns they have. Finally, a variety of possible strategies for resolving the conflict would be identified and it was hoped, an agreement could be reached. Bill made it clear that what was said in the mediation session was confidential and would not be placed in personnel files or even reported to anyone else, except for whatever agreement was reached.

Bill asked Carol to tell Steve what had occurred from her perspective. She said his comments about her being Barbie did not bother her initially. She didn't like it, but it didn't seem to be a big deal. When it happened more frequently, she became frustrated and told Steve to stop calling her Barbie. When he continued to do so, she became infuriated. His behavior indicated no respect for her and she experienced an increasing sense of anger and victimization. Carol even stated that she was beginning to feel as though she was being sexually harassed.

Steve began his story by emphatically declaring that he had not intended to hurt her. He was just being playful; after all, that's the way guys are to girls. Carol should lighten up. It's not that big a deal. He certainly didn't understand this business about sexual harassment. He never touched Carol and was only being friendly. If she interpreted his behavior as sexual harassment, that's her problem.

Bill intervened at this point by saying, "Excuse me, but I need to clarify something that is very important about the legal context of this conflict. The laws of this state would in fact define the type of behavior described by Carol as a mild form of sexual harassment. I say this only to clarify the meaning of the term, not to make any judgment that such behavior occurred."

After Steve completed his statement, Carol asked him why he continued to call her Barbie after she had told him not to. Just last week, she had nearly yelled at him. Still he had continued.

Steve said she should lighten up. Here he is, trying to be nice to her, and now she is getting on his case. He asked her why she didn't like him. Why was she being so mean to him and causing this trouble?

Upon hearing this, Carol got even more upset. She jumped out of her chair, looked straight in Steve's eyes, and shouted, "Can't you hear me? I don't want you to call me Barbie." Steve responded by becoming defensive and saying that he had done nothing wrong. He understands human relationships and has worked with many people; Carol was just taking the whole thing too personally. After going back and forth about their mutual concerns, Bill intervened: "I sense that the two of you are not going to agree on the explanation of why the conflict is occurring. That's okay and its not unusual to have two entirely different perspectives on the same incident. The more important issue is to consider ways of preventing this conflict in the future so that you both feel that it can be managed more effectively. Does either of you have some ideas?"

Steve said that he could request that he work in a different classroom so that he wouldn't be present when Carol was there. Carol said that sounded good and that she would avoid talking with Steve during the few times that they were both present for staff meetings. Steve said he would also avoid talking with Carol and would not ever again call her Barbie. No other ideas for possible resolution were put forth by either Carol or Steve. Bill probed a bit to see if a more collaborative solution could be found. None emerged. It was clear that the two parties simply wanted to avoid each other.

Bill wrote up the agreement, read it back to Carol and Steve, and after they indicated that it sounded good, he asked them to sign it. The meeting ended with both parties quickly leaving the room and Bill feeling that the mediation was not very successful. There was clearly no increased understanding or acceptance between the two of them. Their relationship seemed as strained after the mediation as it had been before.

One week later, Bill checked with Carol to see how the agreement was working. Bill said then that he had hoped the mediation would go better. To his surprise, Carol indicated that she thought it went very well. She was far less distressed and felt more energetic. Bill then checked with Steve and he also indicated that the mediation was effective. He felt it had resolved the conflict with Carol.

The conflict between Carol and Steve is a good example of how even when the mediator perceives the process to be having very little impact, from the disputants' perspective it may be experienced as quite effective. It is also a good example of how an appropriate mediator may be found in public institutions. Although Bill was an employee of the high school, he truly served as an impartial third party mediator because he had had no involvement with the disputants prior to the mediation process.

Supervisor as Mediator

Jim was the director of a community mediation center. He was responsible for supervising two other staff mediators, including Dan. Dan had just recently joined the staff and was very new to the field. After receiving his initial training in mediation and learning more about the program, he became increasingly committed to the concept of mediation. In fact, he was becoming so confident of his ability that he had a difficult time responding positively to the supervision provided by Jim. By his fourth monthly supervisory meeting with Jim, Dan was convinced that Jim did not like him and certainly did not appreciate his effort and skills. In Dan's mind, Jim had become the problem. From Jim's perspective, he was trying to provide supportive supervision. After sitting in on several of Dan's mediations and assessing his skills, Jim thought it important to provide clear feedback to Dan about the strengths and limitations of his mediation skills, but whenever he did so, Dan became defensive. Jim sensed that Dan was not responding well to his supervision but was not confident that further meetings would be productive. The fact that Jim and Dan were trained mediators and did a good job of working with their clients had little impact on their ability to deal effectively with the conflict between them. Out of a growing sense of frustration, Jim finally decided to ask his supervisor if she would mediate the conflict.

As the deputy director of the agency, Sharon was a highly respected staff member and had many responsibilities in addition to occasionally serving as a mediator in referred cases. When approached by Jim, she agreed to perform a mediator-type function, pointing out that she was not an impartial third party with no control or power over the disputants. Jim was still confident that she could play a helpful role in resolving the conflict. Sharon said she would first need to talk with Dan in order to learn his perspective on the conflict and whether he was interested in having her serve as a mediator. Despite her position of authority, Sharon did not want to coerce either party into mediation.

Sharon learned from Dan that the conflict with Jim was getting so intense that he was considering resigning. Dan felt good about his work with clients, but the increasing tension he was experiencing with Jim was getting to be too much. It was his first job since graduating from college and he did not like the supervision that he was receiving. Jim was too critical and judgmental, and obviously did not like him. Mediation sounded okay to Dan, although he was not very confident that it would accomplish anything.

After having met with Jim and Dan separately to hear their perspectives and concerns, Sharon scheduled a mediation session in a conference room at the center. They sat at a rectangular conference table; Sharon at one end, and Jim and Dan sitting across from each other near her. Sharon made some opening remarks about her role, the agenda for the session, ground rules for communication, and confidentiality of the session, including that no report or notes were to go into the personnel file of either party. First, both parties would have a chance to explain their perspective of the conflict, without interruption, and then they could ask each other questions for clarification. The session would conclude by trying to identify one or more strategies for either resolving or better managing the conflict.

Dan began by stating that he did not feel valued by Jim and that Jim did not seem to like him. During supervisory meetings, Jim was always critical and seemed to want to get rid of him. He tried to explain to Jim why he did certain things, but Jim never understood. Dan thought Jim was insensitive and that his constant criticism was even abusive at times.

When it was Jim's turn to speak, he explained that he felt responsible for providing any new employee, particularly one who has just entered the work force, with constructive feedback and support. This included, when appropriate, direct negative feedback about specific behavior or performance. Jim had supervised many staff over the past five years. He felt that his criticism of some of Dan's performance was actually quite gentle. Jim always tried to emphasize positive aspects about Dan's work, although this apparently wasn't heard. Jim looked directly at Dan and told him that he valued his work, saw many good skills, and hoped that Dan would remain with the agency. The fact that Jim was quite direct in identifying certain deficiencies in some skills had absolutely nothing to do with liking or not liking Dan or wanting to get rid of him. To the contrary, it was because Jim saw such great potential in Dan that he took the time to provide regular supervisory feedback.

After hearing this, Dan began to realize that he had probably taken the criticism by Jim too personally. Dan reminded Jim that this was his first job since college and that he was not yet comfortable working with a supervisor. Jim said he understood. He too had had some problems with his first supervisor.

The session now moved into the problem-solving phase. First, specific problems were identified and listed on paper. These included infrequent supervisory meetings, lack of a regular schedule of meetings, interruptive phone calls to Jim during the meetings, and a judgmental attitude toward supervision. Jim and Dan decided to address all of them in a possible resolution. Each issue was further reviewed and an agreement was developed that Jim and Dan felt good about. A two-hour supervisory meeting would be regularly scheduled every other Friday afternoon, during which Jim would not receive calls. Dan would listen more carefully to Jim's feedback and try not to take it personally. Jim would try not to sound judgmental in what he considered constructive criticism. Jim again told Dan that he respected him and enjoyed working with him. Dan and Jim felt much better after the nearly-two-hour session. Sharon wrote the terms of the agreement on a mediation settlement form and made sure that both later received a copy.

During the remainder of the year, Dan and Jim had no further major conflicts. Dan seemed to respond better to each supervisory session. When negative feedback was provided about specific performance issues, it no longer seemed like a personal attack but was used as a tool to improve skills and job performance. Jim no longer felt that he had to be very careful to avoid comments that Dan could perceive as a personal criticism. Dan was becoming an increasingly productive employee and a valued team member.

As the mediator of this conflict, Sharon was not a true impartial third party. She obviously had considerable power over both disputants in her role as deputy director of the agency. In a technical sense, then, Sharon was not a mediator. She did, however, fulfill the basic tasks of a mediator, among them verifying the voluntary participation in the mediation process by both parties and assuring confidentiality, providing a mediation-type intervention to her staff.

Impartial Outside Mediator

The Youth Residential Center is a twenty-bed alternative treatment program for juvenile offenders who are on probation. It was developed by a community-based nonprofit organization committed to youth advocacy. Rather than sending such youths away to one of the overcrowded correctional facilities, the county believed it was more appropriate to work with them in the community.

For the past eight months the Youth Residential Center had an average of twelve offenders in its program. In addition to a small foundation grant, which covered only 20 percent of the operating budget, the center had a contract with the county for a per-diem reimbursement for each youth placed in the facility. For the entire budget to be covered by all funding sources, an average of eighteen residents was required throughout the year.

The discrepancy was worrisome to Executive Director Scott and the organization's Board of Directors. The organization had exhausted the small reserve accumulated over the past two years and current operations were dependent on a loan from a local bank. The board had given a mandate to Scott to cut costs and secure sufficient referrals for the program to reach full capacity. During the two previous weekly staff meetings, Scott had told the two case managers, Sue and Dale, that they must immediately contact all referral sources and fill the beds. Scott believed that he had effectively communicated the nature of the emergency and that they would respond appropriately.

The perceptions of the case managers, however, were quite different. Earlier in the year, a third case-manager position had been eliminated because of reduced funding, and for several months they had taken on many additional responsibilities and were feeling burned out. Sue and Dale thought their extra efforts were not recognized or appreciated by Scott. His last order outraged them; he clearly didn't understand the stress they were under.

On three subsequent occasions, between the staff meetings, Sue and Dale met with Scott to express their concerns. Scott consistently responded with a very abrupt statement that the center was in an absolute emergency situation that required such action. He was not interested in listening and had little patience with addressing their emotional needs. Instead of motivating, Scott's leadership style was having the exact opposite impact: Sue and Dale were becoming so disillusioned and stressed that they were considering resigning. Scott himself was becoming very frustrated by what he viewed as resistance from his case managers.

At the next monthly meeting of the executive committee of the board, Scott reported on the staff problems he was facing. He explained how he had done everything possible to motivate his case managers to secure more referrals, but they seemed to resist his efforts. Sue and Dale were highly committed staff and had excellent performance records. He just couldn't understand why they were now resistant to his leadership. One of the committee members asked Scott if he had considered calling on a mediator to help with the conflict. Scott said he was not familiar with how mediation worked. The committee member said that she herself was a trained family mediator and a volunteer at the local dispute settlement center. She described the mediation process, adding that she would not be an appropriate mediator because of her board membership. Scott thought that it might be worth trying if Sue and Dale felt comfortable with it. Scott met with Sue and Dale to present the option of mediation as a technique for resolving the conflict that had been developing. After an informational briefing and learning that a trained mediator from the dispute settlement center could work with them, both agreed it sounded like a good idea.

Jan had worked for three years with the dispute settlement center, and having mediated several agency staff conflicts, she felt quite comfortable handling the case with Scott, Sue, and Dale. The intake worker at the Dispute Settlement Center talked with all three parties separately on the telephone, informing them that Jan would meet with them at the scheduled session. Jan had no prior contact with any of the parties prior to the session, although she had briefly reviewed the case file prepared by the intake worker.

The mediation took place in a conference room at the Dispute Settlement Center, a neutral location. Following her opening statement about the mediation process and ground rules, she asked Sue and Dale to describe the conflict from their perspective. Dale said that he understood the importance of securing more referrals but felt that he and Sue were being treated unfairly by Scott. Sue added that she was strongly committed to the agency and wanted to help with the funding problem but felt Scott was demanding additional work in a way that seemed to indicate little understanding of the increasing stress that she and Dale were experiencing. Her work was not valued, nor-more importantly-were her thoughts on how to address the problem of low residency.

Scott had a difficult time taking in what Sue and Dale were saying. He had thought his leadership was appropriate. As he began to relate events from his perspective, he spoke of the enormous amount of stress he had been under, how he had not been sleeping well and was continually worried about funding for the program. He had no idea that his directive to Sue and Dale to increase referrals to the program had triggered such resentment and hurt feelings. Also, he felt misunderstood and unappreciated by his staff, particularly because he had been putting in twelve-hour days for the past two months.

Sue and Dale began to understand where Scott was coming from and the pressure he was under. And Scott too realized that the staff whom he relied on the most were very frustrated and stressed out. After further discussion and clarification of the issues related to the conflict, the three began to identify several possible options for resolving it. With the help of Jan, they agreed upon a plan to share responsibility for securing additional referrals, to meet on a weekly basis to review progress toward achieving that objective, and to have a follow-up mediation session with Jan in one month.

What We Have Learned from These Examples

As the three cases illustrate, the mediation intervention can be applied in a variety of manners within the context of agency staff conflict. Mediation, however, is not an option that is always available. Direct communication and negotiation between the involved parties, without the assistance of a third party, can often be more effective and desirable. Twelve strategies for managing workplace conflict successfully that are consistent with the principles of negotiation and mediation have been identified:[1]

- Choose the time and place carefully
- Change behaviors, not people
- Agree on something
- Use "I" statements
- Figure out where you went wrong
- Criticize with precision
- When someone attacks, agree
- Bow out for a while
- Have more conflicts
- Find the third option
- Agree on the future
- Work it out on paper

Conflict among workers in human service agencies

---

1. Calano & Salzman, 1988.

is an ever-present reality. Prior training in human relations, communication skills, problem solving, and client empowerment have little impact on the ability of most workers to deal with their own conflict. Through either direct negotiation between the involved parties or third-party-assisted negotiation (mediation) workers in human service agencies can become empowered to manage more effectively, and at times resolve, the many conflicts with which they are confronted. The examples in this chapter represent only a fraction of the full potential of negotiation and mediation as employee skills for openly dealing with interpersonal conflict in the workplace. Far more experimentation is needed in this very promising area of conflict management.

Summary

Informal workplace mediation began out of a need to deal more effectively with staff conflicts within human service agencies. Human services professionals are often well trained to deal with others' emotions and conflicts in a nurturing and direct way, but are often poorly equipped to handle workplace conflict. Instead of dealing openly with conflict in a healthy manner, they tend to overpersonalize disputes.

Workplace mediation utilizes the same phases as the generic mediation model; however, the selection of a mediator is different. When conflict occurs within the workplace, the mediator may be a supervisor, an impartial staff person, or an impartial outside mediator, depending upon the agency and situation.

9
DANGERS AND OPPORTUNITIES

The use of mediation in resolving a wide range of interpersonal conflicts has been found to be highly effective. Mediation is grounded in values that emphasize the importance of client self-determination and empowerment. It provides an opportunity for people who are in conflict with each other to confront the issues directly, express their concerns, search for common interests, negotiate a mutually acceptable agreement, and, often, to enhance their relationship. However, as the field of mediation continues to grow, it faces a number of potential challenges as well as opportunities. The major dangers relate to devaluing the contributions of volunteers, monitoring quality control, and the privatizing of social conflict. The major opportunities relate to mediation of staff conflict, mediation in severely violent offenses, training an entire generation in conflict resolution, public policy impact of moving mediation from the margins to the mainstream within our society, and the contribution of social workers and other human services professionals as mediators.

Dangers

Devaluing Contribution of Volunteers
When the contemporary development of mediation began in the late 1960s, it was often driven by the activism of volunteers. As the application of mediation expanded

from neighborhood disputes to victim-offender, family, and school conflicts, volunteers continued to play a central role. The use of trained community volunteers as mediators was grounded in two factors. One, the various approaches to mediation contained a strong belief in the values of individual and community empowerment. Mediation's focus was on community conflict-resolution programs rather than bringing conflicts to large impersonal governmental institutions, such as the courts. Having local volunteers serve as mediators was consistent with these values. Two, most mediation programs began with very small budgets, and many continue to operate today with quite limited financial resources. It costs a good deal less to operate with trained community volunteers than with paid professionals.

Professionalization of mediators presents a double-edged challenge in that there is a need to utilize the valuable resources that volunteers offer, and yet there is also the need for quality standards in the provision of mediation services. Quality standards concerns are addressed in the next section.

The rapid growth of mediation during the past two decades and its movement toward professionalization may lead to a devaluing of the important role of volunteers. International organizations, such as the Academy of Family Mediators and the Society for Professionals in Dispute Resolution, among others, have been actively involved in the development and promotion of mediator qualifications, which will likely lead to certification and licensing. Many states require a certain minimum number of hours of mediation training and certification of trainers.

Already, there are examples occurring in several

states that for all practical purposes allow little or no room for the involvement of volunteer mediators. However, volunteer mediators, many of whom are highly trained professionals in related fields, have a great deal to offer in terms of energy, vitality, and commitment. As stated before, the use of volunteers mediators yields both financial benefits to the programs and stronger community involvement. Many volunteers in the community mediation programs described in Chapter 3 do not possess the type of formal credentials that are increasingly being required for mediators, yet they are gifted mediators. Their contribution in the application of mediation does not need to be diminished or devalued in the rush toward professionalization.

Monitoring Quality Standards

Another danger facing mediation practice is that in formulating and monitoring quality standards the possibility of expanding services or creating innovative approaches may be diminished. In most jurisdictions it is possible for a person with little or no training to present and market him or herself as a mediator. This could lead to poor-quality mediation, and for this reason, a growing number of states require a minimum number of hours of training in order to practice specific types of mediation. For example, the Minnesota Supreme Court requires that its family mediators receive forty hours of training from a trainer certified by the court. Victim-offender mediators in Minnesota must receive a minimum of twenty-four hours of training; community mediators, twenty-six hours. These requirements, however, apply only to programs receiving funding from the state or seeking state certification.

The Academy of Family Mediators and the Society of Professionals in Dispute Resolution, along with many other related regional and national organizations, are actively involved in developing appropriate standards and qualifications for mediators. For example, the academy requires forty hours for basic divorce mediation training, including segments on relationship skills, communication skills, problem-solving skills, ethical decisionmaking, family systems, domestic violence, and family law. The extent to which these efforts should lead to eventual formal certification or licensing remains controversial to many.

Some argue that in order to maintain quality within the field of mediation practice, formal certification and/or licensing are not only inevitable but desirable. Without them, they suggest, mediation services will not be recognized by other professions and will remain vulnerable to poor quality and unethical practice.

In contrast, mediators who are strongly grounded in the values of individual and community empowerment through the active involvement of trained volunteer mediators are not likely to embrace the rush toward formal certification and credentials. Although concerned about promoting and maintaining high-quality mediation services, they are more likely to advocate within-program evaluation of mediators and competency-based assessment of skills rather than a focus on length of training.

For example, the Victim Offender Reconciliation Program in Langley, British Columbia, has developed its own process for certification of mediators in its program, most of whom are volunteers. Three levels of certification are available. Level One Mediator requires completion of a twenty-four hour training program that includes an assessment of the mediator, at least one observation of a mediation, and the conducting of at least one mediation session that is supervised by a senior mediator. Level Two Mediator requires all of the above plus completion of mediation with seven case referrals, six additional hours of in-service mediation training, and conducting an additional mediation session that is supervised by program staff or a senior mediator. Senior Mediator certification requires all of the above plus completion of mediations with seven additional case referrals, one of which must involve an assault charge, six additional hours of in-service mediation training, conducting an additional mediation that is supervised by program staff or a senior mediator, and completion of at least ten hours of work in the mediation training program as a coach for other trainees.

A framework for self- evaluation, or within-program evaluation, of mediators within many different areas of mediation has been developed and advocated.[1] It involves assessment along seven parameters of effectiveness (see Table 9.1).

Privatizing of Social Conflict
The strength of mediation is its ability to resolve a wide range of disputes between individuals and groups effectively and consistently. The conflict is removed from the formal and public process of the courts and lawyers and the involved parties are empowered to resolve the dispute directly through an informal process involving an impartial

1. Honeyman, 1989.

Table 9.1
Framework for Self-evaluation of Mediators

1. *Investigation skills* relate to the ability of the mediator to obtain appropriate background information about the case.
2. *Empathy skills* focus on the conspicuous awareness and consideration of the needs of others.
3. *Inventiveness and problem solving* center on the active search for collaborative solutions, including helping the disputants to generate ideas and proposals that can effectively address the interests of both parties.
4. *Persuasion and presentation* relate to the degree to which the mediator is effective with verbal and nonverbal communications with parties in the dispute.
5. *Distraction skills* help reduce tensions at appropriate moments in the mediation process by temporarily diverting the attention of the disputants.
6. *Managing the interaction* requires skills in developing the strategy for the mediation, managing the actual process, and working with other professionals who may become involved in the mediation or its outcome.
7. *Substantive knowledge* and expertise is required in the issues and specific type of dispute being mediated.

third party, the mediator. As noted in Chapter 3 however, many argue that certain disputes between individuals and groups should not be taken out of the public domain because the issues involved are far greater than the specific conflict. Here the moral issue of individual rights versus social needs and rights enters the picture. If mediation can more quickly alleviate the individuals' pain and suffering, who is to decide that such aid should be withheld in pursuit of a higher social good? Through the privatization of disputes in the mediation process, the larger contributing factors of social conflict and oppression are masked. Referral to mediation absorbs the discontent before it might erupt as a much larger organized collective action or spontaneous revolt.[1] For example, the referral of cases involving domestic abuse to family mediation runs contrary to the social justice concerns of most activists against domestic abuse. This position is well stated by a leading advocate for battered women in Minnesota:

> Mediation does not address or punish past behavior. At best, it only seeks to change future behavior. There is nothing to negotiate or compromise about with respect to woman abuse, child custody, or child abuse. Mediation promotes the "privatization" of battering by removing this serious civil and criminal problem from the only forum which is empowered to enforce the laws: the courts.[2]

The activists argue that the issues involved in domestic abuse are far larger than the individual victim. Violence against women is rampant and must be addressed through aggressive, well-planned advocacy efforts that can ultimately change the policy of public institutions and

1. Hofrichter, 1978.
2. Frederick, 1991.

attitudes.

At a time when women's rights are beginning to be recognized in the courts, many advocates argue that referral of domestic abuse cases to mediation rather than the courts is tactically stupid and potentially dangerous. They point out that domestic abuse often involves a long-term terroristic-type of relationship that is hardly amenable to being resolved through the short-term problem-solving process called mediation. By reframing domestic abuse as an individual conflict to be resolved through an informal and private process, rather than the public process of the courts, attention and energy may be diverted from addressing the larger societal issue of violence against women. Changes in the policies of the courts and other social institutions are desired, along with greater legal protection for women. Achievement of such social-justice and public policy goals is likely to be weakened by allowing a response to domestic violence that privatizes the conflict.

Another example of the privatization of social conflict can be seen in the context of neighborhood conflict related to poor and exploitative housing conditions. When individual tenants enter a mediation process with a slum landlord, the conflict is framed as an individual and private matter. From a community-organizing and social-justice perspective, the conflict demands a collective response to a social injustice that oppresses the poor. Confrontational tactics are likely to be required, and the more public and publicized the conflict, the better. Mediation may be helpful at a later point, once the power imbalance between the landlord and tenants has been leveled through more assertive collective tactics. Such mediation, however, would likely be of a collective nature in which representatives of the tenants negotiate with the landlord.

If the conflict experienced by individuals involves perceived disparities of power in relationship to larger social institutions or organizations, mediation may not be the most effective technique for seeking redress. Mediation could actually be used by the more powerful party as a political tool to appease individual concerns rather than to address and change the structural problems driving the conflict. Some argue that mediation seems to always benefit the side of authority.[1]

> Since a mediator lacks the ability to enforce his decisions, he must find one which both parties will accept. A mutually acceptable solution tends to be one in which the less powerful tolerates a less satisfactory solution since the mediator cannot impose an unfavorable decision on the more powerful party. The greater the power of the mediator, the wider the leverage he has to impose a solution which does not consider the inequality of the parties.

Consideration of the larger social-justice and policy implications of mediating interpersonal conflict is important. Mediation is not benign. Instead of a simplistic position of being for or against all mediation, it is critical to determine for whom, at what time, and under what circumstances and protections the mediation process can be

1. Merry, 1982.

effective. Many argue that advocacy of social-policy-reform goals often needs to be tempered by embracing the importance of allowing vulnerable individuals the right of self-determination and choice in their specific circumstances, even if that choice differs from that of the reform advocates.

Opportunities

Exciting opportunities to broaden the impact of mediation as a technique for resolving interpersonal conflict abound. These opportunities include use of mediation in staff conflict; availability of mediation in cases involving severe and violent criminal conflict; mediation as part of a socialization process through schools; stronger public-policy support of widespread use of mediation; and increased contributions by social workers and other human services professionals to the field.

Mediation of Staff Conflict

Many of the most painful and difficult conflicts faced by individuals and groups center on their jobs. Low morale among staff can lead to unnecessary stress and low productivity. Although mediation and arbitration have a long history of use in labor relations and mediation is now being applied in a wide range of conflicts in other areas of life, it remains greatly underutilized in regard to interpersonal staff conflict in workplace settings.

During recent years a growing number of employees have received training in conflict management and negotiation, which can be highly effective in empowering individuals to manage conflict experienced on the job more effectively. If they get stuck, however, a third party is required. Unfortunately, very few companies or agencies have policies and procedures that allow for easy access to securing a mediator. A clear opportunity exists to advocate greater use of mediation in resolving staff conflict, and also to assist in the design and implementation of entirely new personnel procedures for resolving conflict in human services agencies and other job settings. The richness of the mediation experience in so many other areas of life should enhance the likelihood of developing effective programs for employees.

Mediation of Severely Violent Offenses

A boundary that has long existed in the field of mediation is now being crossed at the request of individuals whose lives have been shattered by a violent crime. As a result of the increased prevalence of such crime mediation is now being offered to help resolve the emotional issues related to the trauma of the offenses. Some victims of attempted homicide and sexual assault, and family members of homicide victims have stated that the mediation process with the offender played a pivotal role in their journey of achieving a greater sense of healing and closure. Offenders have reported a far greater understanding of the devastating impact of their behavior and a desire not to commit a similar crime in the future.

Precisely because the application of mediation to violent crime crosses an early established boundary in the field, many argue that it is therapy rather than mediation that is occurring in these instances. Others argue that the fact that clear therapeutic benefits ensue from such mediation does not alter the fact that a modification of the basic mediation intervention was employed. Traditional psychotherapy would not lead to that kind of intervention nor employ the same techniques.

Few conflicts in life involve the trauma and pain that are left in the wake of severely violent crimes. A handful of mediators have worked effectively with these cases, nearly always at the request of the victim. Their pioneering work illustrates a challenging opportunity. Mediation could have an important impact upon one of the major problems plaguing industrialized societies: the escalation of violent crime. Although unlikely to have a large or dramatic effect on crime overall, mediation for victims who request it could offer a unique intervention to address the human consequences of violent crime. Perhaps, it could also make a modest contribution to reducing recidivism among offenders involved in mediation. However, far more advanced training in victim-offender mediation for practitioners would be required prior to offering mediation on a more routine basis. In fact, as noted in Chapter 7, a reconceptualization of mediation is required, focusing less on negotiation and far more on the mediator's facilitating the process of dialogue and mutual aid after lengthy preparation of the involved parties through multiple separate meetings.

Training an Entire Generation in Conflict Resolution

School mediation is the fastest-growing area of conflict resolution and mediation. School mediation programs are flourishing at a rate well in excess of the monitoring ability of the National Association of Mediation in Education (NAME). Approximately two thousand school mediation programs have been identified by NAME. Many people in the field suggest that the number being developed is probably four to five thousand. The value of these programs in helping to reduce violence among youths, including gang conflicts, has been recognized by a growing number of politicians at the federal level who are advocating a major increase in funding to support a broad expansion of school mediation programs. Will this strong interest in the benefits of conflict resolution and mediation skills in elementary and secondary school settings become another passing fad, or will the movement become institutionalized in such a manner that negotiation and mediation skills gain a place in the curricula? The opportunity faced by advocates of nonviolent conflict resolution skills in schools is truly enormous. It represents a rare opportunity to educate a new generation of children and youth in conflict resolution skills, through a systemic change in educational institutions and curricula

Public Policy Impact: From the Margins to the Mainstream

Mediation is being used in a wide variety of conflicts in hundreds of communities throughout North America and Europe. Many thousands of cases are referred to mediation each year. Although school mediation has experienced the largest growth in recent years, nearly all other areas of mediation practice have also thrived. For example, in the late 1970s, there were only a handful of victim-offender mediation programs; today, there are more than 125.

The many benefits that flow from mediation and the related growth of the field are increasingly recognized. The practice of mediation has mushroomed over the past two decades. Yet, with rare exceptions mediation remains on the margins of how we understand and approach conflict in Western culture. Law and the adversarial process remain the pillars upon which the dominant system of conflict resolution rests. For the field of mediation to move from the margins to the mainstream of conflict resolution in Western culture, it must become far more active and assertive in the political sphere. Its advocacy must move beyond pilot projects and local efforts to broad ventures in the public policy arena that will provide the framework and resources to make mediation available to all citizens. The Community Dispute Resolution Centers Program administered by the Unified Court System of the State of New York (described in Chapter 3) is an excellent example of such an effort. It is a public-private partnership in which the state provides leadership and financial support to private community-based organizations that offer an increasingly broad range of mediation services to citizens in every county.

Contribution of Social Workers and Other Human Services Professionals

When the contemporary development of the field of mediation began in the late 1960s, it was based upon a strong critique of the adversarial legal process and the legal profession specifically. This theme has permeated the movement as it has continued to grow. More and more people have recognized the severe limitations of the adversarial legal process in resolving many interpersonal disputes, particularly when the parties will have contact in the future. The field of mediation, however, has been dominated by the legal profession. Although many lawyers have made important contributions, the profession does not offer a strong foundation to serve as an alternative to itself.

Social workers and other human services professionals can offer a valuable counterbalance to the important and overly influential role that lawyers continue to play in the field. The basic social work skills and processes of working with individuals and groups provide a solid foundation for later development of mediation skills. Many social workers have already been involved in various applications of mediation, yet mediation is little known and understood in the mainstream of social work education and practice.

The opportunity for social workers and other human services professionals (i.e., nurses, teachers, pastors, rabbis, counselors) to have a greater impact in the field of mediation as it continues to grow in North America and Europe is huge. The basic values of human services professions are a rich contribution, particularly through the lens of understanding the essence of mediation as that of empowerment and mutual recognition of the parties in conflict. For example, the social-work tasks of working with individuals and groups require good communication skills, relationship building, and problem solving, which are an excellent foundation for the use of an empowering style of mediation that addresses the emotional and material dimensions of conflict.

10
Moving to a Higher Plane: A Humanistic Mediation Model

The impact of mediation in resolving a wide range of conflicts is well documented. The use of mediation consistently results in high levels of client satisfaction and perceptions of fairness, within families, among co- workers, in neighborhoods and schools, and in the criminal justice system. The achievement in mediation of a written, mutually agreed upon settlement between the involved parties is usually an important outcome. However, if the field of mediation becomes driven by the desire to reach settlements in the quickest way possible, at the expense of understanding and addressing the emotional context of the conflict, it may evolve into little more than another impersonal, mechanical and routine social service.

Although some conflicts, such as complex commercial disputes, require a primary focus on reaching an acceptable settlement, most conflicts develop within a larger emotional context characterized by powerful feelings of disrespect, betrayal, and abuse. When these feelings are not allowed to be expressed in a healthy manner, an agreement might be reached but the underlying emotional conflict remains. Little healing of the emotional wound is likely to occur without an opening of the heart through dialogue and a recognition of one's own possible contribution to the conflict.

After many years of being applied in diverse settings, the field of mediation is presented with an opportunity to build upon the many anecdotal stories of how mediation periodically has been far more than simply working out a settlement. With mediation, relationships have been repaired; anger has been reduced. While not forgetting the conflict, one's adversary has taken on a far more human quality. Mediation can now move toward a higher level of practice through a humanistic model that more intentionally taps into its transformative and healing powers. As noted in Appendix 3, its healing powers are intrinsic to the process of mediating conflict between individuals but need to be consciously drawn out and utilized.

A humanistic mediation model is not based upon a series of prescriptive steps and techniques that must be adhered to in the proper sequence. Instead, it is grounded in a different paradigm of conflict resolution, one that acknowledges brokenness, affirms common humanity, and embraces what Lois Gold calls "a preference for peace." As Gold notes, the paradigm of healing, rather than problem solving, requires the language of the soul. It requires a "caring, non-judgemental acceptance of the person's humanity (1994)." While acknowledging brokenness in relationships is central to a humanistic mediaton model, it is important to note that it is the role of a therapist to work on the brokenness. Seven elements of the language of the soul are identified by Gold (1994):

1. Generating hope ("with support, you can do it")
2. Tapping into the desire for wellness

3. Speaking from the heart
4. Thinking of clients in their woundedness
5. Being real and congruent
6. Creating a safe space for dialogue
7. Creating a sacred space for the healer within

Some mediators might argue that such a humanistic model may be good but it is certainly not mediation. It appears to focus little on obtaining settlements and much on the emotional component in conflict. The primary purpose of mediation, however, is ultimately to be found in the values of the mediator and the lens through which mediation is seen and understood.

Understandings of Mediation

The manner in which the process of mediation occurs depends a great deal upon the lens through which mediation is understood and viewed. Three distinct understandings of the primary purpose of mediation have been identified: (1) efficiency, (2) protection of rights, and (3) empowerment and recognition.[1]

An efficiency understanding of mediation focuses primarily on the needs of the trial courts: to settle quickly as many cases as possible, and thereby reduce pressure on the courts. Mediation is a practical alternative to court intervention for a wide range of relatively minor civil and criminal disputes. Scarce judicial time and resources are freed up to address more serious cases. Court congestion and overcrowding are markedly alleviated. If efficiency is deemed the primary value of mediation, it is likely to result

1. Bush, 1989.

in relatively short sessions involving a mediator who is fairly directive, with little patience for silence or the expression of feelings.

Safeguarding the rights of the disputing parties is the primary concern from a protection of rights understanding of mediation. The mediation process focuses on insuring procedural protections that lead to fairness. All mediation is based on informed consent. While mediation is less formal than court adjudication, there is a highly structured process adhered to during the mediation session. The mediator requires the disputants to obtain representation by an attorney who may even be present during the session. Mediation is viewed as a more principled alternative to the disputants simply negotiating with each other directly, with no constraints or protection being present. If protection of rights is the major value and lens through which the mediation intervention is viewed, the process is likely to be fairly rigid, legalistic and perhaps even directive and judgmental. For example, from this perspective, the mediator may choose to terminate the mediation session if movement toward a final agreement is perceived as unfair to one of the parties.

An empowerment and recognition understanding of mediation focuses on the power of mediation to humanize the conflict between the parties through a process of dialogue and mutual aid. This perspective emphasizes the need of the disputants to exercise autonomy, choice and self-determination. The mediator facilitates a unique and creative resolution of the conflict that is grounded in the parties' expressed needs. An empowerment and recognition understanding of mediation is more likely to result in the parties experiencing their common humanity, empathy for the other and a perspective of caring and interconnection. In short, this perspective comes the closest to viewing mediation as a journey of the heart. Despite their current conflict, disputants are viewed first as human beings in the common journey of life. By emphasizing the values of empowerment and mutual recognition the primary role of the mediator is quite different than when efficiency or protection of rights are emphasized.

> The mediator's role is (1) to encourage the empowerment of the parties-i.e., the exercise of their autonomy and self-determination in deciding whether and how to resolve their dispute; and (2) to promote the parties' mutual recognition of each other as human beings despite their adverse positions. It is not the mediator's job to guarantee a fair agreement, or any agreement at all: it is the mediator's job to guarantee the parties the fullest opportunity for self-determination and mutual acknowledgement.[1]

Other forms of dispute resolution can be viewed within the context of the three concepts just discussed: efficiency, protection of rights, and empowerment and recognition. Interventions such as arbitration and court adjudication are far more likely than mediation to advance the values of efficiency and protection of rights. The one thing that mediation alone can offer in dispute resolution is that of empowerment and recognition. No other form of

1. ibid. pg. 200.

dispute resolution can provide an opportunity for such an experience-initial anger and hostility often are transformed into greater empathy and acceptance. From this perspective, the full power of mediation is tapped into only through an understanding of its intrinsic ability to be transformative and healing (see Appendix 3). Although clearly more dominant in Western culture, settlement-driven mediation with its efficiency focus is not the only acceptable understanding of mediation.

Humanistic Mediation Model

People concerned about promoting social harmony and building more peaceful communities can play an active role in pushing the field of mediation to a higher plane through advocacy of a humanistic model of mediation. Instead of being settlement driven, such a model is driven by facilitating a journey of the heart through a process of dialogue and mutual aid between people in conflict. The emphasis is upon the mediator's empowering each individual to own the conflict, to discuss its full impact with the other party, to assist each other in determining the most suitable resolution, which may or may not include a written agreement, and to recognize each other's common humanity, despite the conflict.

A humanistic model of mediation in some respects parallels humanistic styles of teaching or psychotherapy, which emphasize the importance of the relationship between the teacher or therapist and the student or client, while embracing a strong belief in each person's capacity for growth, change, and transformation. It is important to note, however, that although parties in conflict may be more likely to experience emotional benefits from a humanistic mediation model, the process is not psychotherapy, nor does it require a mediator to have training in psychotherapy. Although a humanistic mediation model may not be effective or even appropriate in all conflicts, it can be applied in a multiplicity of conflicts in families, communities, schools, workplaces, and even in conflicts having to do with criminal offenses.

A humanistic mediation model is grounded in a number of underlying values and beliefs about the nature of human existence, conflict, and the search for healing and closure (see Table 10.2).

To embrace consistently a more humanistic model of mediation, a number of significant changes in the dominant settlement-driven mediation model in Western culture are required. Individual components of the humanistic model have been used periodically by many mediators over time, particularly in the early years of community mediation and victim-offender mediation, as well as a growing number of family mediators. The humanistic mediation model presented builds upon what we have learned and offers a comprehensive and integrated approach to tap into the transformative and healing powers of mediation more regularly and intentionally. These changes in the practice of mediation to more closely follow the humanistic model will be discussed later in greater deatil but are listed in Table 10.3.

Table 10.2
Values and Beliefs: Humanistic Mediation Model

1. Belief in the connectedness of all things and our common humanity.
2. Belief in the importance of the mediator's presence and connectedness with the disputants in facilitating effective conflict resolution.
3. Belief in the healing power of mediation through a process of the disputants helping each other through the sharing of their feelings (dialogue and mutual aid).
4. Belief in the desire of most people to live peacefully.
5. Belief in the desire of most people to grow through life experiences.
6. Belief in the capacity of all people to draw upon inner reservoirs of strength to overcome adversity, to grow, and to help others in similar circumstances.
7. Belief in the inherent dignity and self-determination that arise from embracing conflict directly.

Centering of Mediator

A humanistic mediation model emphasizes the importance of the mediator's clearing away the clutter in his or her own life so that he or she can focus intensely on the needs of the people in conflict. Prior to initiating contact with the parties, the mediator is encouraged to take a few moments of silence through reflection, mediation, or prayer to reflect on the deeper meaning of his or her peacemaking work and the needs of the people in conflict.[1] To be fully present for those involved in the conflict, the mediator needs to be centered.

Table 10.3
Practice Implications: Humanistic Mediation Model

1. Centering of mediator
2. Reframing of the mediator's role
3. Premediation sessions
4. Connecting with the parties
5. Tapping into individual strengths
6. Coaching of communication
7. Nondirective style of mediation
8. Face-to-face seating of parties in conflict (if culturally appropriate)
9. Recognition and use of the power of silence
10. Follow-up sessions

Reframing of the Mediator's Role

Tapping into the full power of mediation in resolving important interpersonal conflict reframes the mediator's role. Instead of actively and efficiently guiding the parties toward a settlement, the mediator initiates a transformative process in which the parties are given the opportunity to enter into a dialogue, experience each other as persons, despite their conflict, and seek ways to help each

1. Gold, 1993; Zumeta, 1993.

other find peace, which may or may not involve a formal written settlement agreement. This often requires the mediator to slow down the process so that those present can get in touch with their underlying and deeper interests and needs, rather than focusing only upon resolution of the most immediate issue(s) that they are facing. As Lois Gold (1994) has pointed out, the mediator helps the parties to listen to their inate wisdom, their preference for peace, despite the intensity of the conflict. Through a humanistic mediation model, there is a sharing of pain and an acknowledgement of brokenness, all of which occur prior to any problem solving and resolution. It is important to note a critical boundary issue. A humanistic mediation model facilitates such an acknowledgement of brokenness among the parties but a therapist is required to work on the brokenness with one or both of the parties.[1] Once the parties are engaged in a face-to-face dialogue, the mediator intentionally gets out of the way by not verbally intervening frequently. It should be noted that rarely does the mediator entirely stand aside especially during the later stages of mediation when the parties in conflict may need assistance to construct a formal settlement agreement. In all cases, it is important that the mediator provide a brief closing statement that thanks the parties for their work and schedules a follow-up meeting if necessary.

Use of Premediation Sessions

Routine use of separate sessions with the involved parties prior to the face-to-face mediation session is standard practice in a humanistic model. The individual

1. Gold, 1994.

sessions occur at least a week or more before the mediation session. Although collecting information, assessing the conflict and describing the mediation program are important tasks to complete, the first and most important task is that of establishing trust and rapport with the disputants. Trust and rapport enhance the dialogue process and are very beneficial in intense interpersonal conflicts-and can also be beneficial in less intense disputes. For this reason, the mediator needs to get into a listening mode as quickly as possible during the initial meeting by inviting the disputants to tell their stories of the conflict and how it affects them. Clearly explaining how the mediation process works and what they might expect to experience is likely to put the involved parties at ease. Effective use of pre-mediation sessions can pre-empt potential obstacles to a humanistic approach by aligning the parties with their highest intentions, their "preference for peace".

Connecting with the Parties

A very strong emphasis on the mediator's connecting with the parties in the conflict is characteristic of the humanistic mediation model. Instead of viewing mediators as technicians who are emotionally distant and uninvolved with no prior contact with the disputants, emphasis would be placed on mediators establishing trust and rapport with the involved parties before bringing them to a joint session. A mediator does not need to lose his or her impartiality to effectively connect with the involved parties before bringing them together. The art of mediation, as well as of teaching, nursing, therapy and social work, is found in connecting with people at a human level through the expression of empathy, warmth and authenticity. It requires listening with the heart as well as the head. It also requires the mediator to generate a sense of hope and to encourage the parties to speak from their heart in terms of their deeper needs, what Lois Gold refers to as their "yearning for wholeness and wellness".

The late Virginia Satir, a world-renowned family therapist and trainer, recognized the supreme importance of the "presence" of the therapist. She regarded authentic human connection as fundamental to change processes. Making contact with people on a basic human level requires "congruence," a condition of being emotionally honest with yourself in which there is a connectedness of your words, feelings, body and facial expressions, and actions. Authentic connection with others first requires looking inward:[1]

1. How do I feel about myself? (self-esteem)
2. How do I get my meaning across to others? (communication)
3. How do I treat my feelings? (rules)
   • Do I own them or put them on someone else?
   • Do I act as though I have feelings that I do not or that I have feelings that I really don't have?
4. How do I react to doing things that are new and different? (taking risks)

Connecting with those involved in mediation takes energy; it requires that we make ourselves responsible for what comes out of us. Although Satir developed her concepts of making contact and congruence within the

1. Satir, 1976.

context of family therapy, her material is highly relevant to a humanistic model of mediation. Humanistic mediators can have a powerful presence with their clients, as Satir did, through a more spiritual understanding of life that embraces the connectedness of all people along with the connectedness of the mediator's actions and belief system with the core of his or her being.

Four specific elements of presence that can increase the effectiveness of mediators have been identified:[1] (1) being centered, (2) being connected to one's governing values and beliefs and highest purpose, (3) making contact with the humanity of the clients, and (4) being congruent.

The transformative and healing power of humanistic mediation is grounded in the process of connecting with the parties in conflict, being fully present in their woundedness and encouraging all present to acknowledge their brokenness.

Tapping Into Individual Strengths

When people are in conflict, it is common for them to communicate and interact in highly dysfunctional ways. The expression of intense anger and bitterness, along with the inability to listen to the other parties or effectively communicate their own needs, can mask many strengths that they may have. It is the mediator's job, during separate premediation sessions, to identify specific strengths in an individual party that may directly assist in the mediation process and to encourage the expression of those strengths in mediation.

To identify strengths, the mediator needs to listen

1. Gold, 1993.

with his or her heart, as well as their head. This requires looking beyond the intensity of the immediate issue and not getting totally distracted by the strong negative energy that is often present. What is their deeper desire for wholeness and peace? How can a sense of hope be generated, that with some additional support the party in conflict can move closer toward their deeper needs? Once the nature of the party's preference for peace is identified, strengths of the individual are more clearly able to be found.[1]

Tapping into the strengths of individuals and coaching them in how to communicate their feelings effectively can contribute greatly to the mediator's ability to use a nondirective style of mediation, as noted below. For example, one of the parties in conflict may have very limited verbal skills and little ability to express feelings, although he or she is able to describe in detail past events. The mediator can build upon this capability by emphasizing very clear and concrete communication, particularly communication where this individual can bring his or her highly descriptive skills into play.

Coaching of Communication

The open expression of feelings related to the conflict is central to a humanistic mediation model. Because of the extreme intensity of such feelings, it may become necessary during the separate premediation session for the mediator to coach each disputant in ways of communicating the feelings so that they can be heard by the other party. The coaching centers on how to own one's feelings rather than projecting them upon the other party. Projecting

1. Gold, 1994.

intense feelings through aggressive communications often triggers defensiveness and shuts down honest dialogue. To avoid this foreclosure requires that feelings be owned by the speaker and communicated as an "I" statement, rather than attacking the other party. Furthermore, coaching helps identify and tap into the strengths of each of the parties in conflict, despite any emotional baggage that is present. Coaching, however, is not suggesting what should be said.

Nondirective Style of Mediation

Moving mediation to a higher plane requires a nondirective style of mediation whereby the mediator assists the involved parties in a process of dialogue and mutual aid. The mediator opens the session and sets a tone that will allow the parties to feel safe, understand the process, and talk directly to each other. The mediator's ability to fade into the background is directly related to connecting with the parties before the joint session and having secured their trust. Without the routine use of separate premediation meetings with the parties, it is unlikely that a truly nondirective style of mediation can be employed. The parties ability to participate in a process of dialogue and mutual aid will be difficult to experience unless they trust the mediator, feel safe and reasonably comfortable, and the mediator fades into the background until he or she is needed.

A nondirective style of mediation should not be confused with a passive style in which the mediator provides little direction, leadership, or assistance. Instead, the mediator remains in control of the process and, although saying little, is actively involved nonverbally in the encounter and is able either to respond or intervene at any point, particularly when people get stuck and indicate a need for assistance. By setting a clear and comfortable tone, that puts the parties at ease so that they can talk directly, the mediator enables an empowerment-and-recognition understanding of mediation. This style of mediation, which can be used effectively only if the mediator conducts separate premediation sessions with the involved parties, frequently has the mediator saying very little after the opening statement.

When a nondirective style of mediation is used, a fairly typical flow of the meeting consists of three phases. First, in an opening statement the mediator welcomes the parties, clarifies the role of the mediator, presents the agenda for the session, and lays out the communication ground rules. This opening statement is likely to be no more than three to five minutes. The main concern is to project a sense of openness, safety, and leadership so that the parties in conflict can enter into a dialogue with each other; the mediator does not repeat the factual context of the conflict. The mediator then facilitates the process by which each disputants gives his or her account of the conflict to the other disputant. During the storytelling phase, the mediator fades into the background, rarely saying much.

Second, the mediator makes a few brief comments to assist in the transition to the problem-solving phase, which may include negotiation of a written agreement. The mediator is now likely to be more active, particularly if the disputants indicate a need for the identification of options for resolution. It is extremely important that the mediator, if asked, present a range of options rather than advice on what he or she believes is the best solution. Even during this phase, the mediator strives to be nonintrusive so as not to hinder or direct the dialogue. Third, if an actual written agreement is desired, the mediator will find it necessary to step in to clarify specific issues, prepare the document, and secure signatures.

In summary, the nondirective style of mediation is most likely to require the mediator to speak at three points: the opening statement; when the transition from storytelling to problem solving is being made; and during the final negotiation.

Face-to-Face Seating of Disputants

Seating during a mediation session is important. Routine use of an arrangement in which the parties sit across from each other with natural eye contact is central to direct communication and dialogue if culturally appropriate. If a table is used, the mediator sits at one end and the parties at the sides. A major blockage to mediator-assisted dialogue and mutual aid is having the parties sit next to each other on one side of the table, facing the mediator on the other side.

It should be noted, however, that face-to-face seating is not always desirable at first. If the parties have an extremely high level of hostility toward each other, despite the work done by the mediator during premediation individual sessions, it may be more productive if they initially sit next to each other, facing the mediator. If their hostility seems to decrease during the mediation session, the parties could be asked to turn their chairs and face each other. Some mediation programs routinely start with the disputants facing the mediator rather than each other. A humanistic mediation model would always start with the parties facing each other unless great hostility or anger worked against the arrangement, or if the culture of one or both parties precluded it (e.g., Native American).

Recognition and Use of the Power of Silence

It is not uncommon for moments of silence to occur even in the midst of a heated conflict. People simply run out of things to say, or they become emotionally exhausted. When this happens during the course of a mediation session, there is a tremendous temptation for the mediator to fill the void with some comments or guidance.

Moments of silence in the process of dialogue and conflict resolution is inherent in a nondirective style of mediation; it is essential to being fully present and acknowledging brokenness. Recognizing, using, and feeling comfortable with the power of silence is important for the mediator. When silence drags on for an extended period, it may actually lead to a higher level of tension. Allowing for ten to twenty seconds of silence, however, can both provide a space for the disputants to reflect on the conflict and encourage them to carry on with the discussion without the assistance of the mediator. Through resisting the urge to interrupt silence with guidance and having the patience to make use of silence, as well as extended conversation, the mediator is more consistently able to assist the disputants in experiencing mediation as a process of dialogue and mutual aid-a journey of the heart in harmony with the head.

Follow-up Sessions

The importance of follow-up joint sessions between the parties in conflict is recognized as central to a humanistic mediation model. The nature of conflict and human behavior is usually far too complex to resolve in only one session, particularly when the conflict involves a significant relationship. Oftentimes, the full range of issues and concerns cannot be addressed in only one session. Even in cases when the conflict is largely resolved in one session, conducting a follow-up session several months later to assess how the agreement is holding or to resolve any issues that may have emerged since can be important in the overall process of healing and closure.

Summary

The dominant model of settlement-driven mediation in Western culture is clearly beneficial to many people in conflict and superior to the adversarial legal system and court adjudication in most cases. Moving to a higher plane, which embraces the importance of spirituality, self-esteem, and our common humanity, is even better (see Appendix 4). A humanistic mediation model can lay the foundation for a greater sense of community and social harmony. With its focus on the intrinsic healing power of mediation, this model can bring about a more complete resolution to conflict. Through a process of dialogue and mutual aid between the involved parties, the humanistic mediation model facilitates the achievement of outer peace through resolution of the immediate conflict, while also facilitating a journey of the heart to find inner peace, which brings forth the true goal of mediation-real peace.

REFERENCES

Ahrons, C., & Rogers, R. H. (1987). Divorcing Families. New York: Norton.

American Bar Association (1990). Directory of Alternative Dispute Resolution Programs. Washington, DC: American Bar Association.

Araki, C. T. (1990). Dispute management in the schools. Mediation Quarterly, 8(1).

Austin, J., & Krisberg B. (1982), The unmet promise of alternatives to incarceration. Crime and Delinquency, 28 (3).

Bush, R. B. (1988). Defining Quality in Dispute Resolution: Taxonomies and Anti-Taxonomies. Working Paper Series 8-7. Madison: Institute for Legal Studies, University of Wisconsin Law School at Madison.

Bush, R. B. (1989a). Efficiency and protection, or empowerment and recognition? The mediator's role and ethical standards in mediation. Florida Law Review, 41.

Bush, R. B. (1989b). Mediation and adjudication, dispute resolution and ideology: An imaginary conversation. University of San Diego School of Law, 3 (1).

Calano, J., & Salzman, J. (1988). How to turn heat into light. Working Woman, March.

Clark, S. H., Valente, E., & Mace, R. R. (1992). Mediation of Interpersonal Disputes: An Evaluation of North Carolina's Programs. Chapel Hill: Institute of Government, University of North Carolina.

Coates, R. B. & Gehm, J. (1989). Victim meets offender: An evaluation of victim offender reconciliation programs. In Martin Wright and Burt Galaway (eds.), Mediation and Criminal Justice. London: SAGE.

Community Boards Program. (1984). Community Boards Training Manual. San Francisco: Community Boards Program.

Coogler, J. O. (1978). Structured Mediation in Divorce Settlement. Lexington, MA: Heath.

Cook, R., Roehl, J., & Sheppard, D. (1980). Neighborhood Justice Centers Field Test: Final Evaluation Report. Washington, DC: Government Printing Office.

Crosson, M. (1990). The Community Dispute Resolution Centers Program Annual Report, April 1, 1989--March 31, 1990. Albany: Community Dispute Resolution Centers Program of the Unified Court System of the State of New York.

Davis, A., and Porter, K. (1985). Dispute resolution: The fourth 'R'. Missouri Journal of Dispute Resolution.

Davis, R., Tichane, M., & Grayson, D. (1980). Mediation and Arbitration as Alternative to Prosecution in Felony Arrest Cases: An Evaluation of the Brooklyn Dispute Resolution Center. New York: VERA Institute of Justice.

Depner, C. E., Cannata, K. V., & Simon, M. N. (1992). Building a uniform statistical reporting system: A snapshot of California Family Court services. Family and Conciliation Courts Review,. April.

Dignan, J. (1990). Repairing the Damage: An Evalauation of an Experimental Adult Reparation Scheme in Kettering, Northamptonshire. Centre for Criminological and Legal Research, Faculty of Law, University of Sheffield, England.

Dittenhoffer, T. and Erickson, R. (1983). The Victim Offender Reconciliation Program: A message to correctional reformers. University of Toronto Law Journal, Summer.

Dukes, F. (1990). Understanding community dispute resolution. Mediation Quarterly, 8, (1).

Duryee, M. (1992) Mandatory court mediation: Demographic summary and consumer evaluation of one court service. Family and Conciliation Courts Review. April.

Emery, R. E., & Jackson, J. A. (1989). The Charlottesville Mediation Project mediated and litigated child custody disputes. Mediation Quarterly. Summer.

Erickson, S. K., & McKnight Erickson, M. S. (1988). Family Mediation Casebook: Theory Handbook. New York: Brunner/Mazel.

Erickson, S. K., & McKnight Erickson, M. S. (1992). The Children's Book: A Separate Parenting Handbook. West Concord, MN: CPI.

Evaluation Group. (1980). An Evaluation Report on the Suffolk County Communiy Mediation Center. Unpublished.

Fagan & Gehm. (1993). Victim Offender Reconciliation and Mediation Program Directory. Valparaiso, IN: PACT Institute of Justice.

Felstiner, W., & Williams, L. (1978). Mediation as an alternative to criminal prosecution. Law and Human Behavior. 223.

Fisher, R., & Ury, W. (1991). Getting to Yes: Negotiating Agreements Without Giving In. New York: Penguin Books.

Frederick, L.(1991). Comments during class presentation at University of Minnesota.

Galaway, B. (1988). Crime victim and offender mediation as a social work strategy. Social Service Review, 62:668-683.

Galaway, B. (1989). Informal justice: Mediation between offenders and victims. In P. A. Albrecht & O. Backes, (eds.), Crime Prevention and Intervention: Legal and Ethical Problems. Berlin: de Gruyter.

Galaway, B., & Hudson, J. (1990). Criminal Justice, Restitution, and Reconciliation. Monsey, NY: Criminal Justice Press.

Gehm, J. (1990). Mediated victim-offender restitution agreements: An exploratory analysis of factors related to victim participation. In Hudson, J. & Galaway, B. (eds.), Criminal Justice, Restitution, and Reconciliation. Monsey, NY: Criminal Justice Press.

Gold, L. (1985). Reflections on the transition from therapist to mediator. Mediation Quarterly, 9.

Gold, L. (1993). Influencing unconscious influences: The healing dimension of mediation. Mediation Quarterly, 11 (1).

Gold, L. (1994). Comments during presentation at annual conference of Academy of Family Mediators in Eugene, Oregon.

Gustafson, D. L., & Smidstra, H. (1989). Victim Offender Reconciliation in Serious Crime: A Report on the Feasibility Study Undertaken for the Ministry of the Solicitor General (Canada). Langley, B. C.: Fraser Region Community Justice Iniatives Association.

Harrington, C. B., & Merry S. E. (1988). Ideological production: The making of community mediation. Law and Society Review, 22(4).

Hofrichter, R. (1978). Neighborhood Justice in Capitalist Society: The Expansion of the Informal State. Westport, CT: Greenwood Press.

Honeyman, C. (1989). Some notes on self-evaluation for mediators. Paper presented at the North America Conference on Peacemaking and Conflict Resolution, Montreal, Quebec, March.

Huber, M. (1991). Native mediation model for urban communities. Interaction (newsletter of the network Interaction for Conflict Resolution, Waterloo, Ontario).

Hudson, J., & Galaway, B. (1974). Undoing the wrong. Social Work, 19.

Hughes, S. P., & Schneider, A. L. (1989). Victim- offender mediation: A survey of program characteristics and perceptions of effectiveness. Crime and Delinquency, 35.

Kaslow, F. W. (1988). The psychological dimension of divorce mediation. In Milne, A. & Folberg, J. (eds.), Divorce Mediation: Theory and Practice. New York: Guilford Press.

Kaslow, F. W., & Schwartz, L. L. (1987). The Dynamics of Divorce. New York: Brunner/Mazel.

Katz, N. H., & Lawyer, J. W. (1985). Communication and Conflict Resolution Skills. Dubuque, IA: Kendall/Hunt.

Kelly, J. B. (1983). Mediation and psychotherapy: Distinguishing the difference. Mediation Quarterly, 1.

Kelly, J. B. (1989). Mediated and adversarial divorce: Respondents' perceptions of their process and outcomes. In J. B. Kelly (ed.), Empirical Research in Divorce and Family Mediation, special issue, Mediation Quarterly, 24.

Kelly, J. B. (1990). Final Report, Mediated and Adversarial Divorce Resolution Processes: An Analysis of Post Divorce Outcomes. Prepared for the Fund for Research in Dispute Resolution. December.

Kolb, D. M., & Rubin, J. Z. (1989). Mediation through a disciplinary kaleidoscope: A summary of empirical research. Dispute Resolution Forum, Washington DC: National Institute for Dispute Resolution.

References

Marshall, T. F., & Merry, S. (1990). Crime and Accountability: Victim Offender Mediation in Practice. London: Home Office.

McEwen, C. A., & Maiman, R. J. (1981). Small claims mediation in Maine: An empirical assessment. Maine Law Review, 33.

McGillis, D. (1986). Community Dispute Resolution Programs and Public Policy. Washington, DC: National Institute of Justice.

Mediation Services. (1993). Mediation Training Manual. Winnipeg, Manitoba: Mediation Services, A Community Resource for Conflict Resolution.

Merry, S. (1982). Defining "Success" in the neighborhood justice movement. In Roman Tomasic and Malcolm M. Feeley (eds.), Neighboorhood Justice: Assessment of an Emerging Idea. New York: Longman.

Merry, S. E. & Rocheleau, A. M. (1985). Mediation in Families: A Study of the Children's Hearings Project. Cambridge, MA: Cambridge Family and Children's Service.

Milne, A. L. (1983). Divorce mediation: The state of the art. Mediation Quarterly, 1.

Mnookin, R. H., & Maccoby, E. E. (1992). Dividing the Child: Social and Legal Dilemmas of Custody. Cambridge: Harvard University Press.

Moore, C. W. (1986). The Mediation Process: Practical Strategies for Resolving Conflict. San Francisco: Jossey-Bass.

Moore, P., & Whipple, C. (1988). Project Start: A School- Based Mediation Program. New York: Victim Services Agency.

Moriarty, W. F., Jr., Norris, T. L., & Salas, L. (1977). Evaluation: Dade County Citizen Dispute Settlement Center. Dade County Criminal Justice Planning Unit.

Morris, M. (1983). Parent Child Mediation: An Alternative That Works. New York: Children's Aid Society.

Phear, P. W. (1985). Parent-child mediation: Four states, four models. Mediation Quarterly, 7.

Satir, V. (1976). Making Contact. Berkley: Celestial Arts.

Shonholtz, R. (1984). Neighborhood justice systems: Work, structure, and guiding principles. In J. A. Lemmon (ed.), Community Mediation, special issue, Mediation Quarterly, 5.

Shulman, L. (1984). The Skills of Helping Individuals and Groups. Itasca, IL: Peacock.

Silbey, S. S., & Merry, S. E. (1986). Mediation settlement strategies. Law and Policy, 8(1).

Singer, L. (1990). Settling Disputes: Conflict Resolution in Business, Families and the Legal System 120.

Slaikeu, K. A., Person, J., & Thoennes, N. (1988). Divorce mediation behaviors: A descriptive system and analysis. In Milne, A. & Folberg, J. (eds.), Divorce Mediation: Theory and Practice (New York: Guilford Press).

Slater, A., Shaw, J. A., & Duquesnel, J. (1992). Client satisfaction survey: A consumer evaluation of mediation and investigative services. Family and Conciliation Courts Review. April.

Smith & Sidwell (1990). Training and Implementation Guide for Student Mediation in Secondary Schools. Albuquerque: New Mexico Center for Dispute Resolution.

Stahler, G. J., DuCette, J. P., and Povich, E. (1990). Using mediation to prevent child maltreatment: An exploratory study. Family Relations, 39.

Stern, M., Van Slyck, M., & Valvo, S. (1986). Enhancing adolescents' self-image: Implications of a peer mediation program. Paper presented at the annual meeting of the American Psychological Association, Washington, DC., August.

Thomas, K. W., & Kilmann, R. H. (1974). Thomas-Kilmann Conflict Mode Instrument. Tuxedo, NY: Xicom.

Toronto Forum on Women Abuse and Mediation (June, 1993).

Umbreit, M. S. (1985). Victim Offender Mediation: Conflict Resolution and Restitution. Washington, DC: National Institute of Corrections U.S. Department of Justice.

Umbreit, M. S. (1986a). Victim offender mediation and judicial leadership. Judicature, 69. December.

References

Umbreit, M. S. (1986b). Victim offender mediation: A national survey. Federal Probation, 50 (4).

Umbreit, M. S. (1988). Mediation of victim offender conflict. Journal of Dispute Resolution.

Umbreit, M. S. (1989a). Victims seeking fairness, not revenge: Toward restorative justice. Federal Probation 53 (3).

Umbreit, M. S. (1989b). Violent offenders and their victims. In M. Wright and B. Galaway (eds.), Mediation and Criminal Justice. London: SAGE.

Umbreit, M. S. (1991a). Having offenders meet with their victims can benefit both parties. Corrections Today (July).

Umbreit, M. S. (1991b). Minnesota mediation center produces positive results. Corrections Today, August.

Umbreit, M. S. (1991c). Mediation of youth conflict: A multi-system perspective. Child and Adolescent Social Work. Human Services Press.

Umbreit, M. S., (1993a). Crime victims and offenders in mediation: An emerging area of social work practice. Social Work, 38(1).

Umbreit, M. S., (1993b). Juvenile offenders meet their victims: The impact of mediation in Albuquerque, New Mexico. Family and Conciliation Courts Review, 31 (1).

Umbreit, M. S., (1994). Victim Meets Offender: The Impact of Restorative Justice and Mediation. Monsey, NY: Criminal Justice Press.

Umbreit, M. S., & Coates, R. B. (1992). The impact of mediating victim offender conflict: An analysis of programs in three states. Juvenile and Family Court Journal, 43 (1).

Umbreit, M. S., & Coates, R. B. (1993). Cross-site analysis of victim offender mediation in four states. Crime and Delinquency, 39.

Wahrhaftig, P. (1981). Dispute resolution retrospective. Crime and Delinquency, 27.

Wallerstein, J., & Kelly, J. (1980) Surviving the Breakup: How Children and Parents Cope with Divorce. New York: Basic Books.

Wright, M. (1991) Justice for Victim and Offenders. Philadelphia: Open University Press.

Wright, M., & Galaway, B. (1989). Mediation and Criminal Justice. London: SAGE.

Zehr, H. (1980). Mediating the Victim Offender Conflict. Elkhart, IN: Mennonite Central Committee Office on Criminal Justice.

Zehr, H. (1985). Retributitive Justice, Restorative Justice. Elkhart, IN: Mennonite Central Committee Office on Criminal Justice.

Zehr, H. (1990). Changing Lenses: A New Focus for Criminal Justice. Scottdale, PA: Herald Press.

Zehr, H., & Umbreit, M. S. (1982). Victim offender reconciliation: An incarceration substitute? Federal Probation 46 (4).

Zetzel, G. W. K. (1985). In and out of the family crucible: Reflections on parent-child mediation. Mediation Quarterly, 7.

Zetzel, G. W. K. & Wixted, S. (1984). Parent Child Mediation. Cambridge, MA: Children's Hearings Project.

Zumeta, Z. D. (1993) Spirituality and mediation. Mediation Quarterly, 11(1).

APPENDIX 1

The Dynamics of Power in Mediation and Negotiation

Bernard Mayer

For people in the business of solving disputes in a collaborative manner, power is sometimes viewed as a dirty word. Power is equated with coercion, a noncooperative spirit, and a breakdown in communication. Yet power also provides the motivation for collaboration and defines the range of settlement options available to the parties. Power is a factor in all interpersonal relations, and it has a significant effect on even the most cooperative dispute-resolution process. All negotiators have some power or influence over other parties and use this influence to pursue their goals. People who have no source of power in regard to a dispute do not have to be dealt with or taken into consideration and are therefore not a party to the conflict.

Mediators are also invested with a great deal of power by the mediation process. Whether or not they consciously choose to exercise it, mediators inevitably use their influence at every point of the intervention. This is neither good nor bad; rather, it is a necessary consequence of the structure of the intervener's role in conflict resolution. What mediators can choose is whether to exercise this power in a deliberate way and with a specific purpose.

An awareness of the ways in which power impacts negotiation and mediation is crucial to the conflict resolver. In order to help parties reach a settlement, the intervener must understand the nature of power as it is brought to bear in the negotiation process and how to manage the use of power in a productive way. This chapter focuses first on the dynamics of power in negotiation and then on the mediator's use of power. The sources of the mediator's power, the different ways in which it can be exercised, and the ethical issues this presents for the mediator are discussed.

Power and Negotiation

A key question for students of the negotiation process is how parties in conflict reach agreement. A number of authors have identified two dimensions to the conflict resolution process: the distributive dimension and the integrative dimension (Thomas, 1976; Walton and McKersie, 1965). The distributive dimension involves the needs or interests of a party that are in conflict with those of another and that can only be satisfied at the expense of the other's needs or interests. A distributive approach to bargaining assumes that the essential issues to be decided involve a distribution of a fixed amount of benefits to the parties involved. The integrative dimension involves the interdependent, or shared, interests of the parties. In the integrative dimension, for one party to meet their interests, the other party's interests must also be met.

To what extent conflicts are resolved along each of these dimensions depends on the nature of the issues involved, the structure within which the parties are operating, the perceptions about the conflict, their relative power, and the process of conflict resolution itself. A distributive approach to conflict resolution emphasizes the use of power to induce the other side to give up as much as possible. There is a tendency to use coercive power and for each party to settle based on their evaluation of their alternatives to a voluntary agreement. An integrative approach seeks to find a common set of interests and to create a way of satisfying each party's needs. Solutions are reached through establishing an effective means of communication and through maximizing the degree to which all parties interests are met. *Getting to Yes* (Fisher and Ury, 1981) presents a practical prescription for how to focus the negotiation process on the integrative aspect of the conflict. Purely distributive or integrative negotiations are rare, and most bargaining involves some elements of both approaches. One of these two dimensions, however, is almost always predominant in any given conflict resolution process.

Although it is easier to recognize the role of power in negotiations that operate primarily along the distributive dimensions, there is a tendency to ignore the role of power in integrative bargaining. Instead, most descriptions of integrative bargaining emphasize the role of objective principles in establishing a fair and mutually satisfying outcome. One of the major criticisms leveled at the integrative bargaining approach outlined in *Getting to Yes* revolved around the inadequacy of the authors' description of the role of power in negotiation (McCarthy, 1985). A purely integrative analysis of bargaining ignores several fundamental facts about the process. The substantive interests of the parties involved are inseparable from their view of their power situation and their desire to protect or enhance it. McCarthy (1985. p. 65) argues that an acceptable outcome is less defined by a mutual realization that the essential interests of all parties have been satisfied than by "the development of a shared view about the outcome of what can only be termed a 'power struggle'--that is, the ability of one side to inflict more damage on the other than it receives in return. This struggle has its own logic and rationale, and the job of the good negotiator is to anticipate its outcome and secure the best deal possible when the power position of his or her own side is at its height."

Fisher (1983, 1985) agrees that the effect of power on negotiation is inescapable and that one cannot either analyze or engage in negotiations effectively without understanding power's role. He argues, however, that power ought not to be equated with the "ability to do damage" but rather with the "ability to influence the decisions of others" (Fisher, 1985, p. 69). Fisher believes that the use of principled negotiating tactics can in fact change the power relationship. Power resides in principle, persuasiveness, relationship, creative problem solving, and commitment as much as in the ability to inflict damage. So, while a negotiator needs to understand power and to work to enhance it, a principled approach is still the most appropriate.

In these two perspectives on power, we can see the essential dilemma underlying the understanding of influence in negotiation. A win-win approach to negotiation is promoted when negotiators employ integrative strategies such as those described by Fisher and Ury. However, negotiation is also a process that involves the development and use of power. Power is both a means to an end in negotiation and an end itself. In fact, negotiators often cannot identify what their real interests are separate from maximizing their power. Although it seems clear that power has a role even in the most integrative of negotiations, it is hard to understand how to reconcile its impact with the principled basis on which collaborative negotiations are assumed to rest.

McCarthy and Fisher's different definitions of power symbolize this dilemma. Is power the ability to persuade or to inflict damage? Can negotiators best maximize their interests by establishing the principled basis of their negotiating stance or by developing their ability to do damage to the other parties? It would be simple if negotiators could always assume that a principled stand would lead to the maximization of their power, to the realization of their essential interests, and to what Fisher and Ury call an "elegant solution," but this is not always a reasonable assumption. A successful negotiator should remain sensitive to the role of both power and principle in negotiation. A successful integrative bargainer will develop his or her sources of power but apply it in an integrative manner if at all possible.

One way of considering the dilemma of power is to realize that a broader definition may be appropriate. Power can be considered to include a variety of approaches to exerting influence over others and may stem from a number of different sources. Kriesberg (1982), Etzioni (1980), Deutsch (1973), Gamson (1968), and others have all suggested three similar but variously defined avenues of influence. These involve the use of rewards, punishment, or persuasion. If power is broken down into these components, then the analytic task shifts to a consideration of when each particular form of influence is appropriate to the participant, the process, and the desire outcome. The negotiator has to determine whether the circumstances indicate that influence based on the ability to reward, to punish, or to persuade is most likely to accomplish his or her ends.

There are many sources of power, but for the most part they can be divided into the following ten categories:

1. *Formal authority.* The power that derives from a formal position within a structure that confers certain decision-making prerogatives. This is the power of a judge, an elected official, a CEO, a parent, or a school principal.

2. *Expert/information power.* The power that is derived from having expertise in a particular area or information about a particular matter.

3. *Associational power* (or referent power). The power that is derived from association with other people with power.

4. *Resource power.* The control over valued resources (money, materials, labor, or other goods or services). The negative version of this power is the ability to deny needed resources or to force others to expend them.

5. *Procedural power.* The control over the procedures by which decisions are made, separate from the control over those decisions themselves (for instance, the power of a judge in a jury trial).

6. *Sanction power.* The ability (or perceived ability) to inflict harm or to interfere with a party's ability to realize his or her interests.

7. *Nuisance power.* The ability to cause discomfort to a party, falling short of the ability to apply direct sanctions.

8. *Habitual power.* The power of the status quo that rests on the premise that it is normally easier to maintain a particular arrangement or course of action than to change it.

9. *Moral power.* The power that comes from an appeal to widely held values. Related to this is the power that results from the conviction that one is right.

10. *Personal power.* The power that derives from a variety of personal attributes that magnify other sources of power, including self-assurance, the ability to articulate one's thoughts and understand one's situation, one's determination and endurance, and so forth.

Some of the sources of power listed above may be consistent with a principled or integrative approach to negotiation, others may not. For example, a party with abundant sanction power but little moral power may find it easier to engage in a distributive approach to negotiation. Successful integrative bargaining will be promoted by the development of sources of power that are congruent with this approach, such as information, moral, personal, and resource power. Other sources of power are also important to the integrative negotiator but primarily as alternatives to be utilized if the negotiation process fails.

Three kinds of problems in the application of power to negotiations are most frequently associated with breakdown in collaborative problem-solving processes. These are the use of inappropriate or ineffective power, the incongruent application of power, and significant imbalances of power.

Appendix 1

The type of power applied may be inappropriate to the process, the desired outcome, the issue being negotiated, or the party toward whom it is directed. Furthermore what is appropriate at one point in the process may be problematic at another. An incongruent application of power occurs when contradictory types of power are exercised during a negotiation.

Power imbalances occur when one party has a great deal more real or perceived power than another. This may be characteristic of the parties' total relationship or relevant only to a particular negotiation or to the specific type of power being utilized. Power inequities cause problems because they lead to rigidity on the part of both the stronger and weaker parties, because they lead to a breakdown in the collaborative process, or because they cause unprincipled agreements to be reached.

The sources of power and the nature of its exercise have crucial implications for the approach taken in negotiation. Without an understanding of the significance of power relations to negotiation, a negotiator is less likely to optimize his or her interests and may even exacerbate the conflict. This does not mean that the principles of interest-based bargaining are not valid. However, negotiators selecting an integrative approach should bargain with an awareness of power dynamics.

Mediators and Power

Although parties to a conflict may turn to mediation for other reasons, the mediator's central objective is normally to handle problems caused by the application of power to the negotiation process. They may engage in problem-solving processes or allow parties to express their emotions safely, but these tactics are often intended to bring about a more constructive application of power.

For mediators to achieve this objective, they need to understand the sources and limits of their power and the strategies that are available to them to influence power dynamics. They must also come to terms with the ethical dilemmas involved in exercising their power.

Sources and Limits of Mediator Power. In most settings, mediators derive their power from the parties with whom they are working. These parties have agreed to participate in a process that is managed by the mediator and to accept his or her procedural expertise. When the parties are no longer willing to grant the mediator this power, then his or her influence is normally at an end. There are several other elements that contribute to the mediator's influence. The mediator usually has personal power in the ability to articulate the issues and interests of concern to the parties and in the rapport established. Frequently, the mediator becomes important to the parties as the one person who has a reasonably decent relationship with the various factions.

People often turn to mediators because of their presumed expertise in the substantive areas involved. This is an important potential source of power, but a dangerous one. Mediators who use their substantive expertise risk losing some of their other sources of influence, particularly the parties' perception of their impartiality. When mediators can use their substantive expertise in an impartial way, they can be effective in helping move parties through the decision-making process.

An important source of mediator power lies in the intervener's alternative to a negotiated solution. Mediators lose nothing but a little prestige when no settlement is reached. To be able to say to parties that "I will do what I can to help, but in the end the results are up to you" gives the mediator a great deal of power. It is very likely that experienced mediators benefit from being able to dissociate themselves from the results of a given case because their professional pride and reputation is built on a larger foundation than one or two negotiations. This source of power is used by mediators repeatedly to get parties to act in a mature and responsible way.

The credibility of the mediation process itself is another major source of the mediator's power. This is a fragile commodity that can easily be damaged if mediators abandon the principles of impartiality and confidentiality.

The mediator's power is limited by his or her role, the nature of the mediation contract, the constraints facing the parties, the social structure within which mediation occurs, and self-imposed ethical restrictions. The role of the mediator is to focus on the process of negotiation and to provide the parties with the structure for arriving at the best possible solution. This limits the mediator's ability to influence the substantive outcome directly, quite apart from ethical considerations. The mediation contract generally requires the mediator to remain impartial as to the conflicting goals of the parties and to maintain a clear standard of confidentiality. If the mediator deviates too much from his or her role or the terms of the contract, the parties may well withdraw their support from the process. Finally, a mediator's power does not normally encompass the ability to come up with solutions that were not in principle obtainable through independent negotiations. The mediator may help parties discover new settlement options, but he or she does not create them.

Mediator's Exercise of Power. Given the mediator's potential sources of power and the constraints on its exercise, what is the appropriate role of mediator power in the mediation process?

The mediator's commitment is to empower the parties by strengthening the process itself. This means exerting influence by advocating the procedures that encourage the development of sound, integrative decisions. These procedures include:

1. Gaining access for all parties to relevant data and information.
2. Ensuring the opportunity for each party to be heard.

3. Helping parties to separate and articulate feelings, values, perceptions, and interests and to identify all relevant interests including those of unrepresented parties.
4. Helping to develop a creative set of options that maximize the parties' individual and collective interests.
5. Helping parties evaluate the options that have been identified and their alternatives to a negotiated agreement.
6. Designing and assisting in the selection of the options that maximize the satisfaction of the parties.
7. Formulating the selected solution in a manner that increases its chances of being mutually acceptable and anticipates to the greatest extent possible the potential for future misinterpretations or manipulations.
8. Assisting in the design of an implementation procedure that promotes compliance and follow through.

It is in the service of the above procedural objectives that mediators are most likely to exert influence within the framework of their role.

There remains the question of what role the mediator has in changing the power relations of the parties and how to address problems in the application of power to the negotiation process. Is it the mediator's role to balance power when a significant imbalance exists? David and Salem (1984) suggest that mediation is ideally suited to address power imbalances in negotiations. From their perspective, handling the imbalances means ensuring that each party's point of view gets a fair hearing and that no party is coerced into agreeing to something that is not in his or her interests. They also point out, however, that a proposed settlement, although unequal, may really be the best option for the weaker party. Thus, the underlying power relations may dictate an unequal result. Mediation, in other words, can provide equality but cannot usually alter the division of resources or the structural conditions that determine the basic power relations between the parties.

Despite the reality of basic power differences between the parties, the mediation process can and should address power imbalances and power dynamics that may hinder productive negotiations. Mediation should promote the exercise of the kinds of power that are congruent with the mediation process, which promote collaborative negotiations, and which are appropriate to the issues and people involved. Generally this means encouraging the use of persuasion, information, appeals to principle, (the sources of power related to a normative orientation), and rewards (the utilitarian basis) and interfering with the use of threats, intimidation, and sanctions, (the sources related to a coercive orientation).

One way in which mediation accomplishes these goals is by helping parties distinguish between their immediate needs and long-term interests. This involves enhancing what Axelrod (1984) has called the "shadow of the future." It is often not in a party's long-term interest to press a perceived immediate advantage or to resort to coercive tactics if this strategy will damage future relations. By helping parties examine their interests in more depth than they might otherwise, the mediator can help them understand the drawbacks of applying their immediate power advantages. Although there are many potential problems with pressing a power advantage, two seem to occur repeatedly in negotiations. Sometimes the only perceived source of power that a weaker party has is to refuse to agree to anything. The perception of being weak and vulnerable is one of the greatest sources of rigidity in negotiations. In addition, agreement forced on a party primarily because of a power differential and not through the satisfaction of the party's interests is likely to be less durable over time and may create unintended future consequences. The mediation process can often make these potential consequences clear to all negotiators and thereby change their approach to bargaining.

There are numerous tactics a mediator can use to change the power dynamics of the parties. Moore (1986) has outlined twelve ways in which mediators use their power to try to promote a satisfactory outcome. These range from guiding the communication and information exchange to managing the doubt the parties may have about their own power and alternatives. Almost anything a mediator does, from inviting one party to speak first to establishing eye contact at a certain point, is an application of their influence in the negotiation. The difficulty is being conscious and intentional in the application of a mediator's power in the negotiation process. It may be helpful for mediators to consider the following principles about the use of their power in mediation:

1. It is better to be conscious about the use of power than to deny its reality in the name of neutrality.

2. Mediators can more effectively give advice, make suggestions, and get parties to think about things they would prefer to avoid by asking the right questions and reframing statements that have been made by others than by stating an opinion or making assertions.

3. It is safer to exert influence in support of the process or the parties' mutual interests than in support of one party. When it is necessary to support one party, it is better to do so by empowering that party, providing an opportunity to be heard, helping to gain access to expert advice or necessary information, and so forth, than it is to support a party by trying to diminish someone else's power or by advocating substantive proposals that support the weaker party's interests.

4. When a mediator decides it is necessary to exert direct influence in support of a substantive outcome, it is best to do so by providing information rather than by stating opinions or putting pressure on the parties.

5. For mediators to be successful, they must trust the process. This means enabling the parties to use the process to discover acceptable results for themselves rather than placing too much emphasis on the mediator's own insights about potential settlements.

6. Exerting influence and maintaining neutrality are not necessarily a contradiction. The mediator loses impartiality only when he or she exerts influence in favor of one party at the expense of the other.

Ethics of Mediator Power. The use of the mediator's power in support of the process itself is much less controversial than the application of that power to achieve specific substantive outcomes or to modify the power relations or relative resources of the parties. The appropriate role of the mediator in influencing the substantive outcome of a dispute or in ensuring adequate representation of key parties has been widely debated. (See McCrory, 1981; Stulberg, 1981; Susskind, 1981.)

The ethical dilemma that faces mediators working in a number of different areas is how to maintain the integrity of the mediation process, which is based on the assumption of mediator neutrality, without letting the process be used to violate important interests of the community or of interested but unrepresented parties. The problem becomes more complicated when the mediator has a great deal of clout. The maintenance of impartiality under these conditions is not an academic question but one that is basic to the credibility of the process. Several considerations may help the mediator cope with this dilemma:

1. The best guide to ethical dilemmas faced by mediators in utilizing their influence is a clear understanding of the purpose of mediation, the role of the mediator, and the explicit or implicit contract under which mediation is entered. The purpose of mediation is to help parties voluntarily arrive at a mutually acceptable decision about issues that are of concern to them. Mediation is not able to correct basic social ills, create social policy where none exists, or make resources available that do not exist. Mediation is also not optimally designed to change people's personalities, self-awareness, or insight into other's needs.

2. Although mediator's perform different functions depending on the stage of mediation or the conflict dynamics presented, their overall role is to guide people through the mediation process and to help them arrive at an integrative solution to their conflict. The use of mediator power in support of or adherence to the process as opposed to supporting a particular kind of substantive outcome is always appropriate to the role.

3. When mediators attempt to influence the substantive outcome, they should do this by utilizing the parties' own capacity to take an objective look at the issues and interests of all involved. This generally means asking the right questions and helping parties to think through their choices and alternatives

rather than making substantive recommendations.

4. If a mediator persists in representing concerns that he or she feels to be essential to a good resolution but that other parties are unable or unwilling to consider, the mediator may lose effectiveness and the process itself may be discredited. The choice therefore may be for the mediator to withdraw or to accept that the result of mediator may be a solution that does not incorporate the interests of an unrepresented third party or the larger community or which violates the values of the mediator. If such a choice is necessary, it is often best made in consultation with the parties themselves.

5. It is important for mediators not to misrepresent the capacity of the mediation process to rectify problems that reside in societal structure or social policy. It is equally important to make sure mediation does not exacerbate these problems.

Many critics of mediation feel that, far from equalizing power, mediation adds to the inequality by preempting the use of advocates by weaker parties. It is important to be sensitive to this very real possibility and to ensure that all parties receive the advice and help they need to participate as equally as possible. If the mediator is sensitive to the ways in which mediation can contribute to a power imbalance and takes steps to address this, then it is more likely that mediation will equalize power.

When basic structural inequalities in power do exist, mediation may be the vehicle through which a weaker party has to choose between two unfavorable outcomes. Such a choice may be inevitable regardless of the conflict resolution process used. If mediation provides someone with the best (albeit still not entirely favorable) outcome, then this process may still be the preferable one. If, however, mediation increases the power differential, it should probably not be used.

Mediation is not a substitute for institutional safeguards that protect the interests of the public, the unrepresented, or the disempowered. When safeguards exist, mediators should see to it that they are not bypassed or subverted. When they do not, mediators should be clear that their services cannot substitute for the procedures and polices that protect individual rights and the public interest.

Conclusion

The impact of power on negotiation and mediation is inescapable, and neither the parties nor the mediator can constructively handle the conflict resolution process if this reality is avoided. A principled approach to negotiation is the most desirable procedure in most circumstances, but the principled negotiator must analyze power relationships, develop his or her power, and understand the limits that the power relationship poses for the process.

A mediator has considerable power in mediation. The exertion of substantive influence by the mediator presents many ethical concerns. It is the mediator's responsibility to see that the mediation process is not used to violate the rights of weaker or unrepresented parties. However, mediation cannot address basic inequities fostered by unequal power relations or by social policy. Perhaps the most that should be expected of mediation is that it does not exacerbate inequities or prevent people from attaining support, redress, or assistance that might otherwise be available to them.

When a mediator understands the dynamics of power in mediation and negotiation, is clear about how to develop and utilize his or her own power, and does not equate neutrality with the absence of influence, he or she will be best able to empower the parties to engage in a collaborative negotiation process.

References

Axelrod, R. *The Evolution of Cooperation.* New York: Basic Books, 1984.

Davis, A.M., and Salem, R.A. "Dealing with Power Imbalances in the Mediation of Interpersonal Disputes." In J.A. Lemmon (ed.), "Procedures for Guiding the Divorce Mediation Process." *Mediation Quarterly,* no. 6. San Francisco: Jossey-Bass, 1984, 17-26.

Deutsch, M. *The Resolution of Conflict: Constructive and Destructive Processes.* New Haven: Yale University Press, 1973.

Etzioni, A. "Compliance Structures." In A. Etzioni and E.W. Lehman (eds.), *A Sociological Reader on Complex Organizations.* New York: Holt, Rinehart & Winston, 1980.

Fisher, R. "Negotiating Power." *American Behavioral Scientist,* 1983, 27 (2), 149-166.

Fisher, R. "Beyond Yes." *Negotiation Journal,* 1985, I (1), 67-70.

Fisher, R. and Ury, W. *Getting to Yes.* Boston: Houghton Mifflin, 1981.

Gamson, W.A. *Power and Discontent.* Homewood, Ill.: Dorsey Press, 1968.

Kriesberg, L. *Social Conflicts.* (2nd edition). Englewood Cliffs, N.J.: Prentice-Hall, 1982.

McCarthy, W. "The Role of Power and Principle in Getting to Yes." *Negotiation Journal,* 1985, I (1), 59-66.

McCrory, J. "The Mediation Puzzle." *Vermont Law Review,* 1981, 6 (1), 85-117.

Moore, C.W. *The Mediation Process: Practical Strategies for Resolving Conflicts.* San Francisco: Jossey-Bass, 1986.

Stulberg, J.B. "The Theory and Practice of Mediation: A Reply to Professor Susskind." *Vermont Law Review,* 1981, 6 (1)m 85-117.

Susskind, L. "Environmental Mediation and the Accountability Problem."

Vermont Law Review, 1981, 6 (1), 1-48.

Thomas, K. "Conflict and Conflict Management." In M.C Dunnett (ed.), *Handbook of Industrial and Organizational Psychology.* Chicago: Rand McNally, 1976.

Walton, R.E., and McKersie, R.B. *A Behavioral Theory of Labor Negotiations.* New York: McGraw-Hill, 1965.

APPENDIX 2

Mediation and Therapy

As an emerging area of practice, mediation has evolved from a multidisciplinary base. This has enriched the profession and also created confusion as to its identity. The knowledge base of theory, practice and techniques of mediation derive from a variety of disciplines and the experience of practitioners from different professions. Law, labor relations, religion, sociology, psychology, psychotherapy, social work and education have all contributed to the development of mediation. As mediation evolves into a distinct field of practice, enriched by the integration of these diverse approaches to conflict resolution, it offers a more creative and comprehensive means to meet client needs than can be offered by any one approach or traditional adversarial forms of dealing with conflict. Just as mediation has distinguished itself from law, it must now distinguish itself from psychotherapy.

Although there are similarities in techniques, process and outcomes between therapy and mediation, mediation is not a new form of psychotherapy. Misunderstanding about mediation may blur boundaries so that the process of mediation and psychotherapy become indistinguishable. If mediation becomes another type of therapeutic treatment, the unique power of mediation as a means of resolving conflict and a genuinely different service is lost. Increased clarity regarding the purpose of mediation is essential in order to develop mediation models that are appropriate for different types of disputes and for the identification and referral of appropriate clients to psychotherapy. Confusion and blurring of roles, goals and techniques are most frequent in areas of interpersonal conflict, parent-child relations, custody and divorce. This is particularly true for psychotherapists from mental health and family therapy backgrounds who provide mediation services.

This paper will present a model for understanding the relationship between mediation and psychotherapy and compare their similarities and differences in five areas: goals, roles, assessments, processes and interventions. Suggestions will be made on how psychotherapeutic methods may be integrated into mediation to facilitate its process, and creative new areas of mediation will be described which challenge traditional understandings of the relationship between mediation and psychotherapy.

Used by permission--William Bradshaw, MSW, Assistant Professor, Department of Social Work, College of St. Catherine, University of St. Thomas, St. Paul, Minnesota.

Mediating Interpersonal Conflicts: A Pathway to Peace

Definitions for Mediation and Therapy Comparisons

Mediation is a means of resolving conflict through a neutral third party who facilitates communication to help define the issues, develop alternatives and reach resolution. The mediator helps the disputants negotiate with one another to resolve the dispute and develop an agreement. Frequently the agreement is in written form and legally binding. The work is task focused, issue oriented and emphasizes problem-solving. The purpose of psychotherapy is the development of insight, personality and behavioral change. Psychotherapy involves a unique helping relationship which uses interpersonal and psychological methods to resolve crisis, improve relationships, reduce symptoms, improve social and psychological functioning, and enhance well-being. The work is client focused, generally emotion oriented and emphasizes behavioral change.

The practice of mediation includes a variety of styles, some of which are more appropriate for certain types of conflict. Underlying the various styles, there are two distinct approaches: "therapeutic," which is non-directive and empowering, and "bargaining," which is directive and controlling (Umbreit, 1988; Sibley & Merry, 1986). In therapeutic styles the mediator is less active and directive, encourages communication in which parties express emotional concerns and exploration of issues which may go beyond the immediate complaint. More attention is paid to enhancing the process of mutual aid between the parties than simply emphasizing settlement issues. Therapeutic styles of mediation are sometimes confused with therapy. Bargaining styles of mediation focus on the bottom line of settlement issues and the bargaining process. The mediator is highly active, directive and emphasizes accomplishment of tasks and avoids emotions and relationship issues as much as possible. The therapeutic and bargaining styles represent extremes on a continuum of mediation styles and suggest the richness and variety of mediation practice.

While there are numerous approaches to psychotherapy, two distinct categories will be used in this chapter--insight and action. Insight includes psychodynamic, non-directive, interpersonal approaches to treatment. These therapies are generally long term and emphasize expression of emotions and the development of insight. Therapists are less directive and the process of therapy is emphasized over goals and tasks. Action therapies include cognitive-behavioral, task-centered, strategic, solution based, and brief therapy. In these, the therapist is more active, directive and task oriented. Treatment is brief, goal focused and involves clients in many task assignments as part of therapy.

Appendix 2

Table 9.1
Types of Therapy and Mediation

Problems in Mediation and Therapy Comparisons

There are many aspects of mediation that are clearly different from psychotherapy, however, there are also similarities in process, skills and outcome. Comparisons between mediation and psychotherapy have been made by numerous authors (Milne, 1985; Kelly, 1983; Grebe, 1986; Forlenza, 1988). These comparisons have two major limitations. First, there are numerous mediation and psychotherapy models, of which some are radically different, and others quite similar. Mediation models range from specific focus on the mechanics of dispute resolution and settlement to more therapeutic and educational approaches.

There is a plethora of therapy models including psycho dynamic, cognitive, behavioral, nondirective and brief. On the one hand, attempts to compare them in a general way, frequently using traditional dynamic models of individual therapy, oversimplify the issues and create apparent distinctions which in reality may not exist. On the other hand, a comparison of a single model of therapy that is more compatible with mediation can suggest similarities that are not reflective of the wider fields of psychotherapy.

Second, most comparisons fail to take into consideration differences in a client's need, type of disputes and areas of mediation. For example, a client's characteristics, needs and the content of mediation may vary greatly in mediation of divorce, workplace or victim offender issues. Each may require somewhat different approaches and methods for successful resolution. There may be considerable variation in similarities and differences between psychotherapy and mediation on dimensions of practice in different areas of mediation.

Common Skills and Special Knowledge

Mediation and psychotherapy may be initially compared in terms of common knowledge and core skills, special knowledge, special techniques and application to different areas of mediation. To observe a good mediation or psychotherapy session would be to observe good use of core helping skills.

Common core skills include basic communication and human relationship skills (Shulman, 1984, Hepworth & Larson, 1990). The ability to have a nonjudgmental attitude, ask open ended questions, attend verbally and nonverbally, establish rapport, use empathy, reflection and to use focusing and summarizing skills are essential to both psychotherapy and mediation. The ability to balance task focused work with emotional needs, clarify the nature and process of the work, keep to task, deal with obstacles and break work into smaller manageable pieces are generalist skills pertinent to mediation and psychotherapy.

Both mediation and psychotherapy are enhanced by specialized knowledge in specific areas. For example, the field of divorce mediation may involve special knowledge of financial planning, guidelines for equitable division of family resources, real estate and tax information. In therapy a family systems framework is invaluable in understanding the context of family disputes. Understanding the process of grief and loss, marital dynamics, and dysfunctional communication patterns may assist in dealing with the emotions and resistance that frequently hinder the process of reaching a settlement.

Mediators have special skills in conflict management, negotiation and bargaining strategies which can assist couples in reaching decisions about distribution of family resources. Psychotherapists may be adept in the use of empathy, role reversals and re-framing techniques which can be used to facilitate the mediation process. Transactional analysis, for example, has been successfully applied in mediation to reduce conflict within couples.

The different knowledge base of mediation and psychotherapy can be integrated within specific areas of mediation to provide service to clients that will better meet their needs. Similarly, skills unique to each field can facilitate the mediation process and accomplishment of the mediation goals. For clinically trained mediators therapeutic knowledge and skills are used to facilitate the process and to meet the goals of mediation not therapy.

Common core skills, specialized knowledge and techniques can be applied to specific areas of mediation as a model to examine the relationship, similarities, and differences between mediation and psychotherapy. In addition, points of integration and potential areas of synthesis can be identified which may enhance the development of new mediation models and improve mediation services to clients. Mediation and psychotherapy will be compared in five critical elements of practice: goals, roles, assessments, processes and interventions.

Table 9.2
Divorce Mediation Example

Appendix 2

Comparison of the Elements of Practice

Goals

The goal of mediation is to negotiate agreement of disputed issues in ways that are agreeable and of benefit to all parties (Milne, 1985). The focus of mediation is circumscribed by the context and purpose of mediation--clients contract for mediation service to resolve disputes and get agreements. They are not contracting for psychotherapy. The goals of psychotherapy are cognitive, affective, behavioral, and relationship changes which improve intrapersonal and interpersonal functioning.

In divorce mediation, for example, the goals focus on allocation of property and money, custody and visitation issues, and the disillusion of the marriage contract--not treatment. There is no analysis of the past, exploration of history, development of insight or personal change. The goal is to reach an agreement that handles property, economic and visitation issues with clear and binding guidelines.

While therapeutic changes may occur, in terms of personality change, insight, or resolution of grief as a result of the settlement, these are side effects of the mediation process, not primary goals. Therapeutic interventions may be used, but their purpose is to reach an agreement, not to provide therapy. The specific goal of settlement is a major distinguishing feature between mediation and psychotherapy.

Kelly (1983) has noted that some family mediators have subgoals in addition to the basic mediation goals. These include working with the couple so they can share parenting in a reasonable way after the divorce. Likewise the family may be assisted to adapt to the realities of a divorce. Educating, modeling and practicing problem-solving and communication skills may also be subgoals. Clearly these subgoals represent more therapeutic models of divorce mediation and blur the boundaries between mediation and psychotherapy.

Roles

The role of a mediator or psychotherapist will vary based on the particular model of practice. In general mediators have been described as active, directive and task focused while psychotherapists have been traditionally seen as more passive, non-directive, emotion focused and insight oriented. This may hold true in comparison to individual dynamic treatment, however, these distinctions disappear when comparing mediation to specific forms of therapy such as cognitive, behavioral, and strategic approaches, which are very active, directive, and task focused.

The role of the therapist and mediator is influenced by the agency purpose, the context of service, and the service goals and contract. The mediator is not responsible for the mental health of the client; the agreement is to help resolve a dispute. The mediator also holds a legal or quasi-legal role, especially when their work is connected to the court in some way, as in divorce settlements, custody cases and victim offender restitution. Psychotherapy, for the most part, is a personal event with the client requesting assistance with mental health issues. Both mediators and therapist encourage empowerment of the client in meeting their needs and accomplishing their goals.

The relationship between practitioner and client and the use of self by the practitioner take on quite different meaning in mediation and psychotherapy. In mediation there is little emphasis, analysis, or discussion about the mediator relationship, other than some rapport building. In psychotherapy, the relationship between therapist and client and the therapist's use of self assume much greater importance. This is especially true in interpersonal, psycho dynamic and humanistic models of therapy which assume that much of the healing in therapy comes through the relationship, qualities of the therapist or in corrective experiences which come through interaction with the therapist. The wealth of literature on transference and countertransference highlights the importance of relationship in psychotherapy. In all forms of therapy, however, there is considerably more attention paid to the relationship than in mediation. With the focus on technical aspects of dispute resolution in mediation, the impact of the mediator and the relationship factors have been neglected.

Assessments

Assessment in mediation does not require detailed history of the individuals involved or of the problem to be resolved. External, concrete data is more important than internal, historical, psychological information. History is not necessary for successful agreements, in fact, some feel that too much background information can lead to mediator bias.

Psychotherapy assessments range on a continuum from heavily psychological and historically based to those that focus on current behavior. In general, psychotherapy assessments may utilize much more history and internal psychological information as a basis for assessment.

Assessment is tied to the purpose of mediation and is used to develop strategy. In mediation assessment begins with definition of the issues of the dispute, not in terms of psychological issues, but in terms of mutual interests and needs in the settlement. Defining issues clarify the common ground and mutual interests between the disputants and identifies conflicts which may interfere with the mediation process.

Mediators assess three types of conflict which can interfere with the process: topical, personal and relational (Milne, 1985). Topical conflicts refer to position taking in negotiation and genuine conflicts of interest. Personal conflicts include individual psychological issues such as revenge which may impede divorce mediation. Relationship conflicts are the ongoing issues between the disputants. An essential part of the assessment is to clarify that the topical conflicts are the focus of mediation and that treatment or resolution of personal and relational conflicts will not be on the mediation agenda.

Another area of assessment is that of power differentials among the parties and their communication and negotiation skills (Kelly, 1983). Observed power imbalances, for example between spouses in divorce mediation, are used to develop strategies which support and empower the weaker party in order to ensure fair negotiations and settlements. Communication between disputants, particularly in custody and divorce cases, is often dysfunctional. Assessment of these skills is important for planning intervention strategies in the mediation session.

Psychological assessment is based on the purpose of psychotherapy and may include the use of several formalized instruments. Assessments may include analysis of defenses, psychiatric diagnosis, measurement of symptoms and level of functioning, assessment of the behavior and cognition to be changed, relationship dynamics, stressors, coping mechanisms, and social support.

Process

Mediation and psychotherapy have been described as processes which includes several stages. One mediation approach describes a four stage process: setting the stage, defining issues, processing issues and resolving issues (Milne, 1985). These are comparable to standard counseling stage theories which include preparation, engagement, goal setting and planning, work phase and termination (Shulman, 1984).

Stage descriptions of the process of mediation and psychotherapy are remarkably similar and share a common core of generalist skills in the helping process. Initial work focuses on establishing rapport and engaging the client. Clarification of the role and purpose of the work and identification of needs, interests and goals are done in this stage.

In the work phase problem-solving is preeminent. Options are generated, tasks assigned and obstacles to progress are identified and worked through. In mediation mutual interests are clarified and possible alternatives brainstormed. Common obstacles to progress, that are worked on, include improving communication, use of I statements and paraphrasing which enhances mutual understanding. The management of emotions, personal and relationship conflicts that disrupt the work of reaching an agreement in the dispute, are essential to this stage.

In addition to these generalist methods, psychotherapy in the work phase may differ considerably from mediation in the range of interventions and type of process utilized by different therapeutic schools. Work focusing on cognition, emotions, behavior, dreams or interpersonal issues with the therapist may dominate. Issues of resistance, reinforcers, and motivation or task breakdown are worked with in order to facilitate the change process when progress toward goals falters.

Endings for both mediation and psychotherapy emphasize monitoring of progress, evaluation of goal attainment, maintenance of change or keeping the dispute resolution agreement. Endings in psychotherapeutic work also frequently emphasize dealing with feelings about the therapist and loss of the relationship.

Differences in process between mediation and psychotherapy are most vivid in comparing the role of emotions. The role of emotions in the process of mediation and psychotherapy may be falsely dichotomized as therapy focuses on emotions and mediation focuses on tasks. The human experience of conflict generates many feelings. For example, in divorce mediation, couples will bring considerable emotions to mediation and the tasks of mediation will stimulate more emotions. Important differences occur in the use of emotions and the methods of handling them. In mediation emotions are not the major factor. Emotions may be expressed and considered in mediation if they facilitate the process of dispute resolution. However, if the process becomes dominated by emotional expression and exploration, the tasks of mediation are hindered.

Emotions are of paramount importance in insight therapy and are given major focus in treatment. Working to elicit, identify, explore, express, and understand feelings is common. Other approaches, such as behavior therapy and task-centered approaches, place considerably less importance on feelings and work with them primarily when they obstruct task completion.

In mediation, the mediator must evaluate when to ignore, allow, or re-frame emotional expression in terms of which is the best strategy to further progress in reaching a settlement. She may allow expression of feelings but without exploration of the history or attempts to therapeutically intervene in the situation.

In human interactions affect is important. In therapy, emotions may be worked with for release, understanding, or personal growth, but in mediation they are understood and dealt with in different ways. The mediator doesn't explore or interpret feeling but rather manages emotions to facilitate the process. To manage emotions, the mediator may provide communication skill training to clients or may reinforce the purpose of mediation and explore the mutual needs, interests and issues (Milne, 1985). The therapist doing mediation, who is trained to focus on the internal realities of the client and their emotions, may find it difficult to ignore or avoid emotions while focusing on rational problem-solving.

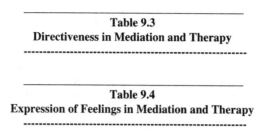

Table 9.3
Directiveness in Mediation and Therapy

Table 9.4
Expression of Feelings in Mediation and Therapy

Interventions

Management of conflict in mediation is essential for effective mediation. Too much conflict can prevent progress and create an adversarial process. In addition to the core skills shared by mediators and therapists, mediators are trained in conflict management, negotiation and bargaining techniques. Conflict management includes separating the person from the problem; being hard on the problem but soft on the person; and focusing on mutual interests (Fisher & Ury, 1991).

Mediators may work with conflict in several ways, including the use of time outs, ventilation outside the session, and training clients in assertive communication. Breaking conflict down into manageable pieces is frequently done. Mediators may also identify dysfunctional responses to conflict, give directives, prohibit certain topics, and reinforce cooperative interactions. All of these conflict management methods serve to contain conflict in order to maintain task focus and reach settlements.

Negotiation strategies are an area of skill in which many psychotherapists have little background. Negotiation techniques like Best Alternative to a Negotiated Settlement (Fisher & Ury, 1991) are commonly used by mediators. Kelly (1983) describes four negotiation methods which have proven effective in mediation: educating clients to understand the details of proposals and the process of mediation; asking clients to explain their demands; asking each client to make a case for why the other should accept their demands; and stressing a win-win approach to negotiation in which mutual interests can be met.

Directive and non-directive therapeutic interventions include useful strategies for conflict resolution which can be used in mediation. For example, commonly used interventions include re-labeling, re-framing, use of metaphors, directives, behavioral contracts, task breakdown and implementation, and changes in cognition and beliefs. While the purpose of mediation is not therapy, there are often therapeutic effects as a result of mediation.

Solution based psychotherapy provides an excellent example of treatment strategies which may be used to enhance mediation. Solution based therapy is a brief, directive, task oriented approach to treatment which emphasizes methods that empower clients to create solutions to their problems. It is especially useful in cases where clients or couples are stuck in negative communication and behavioral patterns. Unique strategies to identify goals and promote doing something new in face of an impasse, instead of doing the same thing over and over, have been successful in helping clients achieve goals and find creative solutions to old problems.

Strategies that shift emphasis away from problem behaviors and towards solutions have great relevance for dealing with the impasses and conflicts in mediation. This type of interdisciplinary collaboration can enrich mediation and assist in creating new therapeutic models and mediation services that can better serve unique populations, problems and needs of clients.

Emerging Areas of Mediation

Two newly emerging areas of mediation highlight the need for creative responses to the unique needs of conflict resolution and mediation. These challenge and expand some of the commonly held beliefs about the distinctions between psychotherapy and mediation. In the field of victim offender mediation, traditional work has focused on the development of restitution plans between victims and offenders involved in nonviolent property offenses. Recently, victim offender mediation has expanded to include mediation of severely violent offenses. For example, in one mediation case, a mother felt the need to confront the man who killed her son and hoped it would bring some healing to her. Similarly, the offender wanted to find some healing for himself. The common purposes of mediation, conflict resolution, restitution, and an agreed upon settlement did not apply in this case. A non-clinician performed the mediation without having goals of therapy, personality or behavior change. To observe the process, one would find similarities to therapy and mediation in the use of the common core skills of helping. The results for both parties were therapeutic. Victim offender mediation of violent crimes, with the goal of achieving a greater sense of closure and healing, extends and adapts the power and potential of mediation to serve distinct human needs.

In child custody and divorce mediation there are families so severely dysfunctional that traditional mediation is inadequate to address the complex psychological and interactive patterns that block efforts to reach decisions and settlements. Unfortunately, attempts to provide family therapy by other workers prior to mediation are often not realistic because of pressing time frames and the intermingling of family dynamics with critical issues of the family which are of a legal nature and require mediation. A therapeutic interactive approach, with a therapist-mediator or a team of therapist, mediator and attorney, focuses on dysfunctional dynamics and patterns of behavior to resolve severe conflicts and determine custody and divorce settlements.

It may be that with such difficult family situations a hybrid of therapy and mediation procedures carried out by a therapist-mediator in a therapeutic context provides the best approach to mediation with severely disable families. Such a role calls for an advanced practitioner and blurs the boundaries of psychotherapy and mediation. It has been suggested that it may be important to consider this a special form of conflict resolution within a psychotherapy context in order to preserve the integrity of traditional mediation. In any case, it suggests another example of integrating mediation and psychotherapy to meet the unique needs of people in mediation and conflict resolution.

Summary

In evolving from multidisciplinary roots, mediation has a growing need to differentiate itself from psychotherapy and to identify principles, methods and strategies from the field of psychotherapy that can be used to facilitate the process of mediation and meet the goals of mediation practice. It is important to distinguish therapy from mediation, although such a task is difficult due to the diverse models and styles within each field.

Mediation styles can be divided into two distinct approaches-- therapeutic, which is non-directive and empowering, and bargaining, which is directive and controlling. For comparisons sake, psychotherapy is also categorized into two approaches--insight, which is psychodynamic, non-directive and interpersonal, and action, which is task-centered and solution based. Both mediation and psychotherapy draw from some common core communication and human relationship skills.

Comparisons between mediation and psychotherapy were made regarding goals, roles, assessments, processes and interventions. The goal of mediation is conflict resolution, while psychotherapy focuses upon helping interpersonal and intrapersonal functioning. The roles of the mediator or therapist vary based on the style of practice and may be quite similar or different. Assessment for mediation does not require a detailed history of the individuals involved, psychotherapy usually does. The process of mediation and therapy are usually described as going through several stages, however, depending up the model practiced, the similarity or differences vary. Interventions of mediation center on conflict management, while therapy interventions focus on individual behaviors. Newly emerging areas of mediation, such as divorce and child custody, or victim offender mediation for severely violent offenses, are challenging the boundaries between mediation and therapy.

Table 9.1
Types of Therapy and Mediation

Models of Psychotherapy

Insight	Action
Psychodynamic	Cognitive-Behavioral
Person-centered	Task-centered
Interpersonal	Strategic
	Solution based

Styles of Mediation

Therapeutic	Bargaining
Therapeutic	Bargaining
Empowering	Controlling
Educational	Legal

Table 9.2
Divorce Mediation Example

Common Skills
- empathy - reflection
- focusing - summarizing
- balance task & emotional needs
- identify common ground
- dealing with obstacles

Mediation: Special Knowledge	Psychotherapy: Special Knowledge
• financial planning	• marital dynamics
• custody procedures	• grief and loss
• divorce laws	• resistance
• conflict negotiation, bargaining, mediation	• reframing - relabeling

Appendix 2

Table 9.3
Directiveness in Mediation and Therapy

Directive	Non-Directive
I--I	
Bargaining styles of mediation	Therapeutic styles of mediation
Action models of psychotherapy	Insight models of psychotherapy

Table 9.4
Expression of Feelings in Mediation and Therapy

Frequent	In-Frequent
I---I	
Therapeutic styles of mediation	Bargaining styles of mediation
Insight models of psychotherapy	Action models of psychotherapy

References

Fisher, R. and Ury, W. (1991). "Getting to Yes: Negotiating Agreements Without Giving In." New York: Penguin Books.

Forlenza, S.G.(1988). "The mental health professional as mediator." Paper presented at the annual meeting of the Eastern Psychological Association, Buffalo, NY.

Gold, L. (1985). "Reflections on the transition from therapist to mediator." *Mediation Quarterly*, No. 9, September.

Grebe, Sarah Childs (1986). "A comparison of the tasks and definitions of family mediation and those of strategic family therapy." *Mediation Quarterly*, No. 13, Fall.

Hepworth and Larso (1990). *Direct Social Work Practice Therory and Skills.* Homewood, Ill: Dorsey Press.

Kelly, J. (1983). "Mediation and psychotherapy: Distinguishing the difference." *Mediation Quarterly*, No. 1.

Milne, A.L. (1985). "Mediation or therapy - which is it?" In S.C.Grege (Ed.), *Divorce and Family Mediation*, Rockville, MD: Aspen.

Shulman, L. (1984). *The Skills of Helping Individuals and Groups*. Itasca, Ill: Peacock.

Silbey, S.S. and Merry, S.E. (1986). "Mediation Settlement Strategies." *Law and Policy*, January.

Umbreit, M.S. (1988). "Mediation of Victim Offender Conflict." *Journal of Dispute Resolution*. University of Missouri School of Law.

APPENDIX 3

Influencing Unconscious Influences: The Healing Dimension of Mediation

Lois Gold

Current role definitions limit the potential for the mediation process to be a healing experience. This article examines the implications of considering mediation within a healing paradigm. Methods to increase the healing potential of the mediation process focus on the quality of the mediator-client relationship, drawing from the mediator's highest consciousness or spiritual center, the use of indirect and embedded suggestion, and strategies that promote self-healing. It is suggested that there is room for a model of mediation incorporating healing, which might be referred to as "holistic" mediation.

To a significant extent the role of the mediator is constrained by the limitations of the negotiating structure and language. We work primarily on a cognitive level, yet 93 percent of all communication is nonverbal, and significant psychological change usually occurs outside conscious awareness.

Beginning with the assumption of divorce negotiations as a multilevel experience, this article will explore the potential for healing in the noncognitive experience of the mediation process. Drawing on the healing arts, Ericksonian hypnotherapy's model of the unconscious as a creative resource, and our own spiritual centers, I will describe how we can augment the healing elements inherent in a collaborative dispute resolution process.

From this perspective, the focus will be threefold: (1) an examination of the concept of mediator "presence," (2) a consideration of mediation within a healing paradigm, and (3) a discussion of indirect interventions and techniques that promote self-healing.

Mediator "Presence"

How we use ourselves and what we bring of our own personal being has largely been neglected in the mediation literature. Narrow role parameters have defined practice without taking into account the relationship between client and mediator or the "presence" the mediation brings to the negotiation session. While this may have been necessary in the nascence of the profession in order to carve a professional identify, develop skills as negotiators, and guard neutrality, we have not had permission to consider our own unique personas in our work. It is almost as though being a "neutral" implies significant constraints on being a person. Mediation is task oriented; for this reason, we have rarely explored the skills and interventions that do not bear directly on negotiating and bargaining.

I first came to think about the concept of "presence" through my association with the late Virginia Satir. An element of her charisma as a teacher, therapist, and pioneer in the field of family therapy was what she described as being "fully present." She was steeped in the humanistic tradition, and her belief in each person's capacity for growth change, and transformation was in her bones. She described it as "feeling these things in every cell of my body." A master reframer, she was able to find positive intention behind even the most maladaptive behavior and never wavered from seeing the potential for change in even the most difficult circumstances. She regarded authentic human connection as fundamental to change processes and perhaps was most remarkable in her ability to make contact with each person on a basic human level.

As mediators, we share a commitment to similar humanistic principles. Satir had a powerful presence because she was connected to her belief system at the core of her being. While the most remarkable example of "presence" is charisma, most of us experience effortless flow when there is a congruence of mind and action, when we lose all self-consciousness, and when we are fully present.

Four elements of presence can increase our effectiveness as mediators: (1) being centered; (2) being connected to one's governing values and beliefs and highest purpose; (3) making contact with the humanity of the clients; and (4) being congruent.

1. *Being centered.* Being centered or grounded refers to the state of physical and mental alignment in which people experience an almost transcendental connection to their being or to the larger universe or cosmos. There is a feeling of harmony, as if boundaries disappear. People empty their mind and simply focus on "what is," observing present experience without interfering with it. A shift of consciousness occurs that makes it possible to see things not ordinarily seen because the focus is outside of the self and thinking and judgement are suspended.

Being centered, however brief, is an altered state of consciousness. In mediation, we usually operate in the linear, analytical mode. However, we shift consciousness all the time, and each state of consciousness produces new opportunities for problem solving, because the mechanisms that operate within it organize experience differently (Lankton, 1985). Working from the center draws from the creative side of our brain, frequently generating new perceptions and perspectives on the problem. At any time during or before a mediation session, the mediator can momentarily shift consciousness by taking a few deep breaths, emptying the mind of all thought, and simply centering on the awareness of the present moment.

When the mediator is centered, this attitude of self-acceptance and self-respect translates into an appreciation of the clients' humanity, enabling the mediator to see them apart from the context of the dispute. A mediator who is centered can inspire trust and allow others to reflect their own truth. When the mediator projects a sense of reverence for what is sacred in this work, is willing to view the clients from the heart, and can speak to the clients' soul, this work will be healing.

2. *Being connected to one's governing values and beliefs and highest purpose.* The more emotionally connected we are to our highest intention in choosing to become a mediator, the more the power of that intention will be expressed in our work. Because the decision to become a mediator for many represented a radical shift in goals and often grew out of a desire to bring about change, this profession is characterized by a sense of purpose and mission. The more the highest intention in making that choice is clarified, made conscious, and amplified, the more it becomes a guiding force. Intention organizes behavior at the unconscious level. Centering on intention, on why we answered the "calling," is empowering and affects the presence we project. To the extent that we convey the highest possibilities of this work, we enable our clients to recognize and clarify their highest possibilities.

A short meditation before a session can be used to clarify and connect to one's central and governing values and highest purpose. Sit comfortably, close your eyes, take several slow deep breaths, and review your belief in mediation, the skills and resources you have acquired as a negotiator, what you respect most about how you work, why you chose to become a mediator, and what you sense are the deepest concerns and hopes of the clients you are about to see.

3. *Connecting with the humanity of the clients.* The third element of "presence" is the ability to connect with the client. Some experts suggest that connection is the key to helping and that the quality of the relationship is what makes the difference in enabling others to bear their pain and garner strength. It has been said that the successes of Carl Simonton, the pioneer in the use of visualization in the treatment of cancer, had as much to do with him and the relationships he established as they did with the techniques he used (Capra, 1988).

This kind of connection comes from being able to acknowledge and simply "be with what is"--the loss, sorrow, pain--and to not need to do anything about it. There is a healing power in just being there. By the very act of entering the world of others and acknowledging experiences they may not have been able to communicate and making these experiences more understandable and real to them, something transformational occurs. A profound feeling of intimacy is created when people feel they have been understood at the deepest level. Rapport is lost if the mediator focuses only on the substantive issues and ignores the body language or other signs of stress in the person.

It is easy to become so absorbed in the negotiation process or caught up in the conflict that the individual person becomes invisible. The mediator should try to step back and look at both parties in their human struggle to survive--seeing the lost hopes, spent dreams, and pain. The compassionate acceptance of each person's humanity that the mediator expresses enables the clients to feel more compassion for themselves and possibly for their partners.

It is interesting to compare mediation cases in which the issues were competently resolved and those in which a real feeling of connection between mediator and clients existed. The difference can be seen in the good-bye. It is in the hug instead of the handshake. Mediators are invited to review their cases and examine what characterized the cases in which they felt an emotional connection with clients. What was that connection rooted in? What part of the mediator's self was allowed into the mediation process? I suspect that these are the couples who were helped at the deepest level.

4. *Being congruent.* A fourth element of presence is congruence. Being congruent is the condition of being emotionally honest, being who you are, and not allowing your anxiety, pride, or ego to be a mask (Satir, 1976). It is being authentic, not having to be perfect and have all the answers. Carl Rogers has said that "there is something I do before a session. I let myself know that I am enough. Not perfect. Perfect wouldn't be enough. But that I am human, and that is enough" (quoted in Remen, 1989, p. 93). The power of congruence comes from the permission to be who you are, unencumbered by "shoulds" and self-consciousness.

A Healing Paradigm

As mediators, it is not our goal to heal our clients, and we do not typically think of ourselves as healers. However, I believe that we could actualize the healing potential inherent in a cooperative process by thinking about mediation in terms of a healing paradigm as well as within a conflict resolution context.

Healing is a complex phenomenon that has physical, spiritual, and emotional components. It is not well understood. We understand the process of disease and dysfunction more than we understand the process of recovery.

Appendix 3

While it is beyond the scope of this article to rigorously define hearing or to create some standard to apply to the mediation process, I would like to draw on the elements of the healing arts that relate to what we do as mediators.

One of the healer's fundamental roles is to help individuals tune into their own healing capacities. People are healed by different kinds of healers and systems because the real healer is within. Different techniques merely activate the inner healer.

Many diverse techniques in the healing arts exist. The threads that unite the various approaches to healing are universals that can be applied to any helping relationship to make it more healing. In the book *Healers on Healing,* Carlson and Shield (1989) draw common elements from the writings of such well-known healers as Carl Simonton and Ram Dass. They describe the major elements of any healing experience in terms of (1) the role of unconditional love and caring, (2) the nature of the relationship--rapport, connection, emotional support--since healing does not occur in isolation, (3) the importance of the return to wholeness, (4) the desirability of listening to innate wisdom--helping clients find and listen to their higher intelligence, (5) the need to develop a healing attitude--believing change is possible and working toward a better future, and (6) the realization that healing is our natural state, since the organism strives toward health and restoration.

Love is the uniting principle in all healing approaches. Healing's opposite is judgement, and any system or practitioner loses effectiveness in becoming judgmental. The true healer merely gives the gift of healing but does not watch over the patient to say what form it should be received in. This frees the healer to heal unhampered by anxiety over the possible results (Prather, 1989). The common denominator in all healing methods is unconditional love that respects the uniqueness of each individual and empowers clients to take responsibility for their own well-being. One aspect of the healer's love is to help clients overcome the fear of change and to align themselves with the process of transformation (Schwartz, 1989). Healing arises out of compassion. Compassion is a genuine concern for another's pain. Suffering is a soulless state. Part of the role of ritual is to coax the soul into participating in a time of need. The compassionate healer whose soul is present awakens the other's soul (Bruyere, 1989). Empathy, nonpossessive warmth, and genuineness create a sense of being "present" with the client. . . genuinely listening to what is occurring at the moment and putting aside any preconceived notions of what needs to be done (May, 1989). The way we stand in relationship to each other fosters healing. My woundedness allows me to connect to you in your woundedness and creates trust. I know what suffering is. I know of your feeling of isolation, loss, and fright. My woundedness allows me to be with you in a nonjudgmental way, and my presence facilitates something. In a true healing relationship, both heal and are healed (Remen, 1989).

Although our work does not typically have healing as a focus, the mediation process shares the fundamental principles just outlined. While we describe what we do differently, mediation, like other helping professions, operates within this core framework. We see ourselves as caring individuals who believe that clients have the inner capacity to find their own solutions. We activate the hope that life can be better, that solutions are possible. We value self-determination and empowerment. We are oriented toward the future, supporting clients in moving forward and in constructively coping with change. We help them work toward the higher good for themselves and their families.

Disputes that are honorably resolved open the way for any wounds to mend. A process that is respectful of each person and that encourages the expression of mutual respect and courtesy heals the ravages of hateful and angry diatribes. A process that supports people in retaining control of the awareness of mutual needs, mutual losses, and shared concerns reduces feelings of victimization and blame. A civilized parting in which the parties retain their integrity honors the marriage and the life that was shared. All this is healing.

In this context, I think we could agree that at its best, the mediation process itself, independent of particular interventions or techniques, has considerable healing potential. Perhaps the unrealized potency of mediation lies in the experience of a collaborative, constructive process, which as a whole, has an integrity and healing power that is greater than the benefits derived in any given session (Gold, 1988).

As an experiment, imagine how your work might be affected if you saw yourself as someone who could help others activate their own healing energies, or if you believed that one of the goals of mediation was to help people heal. How might it change your "presence"? How might you interact with clients differently? How might your interventions be different?

Indirect Interventions and Techniques That Promote Self-Healing

By having a more open and compassionate heart and by making healing part of our consciousness, we can evoke the desire to heal, help create movement toward a healing path, and participate in healing that arises naturally. If we operate from a healing paradigm as well as from a dispute resolution model, we will intuitively bring this dimension into our work more often. This might appropriately be termed *holistic* mediation.

In addition to being aware of the quality of the relationships we establish with our clients and the "presence" we bring to our work, we can use a number of strategic techniques that foster self-healing. The unconscious mind is particularly receptive to suggestions at times of emotional crisis on both a conscious and unconscious level. The indirect references or suggestions the mediator make can have a powerful effect on the subconscious.

1. Frame mediation as a healing process. You can frame mediation in healing terms in many ways. In your informational "monologue," when the clients' attention is usually riveted to you, you can describe how mediation can pave the way for healing by helping parties lay aside old grievances, increase understanding, build trust, become less angry, begin to forgive each other, and so on. Telling an anecdote about other clients or casually stating that other people have experienced mediation as healing can plant a seed without challenging the defenses when there are high levels of conflict. With more receptive clients, you can suggest that if they make healing one of their personal goals, they might find that negotiations go more smoothly. Whenever you refer to the potential for healing in the mediation process, you set the stage for cooperative, healing behaviors.

It is important to remember that while people come to mediation primarily to get matters resolved, a part of them often seeks something more--to be acknowledged, affirmed, have the marriage honored, or say goodbye with dignity. Whenever I describe mediation in terms of these unspoken universals or in terms of paving the way for wounds to heal, I know I have touched a responsive chord. The mediation session is a rare opportunity to respectfully acknowledge profound human concerns at a point where the parties are together, with *both* capable of listening. We speak to the part of the psyche that Gerald Jampolsky (1983, p. 99) describes as "having a preference for peace"--the part that recognizes the sorrow, loss, and broken spirit and longs (in even the angriest clients) to be whole. Do not underestimate the power of tapping into the universal desire for wellness that exists in even the bitterest disputes. You can suggest that clients make self-healing a guiding principle in interacting with each other--that is, that they constantly ask themselves the question, Will this action promote my healing or make things worse? (Gold, 1992).

2. *Reinforce the choice of mediation as a healing choice.* Committing to a cooperative resolution process and moving in the direction of what seems right promotes healing. Help clients to appreciate the full significance of the choice they have made in using mediation. In her book *Healing Choices, Elegant Choices,* Marsha Sinitar (1988) states that "how we do things counts." The act of choosing a peaceful path is a healthy choice. Choice changes us in the quality and direction of the choice. Reinforce the importance of the peaceful choice as a commendable effort toward the higher moral ground.

3. *Clarify the highest intentions.* The more you can help clients become aware of their highest intentions in making positive choices, the more they will be guided by those intentions. Embedded in the choice to mediate are unspoken hopes that can be powerful forces in helping clients get the most out of this process. By helping them clarify their highest intentions and goals in choosing mediation, those intentions become more concrete, visible, and

attainable. In the opening discussion of what they hope to achieve from mediation, probe to help them articulate their highest purpose. To each response, ask questions like the following: "What else?" "What would that be like?" "What are your highest hopes for the family or for the future?" Restate or reframe what has been said, to mirror back and anchor what they have each stated as their most important concerns.

4. *Generate awareness of the sacred in divorce.* In divorce, things that should be held in reverence are often treated like bartered commodities. Couples in conflict can become so narrowly focused on their dispute that they lose all awareness of the larger, more important context. The act of bringing children into the world is a privilege, the creation of life sacred; nothing is ever permanent, we are always having to face change. Help clients relate their experience to the larger contexts that govern life. Perspective comes with seeing our small experience in relationship to the overall human experience. Put divorce in its proper context--the undoing of what were once sacred vows. Help clients remember their dreams for the children, recognize that the love that once existed between them is carried on by the children, and accept the lifelong family connection through these children.

5. *Create a spiritual reframe for grief.* It is helpful to share information about the grieving process with couples who seem locked in anger and battle. The mediator can offer direct information about stages of grieving, a simple preemptive statement about the fact that the rage and blame of intense conflict are often a manifestation of grief, or that sometimes intense grief at the loss in divorce carries within it the loss and grief of the past. The mediator can also allude to wider metaphysical contexts--that no life is without suffering; pain is a great teacher; honoring one's grief can open one's heart to greater levels of compassion; a person's own woundedness can make it possible to appreciate a spouse's woundedness.

The goal is to help the clients unlock their isolated identification with their pain and shift the frame that locks them in the dispute by referencing it to larger metaphysical contexts about pain and suffering.

6. *Make indirect or embedded suggestions about healing.* Indirect or embedded suggestions address change at an unconscious level. They are effective when there are high levels of conflict, resistance to cooperation, or strong positional arguing. These interventions enable shifts in perception or attitudes to take place without challenging the person's defenses.

You can embed suggestions about healing by posing questions that contain a presupposition about healing that must be accepted in order to answer the question (Lankton, 1985). Examples include the following: "What is the most healing way *you know* to handle this parenting dispute?" "How do you see yourselves healing the family?" "How do you want the divorce process to honor what was good in your marriage?" These questions contain a presupposition about the clients' ability to act in healing ways and require parties to search internally for positive solutions without having the opportunity to resist being positive.

Even angry clients can be asked, "What would your higher intelligence say about this dilemma?" (The client cannot logically resist this questions and is required to draw on personal strengths in order to respond).

7. *Reframe negotiations in language associated with healing.* Questions framed in terms of healing words, like harmony, wholeness, peaceful, healthy, or mending, require the answer to be organized around these principles. They alter the accessibility of information consistent with these principles and require parties to reorganize responses in terms of mutual benefits rather than individual posturing. Examples might include the following: "How can this misunderstanding be mended?" "How can you bring more harmony into the transitions between households?"

Questions or potential impasses can be framed in terms of what would be the most healing solution. A concession can be reframed as a healing gesture or as a gift for the "higher good of the family."

8. *Connect with clients' higher intelligence.* The emotional overload of divorce hampers the capacity for rational, mature reasoning. Impulse control is diminished. To the extent that mediation helps shore up rational functioning by the rules and structure it provides, we can specifically address the more resourceful part of the person--the "higher intelligence." For example, a client who was a college professor regularly launched into a diatribe of "I can't believe you are doing this to me" whenever his wife brought an issue to the bargaining table. When I asked if, as a favor, his higher intelligence could address the issue on the table, he understood immediately and offered a reasonable proposal.

In divorce, we are working with a duality of the personality; the part that wants to act out, and the part, however buried, that wants to do the right thing, that longs for healing and wholeness. Often, both parts need to be acknowledged by the mediator, especially with clients who frequently erupt emotionally in the mediation session. You can help clients find and listen to their higher intelligence by posing questions that require them to hypothetically put aside their angry, mistrustful, or other negative feelings and think of a solution as if these feelings did not exist. As an example, you could ask the following question: "If he hadn't had the affair, what solutions do you think could be found for the disagreement about overnight visits?" You can pose questions directly to the "higher intelligence" while acknowledging the feelings and wishes of the angry or hurt side. Ask clients to operate from this part, and as Fisher and Brown suggesting in *Getting Together: Building Relationships That Get to Yes* (1988), be "unconditionally constructive," acting in the direction of good regardless of whether the other reciprocates.

9. *Increase hope and the belief in the potential for success.* Hope

operates to energize and organize a person's resources. The client's confidence and beliefs about the help to be received affect healing. Skillful healers may bolster what Jerome Frank refers to as the healing power of expectant faith (Walsh, 1990). This may account for the frequent reports of improvement between initial phone calls and the first appointment that has been found in a variety of helping professions.

Even on the telephone, be encouraging about the potential for success. Conveying your faith increases theirs. Create pictures of positive future expectancies. Tell stories of other success. Help them see how far they have come. Describe the behaviors and attitudes most associated with success in mediation.

10. *Make the most of the introductory "monologue."* During times of emotional crisis or life transition, the unconscious mind is looking for information to help resolve developmental demands and ease psychological pain. People are more suggestible and are likely to be deeply receptive to suggestions. The introductory informational "monologue" can be strategically used to convey information conducive to negotiating success, cooperation, and healing, because the unconscious is paying close attention. You can embed suggestions about healing and higher purpose as discussed earlier, preempt potential roadblocks by describing a set of behavioral norms associated with successful outcomes (Saposnek, 1983), or describe future possibilities for family life after divorce. You may notice times when the clients' rapt attention to your words is almost trancelike. The intensity of their absorption in what you are saying allows your words to enter their subconscious. In this sense, the introductory "monologue" can be used as an induction into a healing and cooperative process.

11. *Utilize postmediation suggestion.* The unconscious receptivity and search for helpful information are similarly operative at the end of mediation. The mediator can use the closure phase of the last session to seed future growth and healing. In hypnosis, this is referred to as *posthypnotic suggestion*--the suggestion that clients can continue to learn from the experience in a variety of ways. In a closure monologue, you can suggest how the knowledge clients have gained in mediation may help them handle conflict better in the future; how they may find, as time goes on, that this experience has allowed old wounds to heal; or that the mediation experience may enable them to relate to each other differently in the future. By describing the possibilities for future success or change, you create a future expectancy that may increase the likelihood of unconscious behavior supporting that expectancy.

12. *Prescribe leave-taking rituals.* The last strategy is to suggest to clients that at some point in time, they may want to consider a ritual or ceremony allowing them to say goodbye to the old relationship and acknowledge a new basis for relating in the future. It is best to let clients design

the ceremony, because the symbols and action they choose tend to have more meaning than what you could prescribe. You can describe an example of a basic structure for leave-taking rituals or ceremonies as follows (van der Hart, 1983; Gold, 1992):

> Clarifying the purpose--honoring, letting go, burying (what or whom)
> Choosing key symbols--representing the other person, the old or new relationship, or the future (wedding rings, memorabilia, photos, heirlooms held for the children)
> Deciding on a symbolic act--treasured possession exchange; peace offering; burying the hatchet or burning a symbol of the past; exchanging farewell letters; casting objects out to sea.

Conclusion

There is no rigid prescription for using the ideas described in this article, nor do I offer a unified model based on these concepts. Instead, I have tried to present ideas about how mediation can be more healing and to raise awareness about how the quality of the relationships we establish with our clients can foster a more profound experience. Mediation has the potential to be an ever greater healing force than I have suggested here. Future progress is in the hands of each individual practitioner. However, I do believe there is room for us, as a profession, to consider a more holistic approach to mediation. The ideas in this article will hopefully continue to stimulate the creative unconscious of readers who are mediators about their role in the mediation process.

References

Bruyere, R. "The Compassion Factor." In R. Carlson and B. Shield (eds.), *Healers on Healing.* Los Angeles: Tarcher, 1989.

Capra, F. *Uncommon Wisdom: Conversations with Remarkable People.* New York: Simon & Schuster, 1988.

Carlson, R., and Shield, B. (eds). *Healers on Healing,* Los Angeles: Tarcher, 1989.

Fisher, R., and Brown, S. *Getting Together: Building Relationwships That Get to Yes.* Boston: Hougton Mifflin, 1988.

Gold, L. "Lawyer Therapist Team Mediation." In J. Folberg and A. Milne (eds), *Divorce Mediation.* New York: Guilford, 1988.

Gold, L. *Between Love and Hate: A Guide to Civilized Divorce.* New York: Plenum, 1992.

Jampolsky, G. *Teach Only Love.* New York: Bantam Books, 1983.

Lankton, S. "A States of Consciousness Model of Ericksonian Hypnosis." In S. Lankton (ed.), *Ericksonian Monographs No. 1: Elements and Dimensions of an Ericksonian Approach.* New York: Brunner/Mazel, 1985.

Lankton, S. and Lankton, C. *The Answer Within: A Clinical Framework of Ericksonian Hynotherapy.* New York: Brunner/Mazel, 1983.

May, R. "The Emphathetic Relationship." In R. Carlson and B. Shield (eds.), *Healers on Healing.* Los Angeles: Tarcher, 1989.

Prather, H. "Love is Healing." In R. Carlson and B. Shield (eds.), *Healers on Healing.* Los Angeles: Tarcher, 1989.

Remen, R.N. "The Search for Healing." In R. Carlson and B. Shield (eds.), *Healers on Healing,* Los Angeles: Tarcher, 1989.

Saposnek, D.T., *Mediating Child Custody Disputes: A Systematic Guide for Family Therapist, Court Counselors, Attorneys, and Judges.* San Francisco: Jossey-Bass, 1983.

Satir, V. *Making Contact.* Millbrae, Calif.: Celestial Arts, 1976.

Schwartz, J. "Healing, Love, and Empowerment." In R. Carlson and B. Shield (eds.), *Healers on Healing,* Los Angeles: Tarcher, 1989.

Sinitar, M. *Healing Choices, Elegant Choices.* New York: Paulist Press, 1988.

van der Hart, O. *Rituals in Psychotherapy: Transition and Continuity.* New York: Irvington, 1983.

Walsh, R. *The Spirit of Shamanism.* Los Angeles: Tarcher, 1990.

APPENDIX 4

Native mediation model for urban communities
by Marg Huber

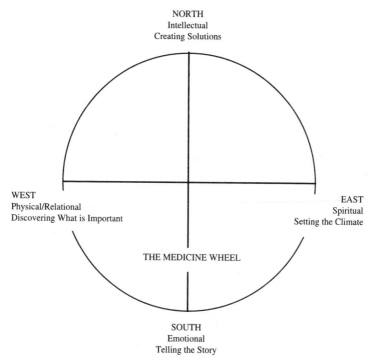

NORTH
Intellectual
Creating Solutions

WEST
Physical/Relational
Discovering What is Important

EAST
Spiritual
Setting the Climate

THE MEDICINE WHEEL

SOUTH
Emotional
Telling the Story

The Medicine Wheel, an ancient spiritual Aboriginal symbol, is the central feature in a mediation model developed in 1990 by a group of B.C. Native community leaders.

Leaders from several different Native tribal groups volunteered their time in weekly meetings over three months to develop the model which is intended for use in urban communities. The project was spearheaded by Cliff White, at that time the Executive Director of the Allied Indian and Metis

Reprinted by permission of The Network Interaction for Conflict Resolution, Conrad Grebel College. Waterloo. ON N2L 3G6

Society in Vancouver.

Historically, Aboriginal people have been expected to use European-North American processes for resolving disputes. With differing reference points, beliefs and values, communications between cultures are often scarred with deep misunderstandings.

In recent years, some Native people have sought mediation training in order to participate more effectively in intercultural negotiations. At the same time, mediators in the "white heritage" society who have worked with parties of Native origin have expressed interest in learning about Native values, beliefs and systems of understanding.

Grounded in Native spirituality and based on Aboriginal cultural values, the model assists Native people to feel more comfortable and empowered in the mediation process, providing for better mediated outcomes.

Mediation around the Medicine Wheel

The medicine wheel is an ancient symbol well-known in North American Native cultures. Developed as a teaching tool, it enables people to understand complex concepts in a holistic way.

In the context of mediation, the medicine wheel, which contains the four sacred directions, provides a visual, spiritual map for the mediation process. The medicine wheel orients clients to the mediation process and provides structure to discussions.

The parts comprising the whole person are represented on the wheel: the spiritual, the emotional, the physical and the intellectual. In mediation of a dispute, the perspectives and qualities associated with the four directions of the wheel become relevant.[1]

The medicine wheel contains the universe. A line is placed across a circle from east to west. Above the line is Father Sky and everything contained in Father Sky: the sun, the stars, etc. Below the line is Mother Earth and everything contained in Mother Earth.

The medicine wheel assigns certain qualities to each direction. While some tribes assign different qualities to each of the points on the circle, the qualities of a complete human being are universal.

Each person who looks deeply into the medicine wheel will see things differently, but will see the tree of his or her unique life with roots buried deep in the soil of universal truths that human beings share in common. The process which develops is circular rather than sequential. Issues emerge from the discussion, instead of being delineated in an agenda. Native people tend to speak deeply from the heart. This can be difficult for a person experiencing

1.The Sacred Tree, a 1984 Four Worlds Development Project publication, the collaborative work of
   North American leaders, articulates and expands on these qualities and others.

conflict or pain. Because the mediation process is grounded in spirituality, emotional expression becomes more comfortable.

Using the wheel, a "journey" through mediation parallels the journey through life. The wheel is travelled as the sun travels across the sky, beginning in the East and moving around the circle to the South, the West and the North. Natural imagery identified with each direction can be used as a guide. Parties are also encouraged to discover their own symbols to represent stages of the mediation journey.

The East: Setting the climate

The place of the East is the spiritual: the direction of renewal, opening, orientation. In mediation, the East is the place for setting the climate. It is associated with warmth of spirit, purity, trust, hope and uncritical acceptance. Here one learns truthfulness, clear speech, self-reliance. One gains the ability to see clearly through complex situations, to focus on the here and now, to see the overall picture. This is the place of faith - of believing without seeing.

The humble mouse and the noble eagle are the twin symbolic teachers of the East. Greatness of spirit and humility are seen as opposite sides of the same reality.

Mediation tasks: The setting

Security and comfort of Native parties are enhanced when sessions are informal and relaxed and take place in a Native facility or organization, with symbols of their culture around them. Seating people in a circle and inviting people to speak in turn enhances equality and helps bring everyone in the room to the present.

Spiritual rituals: "Touching the spirit"

An opening prayer, the smudging of sweetgrass, or other sacred rituals set a tone of respect and security which eases discussion of difficult issues. When mediators "touch the spirit," they assist parties to clear their minds and focus on the present. Anxiety is decreased, strong emotions are diffused and parties relax. Smudging serves further to purify the body, mind and spirit, offer protection and clear negativity. The effects on parties of this spiritual beginning is carried throughout the session.

Describing the Process: "I have walked that way, too"

The mediator can describe the process by putting up a picture of the medicine wheel and giving an overview of mediation as it progresses around the wheel.

"I have walked that road too" is considered a helpful way for mediators to introduce themselves and their role. Native clients are inclined to expect personal perspectives: examples of the mediators' own conflict experiences normalize conflict and humanize the mediators. In the eyes of parties, mediators are then more likely to understand parties' difficulties with both the conflict and the mediation process.

The South: **Telling the story**

The South is the place of the heart: The place of generosity, sensitivity to the feelings of others, loyalty, and the deep love of one person for another. The most valuable gift of the South is the ability to express feelings openly without hurting others.

It is considered that emotions like anger, hurt, and resentment do not merely "happen" to us like a rock dropped on our heads. Feelings can be examined and clarified by an act of will. Until feelings are understood and released, they continue to block capacities for genuine love and warmth, clear thinking and effectiveness.

A symbol of this lesson is the red willow tree, the strongest and most flexible tree in the forest. It yields to forces that would destroy the other trees, but always springs back.

Mediation Tasks

In mediation, the South is the place for telling the story. Expression of feelings is encouraged. Parties are invited to speak openly and directly to one another. Listeners are encouraged to try to really understand what the other is saying, feeling and experiencing. In mediating with Native clients, it is important to allow each party to speak in full before the other has a turn. Mediators must allow a party to finish speaking before intervening.

The West: **Discovering what is important**

The West is the place of the relational and physical. The expression of the South is naturally followed by reflection, the task of the West. This is the place of introspection, listening to one's inner voice, going to the centre of one's being to experience the connection between the human spirit and the Creator.

It is the place of testing. The nearer one draws toward a goal the more difficult the journey becomes. The capacity to stick to a hard and painful challenge is an important lesson of the West.

The West is a place of honesty and sacrifice, where one learns to give and take, and to understand oneself in terms of others. It is the place to learn how to correctly use power: power to heal, power to protect, power to see and know. Here the traveller must learn to manage power in harmony with the great universal teachings.

Two symbolic teachers of the West are the black bear, who possesses great strength from deep within, and the turtle who grants the gift of perseverance.

Mediation Tasks

In mediation, the West is the place for discovering what is important. The task of the mediators is to encourage parties to experience how they are being affected physically by the situation - to focus on feelings as experienced in the body. Clients are assisted to identify what they need and value from each other and the relationship, shared interests, and those interests which must be satisfied in order to reach a resolution.

The North: Creating solutions

The North is the home of the intellect, the place of wisdom and far-sightedness, where one acquires the gift to solve problems, think and imagine, synthesize and discriminate, understand and organize. It is the direction of completion or fulfillment - completing what one has begun. Here are learned the lessons of balance and justice.

The gift of detachment bestows on the traveller the ability to see the past, the present and the future as one. Detachment also means standing apart from strong feelings and beliefs to see them in a different light. Thus one can appreciate the experience of others and find resolutions to differences.

The great mountain is a symbolic teacher of the North: the higher one climbs its slopes, the steeper and more difficult the way becomes. And yet the higher one goes, the more one can see and the stronger one becomes.

Mediation tasks

In mediation the North is the place for creating solutions. When parties are ready to move to problem solving, mediators help them define mutual goals and encourage generation of options for resolution.

Parties jointly select the options which best meet their needs. Mediators must encourage parties to be specific as to who will do what, when, and where, and if appropriate, make a written record of understandings. If necessary, parties should be encouraged to review an agreement with elders or family members before signing it.

Parties must speak from all places on the wheel to truly understand one another and for the process to feel complete. If one party has trouble hearing the other, the other party may be speaking from a different place on the wheel. In discussing the dispute around the wheel, clients may need to revisit one or more places before moving on. This movement allows for flexibility of process within a guiding framework.

At the conclusion of mediation, clients are asked to place themselves symbolically in the centre of the wheel, so they are left with a holistic perspective of their experience. The centre is also the place of volition, where parties put intentions into action. The mediation closes, as it opened, with prayer.

Mediator understanding of Native values crucial

Lack of understanding of Aboriginal values on the part of mediators could result in confusion, unnecessary resistance and potential ethical issues.

A mediation process for Native people must be culturally relevant, yet sensitive to the diverse mix of Native groups and individuals in urban communities. The model was developed according to widely held traditional Native values rather than the particular traits of specific Native groups. This allows for modification to achieve greater relevance for the parties and the dispute.

Mediation bridges differences

Mediation is viewed as a process of bridging difference, bringing people back into harmony. It enables parties to generate sufficient information and understandings for solutions to be reached on which both can agree.

One might consider the image of two pebbles dropped in a pond: concentric circles emerge from each, and as those patterns overlap, an area of turbulence or discord is created between them. Yet the new pattern formed by the overlap can be redefined to create a harmony or relationship within the larger harmony of the pond. The image is one of parts comprising a whole.

The goal of mediation, then, is to restore peace and harmony to individuals, situations and community. In family situations an additional goal is to assist parties to sustain family relationships whenever possible.

In a larger context, mediation is seen as a growth and a healing process. Honoring the spiritual allows people to participate in emotionally charged discussions and resolve differences with integrity. Native communal ties are vital to the individual, so mediation can enhance an individual's sense of belonging and identity, strengthening community relationships as well as relationships between conflicting parties.

Consensus decision making

Values of Native people related to conflict resolution in general include: cooperation, sharing, equality among people, harmony, non-interference in individual matters, consensus decision-making, privacy, a holistic approach to life, age, the relativity of time, and spirituality.

Other values related to a dispute resolution process are patience, moderation in speech, careful listening, avoidance of eye contact, non-verbal or physical communication, and quietness.

Relevant values related to ownership of property and family systems are additional important considerations for mediators of intercultural disputes.

Co-mediation preferred

Mediation is considered best conducted by a co-mediation team, to balance for gender and/or culture. This is also in line with Native procedures. In an urban setting, mediators could be community leaders, professional people or those in management positions with training and competency in the process.

In addition to being non-judgmental and unbiased, it is considered important that mediators be respected in the Native community, and be familiar with community resources. Also important for Native parties is a cultural connection with at least one of the mediators, regardless of the competency or sensitivity of any non-Native mediator.

Pre-mediation assessment

Separate pre-mediation sessions with parties provide an opportunity for mediators to assess the client (level of stress, level of dysfunction, family and community support, spiritual or emotional blocks, abusive relationships). The mediator can then build in safety measures for the process or decide against the mediation. Referral to a spiritual counselor, drug and alcohol counselor, grief counselor or other appropriate community resources may be preferred prior to mediation. Here, mediators assume an advisory role, and must continually assess potential impact on their impartiality as mediator.

Involvement of Elders in the mediation

Potential roles for elders emerge. One or more elders physically present in the session as silent observers could add a spiritual quality to the discussions. They can be called upon as a resource, especially in emotional matters. In this case, elders need to be told ahead what the expectations are of them, and they should be familiarized with the mediation process. An elder could be one of the two mediators, either acting as a silent mediator or providing observations while the other mediator manages the process more actively. Another role for an elder may be to confer with a party prior to decision making, to ensure choices are congruent with the values of the party's own cultural group. The elders included must be aware of relevant happenings in the Native community.

Disinclined to respond with an answer right away, elders need time to reflect. They rarely say anything unless asked. They are respectful of the process and will not interfere, but rather will allow it to unfold. Their comments may be included in an opening stage if they are seated as part of a circle including all parties in the room. Also, elders could begin the mediation process with a spiritual opening.

Presence of chosen family members

The importance of the family in Native groups must not be underestimated. Family members substitute for one another upon death or separation. There are built in mechanisms to indicate who is responsible in the particular circumstance. Native cultures consider many more individuals to be relatives than do non-Native families. This large family network provides much support and security. With one or more family members in attendance at a mediation session, a client may feel more secure in a process that could otherwise seem threatening and isolating.

Seating in a circle: Balance and security

Sitting in circles is customary within many Native groups. The circle is an image for the whole, oneness and unity. Connoting balance and equality, a circle also provides security. In mediation the circle would include everyone present: mediators, parties, family members, and elders.

A circle provides a structure for verbally including all parties to the process at the opening or ending of the session, or at difficult moments during the session. A circle creates a space for everyone to speak in turn. Possibly a talking stick, rock or eagle feather is passed. One may hold the item and choose not to speak, in which case one's space is filled with silence. When each person is finished, the item is relinquished to the next person. It is viewed as highly inappropriate to speak when someone else is holding the item. Verbal contributions of elders who might otherwise be silent can thus be obtained in a respectful way. When emotions are high during a session, speaking around the circle enables those having difficulties with articulation to express themselves with greater ease.

Silence is comfortable, Interruptions inappropriate

Native people tend to prefer a longer, slower process. Silence is comfortable. Individuals may need to talk at some length on unrelated matters before addressing the issue. Native people consider it respectful to allow people to speak one at a time, and for as long as necessary to tell their stories.

Non-linear agenda: The present is infused with the past

Time is viewed as relative, and geared to the activity at hand. The approach to issues and agenda is non-linear. Discourse may appear circular. Time is seen as a continuum. The Native person does not view the past as separated from the present. The present is infused with the past. Past, present and future are often experienced as one.

Symbols and metaphors provide meaningful context

Native cultures are rich in imagery and living examples which can be incorporated into the mediation process to enhance understanding. Metaphors are preferred to definitions. Parables clarify complex ideas. Diagrams assist by making concepts visual.

Native symbols and imagery give a spiritual, integrative quality to the mediation experience. Unity and balance are achieved from consideration of the person and process in a holistic way. Growth and healing result from mutuality of understanding and the courage to address difference and discord with respect, dignity and integrity.

Marg Huber is a mediator, facilitator and trainer of Anglo-Canadian heritage in Vancouver, B.C. She was the facilitator of meetings which resulted in the development of this model.

References:

Bennett, Milton J., "A Developmental Approach to Intercultural Sensitivity,"
   International Journal of Intercultural Relations, Vol. 10 (2), Summer 1986.
Four Worlds Development Project. *The Sacred Tree*, Four Worlds
   Development Press, Lethbridge, Alta., 1984.
Lederach, John Paul. "Assumptions," in *MCS Conciliation Quarterly,* Summer,
   1986, p.2-5.
Lederach, John Paul. "Yes, But Are They Talking?: Some Thoughts On The
   Trainer As Student," in *MCS Conciliation Quarterly*, Summer, 1988, p.10-11.
Lederach, John Paul. "Training on Culture: Four Approaches," in *Conciliation
   Quarterly*, Winter 1990, p. 6-13.
LeResche, Diane. "Training on Culture: A Survey of the Field," in *MCS
   Conciliation Quarterly*, Winter 1990, p. 2-5.
More, Arthur J. "Native Indian Learning Styles: A Review for Researchers and
   Teachers," in *Journal of American Indian Education*, Oct. 1987, p. 17-29.
Stevens, Sam, "An Aboriginal View of the Canadian Justice System," in *Legal
   Perspectives*, Vol. 14, Number 4 May 1990.

APPENDIX 5

Standards of Practice for Social Work Mediators

INTRODUCTION

Social workers sit at the center of many social conflicts. In their role as facilitator of person-to-person, person-to-group, person-to-institution, and institution-to-institution interactions, social workers face the issue of conflict resolution as a normal part of their professional activities. The role of social worker in these conflicts has been variously described as advocate, negotiator, and mediator.

Increasingly, social workers and other professionals have chosen or been asked to play the formal role of mediator, that is, a neutral third party who helps people or groups in conflict arrive at mutually acceptable solutions. Social workers mediate issues such as divorce and postdivorce disputes, parent-child conflicts, child welfare issues, and disagreements concerning care of the elderly. In addition, they mediate neighborhood disputes, community conflicts, and personnel issues. As the use of mediators in a variety of circumstances has increased, a concomitant development has taken place regarding the conceptual framework and skills set within which mediators function. Mediation increasingly is viewed as a powerful intervention tool distinct from--albeit informed by--other approaches to client services.

These developments have led the National Association of Social Workers (NASW) to develop and adopt a set of standards that are intended to guide the practice of social workers who function as neutral third parties. These standards were developed to complement the NASW *Code of Ethics* and to be consistent with the standards of major mediation organizations.

Considered desirable for all social work mediators, these standards are designed to do the following:
- promote the practice of social work mediation
- provide direction and professional support to social work mediators
- inform consumers, employers, and referral sources by providing them with a set of expectations for social worker mediators.

DEFINITION OF MEDIATION

Mediation is an approach to conflict resolution in which a mutually acceptable, impartial third party helps the participants negotiate a consensual and informed settlement. In mediation, decision making rests with the parties.

Reducing the obstacles to communication, maximizing the exploration of alternatives, and addressing the needs of those who are involved or affected by the issues under discussion are among the mediator's responsibilities.[1]

The mediator is responsible to the system of people or groups involved in a decision-making process. The mediator must provide this system with the structure and tools to make mutually acceptable decisions under difficult circumstances. In this sense, the mediator's role is to empower the system so that it does not have to resort to outside parties, such as the courts or arbitrators, to make the decision.

PRINCIPLES GUIDING PRACTICE STANDARDS FOR SOCIAL WORK MEDIATORS

The following principles govern the practice standards for social work mediators:

- Mediation is a method of social work practice.[2]
- The mediator is responsible to the system of parties involved in the dispute or decision-making process, rather than to any single party or client.
- These standards are to be interpreted within the ethical base and values explicated in the NASW *Code of Ethics.*
- Mediators should be familiar with and trained in the theory and practice of mediation. In addition to social work education, the social work mediator needs specific training and practice experience in mediation and conflict resolution.
- Social work mediators should be accountable, both to the client and to colleagues, for the professional and ethical application of their skills and service delivery.
- Because mediation is a growing and developing field, these standards should be reviewed regularly to incorporate new developments in the theory and practice of mediation.

STANDARDS FOR THE PRACTICE OF MEDIATION BY SOCIAL WORKERS.

Standard 1: Social work mediators shall function within the ethics and stated standards and accountability procedures of the social work

1. Adapted from the *Model Standards of Practice for Family and Divorce Mediators.* (Madison, Wisconsin: Association of Family Conciliation Courts, 1984).
2. Method is used to identify specific types of intervention. See Robert L. Barker, The Social Work Dictionary, 2nd ed. (Silver Spring, MD: NASW Press, 1991), p. 144, the term "methods in social work."

profession.

Interpretation: All social workers have a fourfold responsibility: to clients, to the profession, to self, and to society. Social work mediators should identify themselves as members of the social work profession. NASW members shall be familiar with and adhere to the NASW *Code of Ethics* and shall cooperate fully and in a timely fashion with the adjudication procedures of the committee of inquiry, peer review, and appropriate state regulatory boards. They should be aware of and adhere to relevant stated professional standards for social work practices.

Standard 2: Social work mediators should remain impartial and neutral toward all parties and issues in a dispute.

Interpretation: Social work mediators should enter into a dispute as a mediator only when they can maintain a stance of impartiality and neutrality. They should inform all involved parties of any development or circumstances that might contribute to the actuality or appearance of bias or favoritism, or that might interfere in any way with their impartial and neutral role. Impartiality refers to the mediator's attitudes toward the issue and people involved. An impartial mediator acts without bias in word and action and is committed to helping all parties rather than to advocating for any single person.

Neutrality relates to the mediator's relationship to the parties and the issues involved. A mediator should have no relationship with parties or vested interests in the substantive outcome that might interfere or appear to interfere with the ability to function in a fair, unbiased, and impartial manner. Any such relationship must be disclosed to the parties before the start of mediation or as soon as knowledge of such a relationship occurs. If any of the parties or the mediator feels that such a relationship has a potential to bias the mediator's performance, the mediator should disqualify himself or herself from acting as a neutral third party.

It is important that the mediator continue to maintain a neutral stance after the mediation is completed to avoid casting doubt on the legitimacy of the mediation that occurred and to ensure continued availability for future interventions as appropriate.

Standard 3: The social work mediator shall not reveal to outside parties any information received during the mediation process.

Interpretation: As with the success of other social work methods, the success of mediation depends largely on the confidentiality of the process. The mediator should not reveal to other parties any information received during private sessions or caucuses without the express permission of the parties from whom the mediator received the information.

Clients and mediators must be aware that there are legal and ethical circumstances in which confidentiality cannot be maintained. These circumstances include but are not limited to the legally mandated requirement to report suspicion of child abuse or a suspicion of bodily harm or violence to another person. Mediators should be aware of any legal or statutory limits placed on mediation in the jurisdiction in which they practice. Exceptions to confidentiality and any other exceptions that may arise because of the circumstances, legal framework, or institutional structure within which mediation occurs should be disclosed to the parties before or during their initial meeting with the mediator.

The mediator should inform the parties of the possibility that the mediator might be compelled to testify in court or in other ways reveal information gathered during the mediation process. Confidentiality applies to the mediator and the mediator's records.

Standard 4: Social work mediators shall assess each conflict and shall proceed only in those circumstances in which mediation is an appropriate procedure.

Interpretation: Mediation is not appropriate for all types of conflict. Mediators should assess whether each party has the capacity to engage in mediation and has the support necessary to be an effective participant. They should inform parties about alternative dispute resolution processes that are available to them and discuss the appropriateness of mediation at the beginning of the intervention.

If mediation is to be effective, parties at a minimum must have the ability to negotiate for themselves, to assess the information relevant to the case, and to understand the implications of the various agreements being considered. Furthermore,the mediation process should address a potential imbalance of power that might exist between the parties. In those situations in which legal advice or other expert consultation is necessary or would serve parties better, the mediator should make the appropriate referrals. The role of mediator should not be confused with that of an attorney, psychotherapist, or evaluator, even if the mediator also has expertise in one or more of those areas.

Standard 5: The social work mediator shall seek at all times to promote cooperation, to prevent the use of coercive tactics, to foster good-faith bargaining efforts, and to ensure that all agreements are arrived at on a voluntary and informed basis.

Interpretation: Good-faith negotiation means that the parties are making an honest (even if uncertain) attempt to arrive at an agreement, that they are not using the process for destructive purposes, that they are sharing relevant information in a frank and truthful manner, and that they are not using coercive or dishonest bargaining tactics. Although it is not always possible to ensure that all parties are negotiating in good faith, it is the mediator's responsibility to promote and expect good-faith behavior. The mediator should not allow coercive or bad-faith tactics to continue during the mediation process. If the mediator is aware that these tactics are being used and cannot stop their use, the mediation process should be discontinued.

Standard 6: The social work mediator shall recommend termination of the process when it appears that it is no longer in the interest of the parties to continue it.

Interpretation: Mediation should not be used to prolong a dispute unnecessarily or to prevent the use of a more appropriate conflict resolution procedure. Occasionally, it is in the interest of one party to prevent an agreement from being reached. At other times parties are simply unable to agree, and they reach an impasse. The mediator should not continue with the mediation if these situations occur. The mediator should, however, exert every effort to promote the successful conclusion of mediation and should not abandon the effort prematurely.

Standard 7: The social work mediator is responsible for helping the parties arrive at a clearly stated, mutually understood, and mutually acceptable agreement.

Interpretation: It is the mediator's responsibility to conduct the mediation process, not to promote any particular substantive outcome. Frequently, the solution that the mediator believes best meets the interests of the parties is not the one that parties select. The mediator's role is to conduct a fair process, not to promote a particular outcome. The mediator should try to ensure that the agreement, whether partial or full, reflects a fair and good-faith negotiation effort. If the mediator feels that the agreement is illegal, grossly unfair to a participating or unrepresented party, the result of bad-faith bargaining, or based on inaccurate information, the mediator has the obligation to make this known to the parties involved and to try to correct the problem. When parties agree to an unconscionable outcome, an illegal agreement, or one based on dishonesty or misrepresentation, mediators should disassociate themselves from the agreement in accordance with standards of confidentiality.

Standard 8: The social work mediator shall develop an unbiased written

agreement that specifies the issues resolved during the course of mediation.

Interpretation: The written agreements should, to the extent possible, be in the language of the parties themselves, and should be clearly understood by them. The actual determination of whether an agreement is legally binding constitutes a legal judgment. However, it is important for parties to know that any agreement may be legally binding and should not be finalized without the appropriate legal advice.

Standard 9: Social work mediators shall have training in both the procedural and substantive aspects of mediation.

Interpretation: Social workers should mediate disputes only in those areas for which they are qualified by training or experience. If they have no substantive knowledge in a particular area, they should obtain it, work with a qualified co-mediator, have appropriate consultation, or refer the dispute elsewhere. Mediators should obtain formal training in the mediation process, and beginning mediators should work under a qualified supervisor. Formal training is currently available through professional seminars and workshops and university based programs. The standards for training obtained by social work mediators should be in keeping with those currently accepted by the leading professional organizations of mediators in the area in which the social worker is functioning. Social work mediators should upgrade their skills and knowledge in the field of conflict resolution through continuing education programs and participation in relevant professional conferences and seminars.

Occasionally, mediators will be asked to mediate a dispute in which they do not have substantive expertise. If a mediator skilled in that specialty is not available, the mediator either should work with a co-mediator or consultant who is familiar with the substantive area or take the time to become familiar enough with the area to be able to help parties explore their interests and options in an informed manner.

Standard 10: A social work mediator shall have a clearly defined and equitable fee structure.

Interpretation: The fee structure should be presented to all parties at the outset of the mediation. Fees should reflect standards of impartiality and neutrality. All compensation mediators receive for their services should be known to all involved parties, and mediators should accept no side payments or fees based on the outcome of the mediation process.

If at all possible, either a neutral party or agency should cover the cost of mediation of the cost should be split equitably (although not necessarily equally) among the parties. If one party is supposed to pay the entire fee, this should be known and agreed to by all parties at the outset. Under no circumstances should the fee structure give the mediator a vested interest in a particular outcome. Fees should therefore not be contingent on the nature of the agreement or even on the achievement of an agreement.

Standard 11: The mediator shall not use any information obtained during the mediation process for personal benefit or for the benefit of any group or organization with which the mediator is associated.

Interpretation: Mediators are often given access to information that could be used for personal or organizational benefit. It is inappropriate for the mediator to compromise the mediation process by using this information outside the mediation process.

Standard 12: Social work mediators shall be prepared to work collaboratively as appropriate with other professionals and in conformance to the philosophy of social work and mediation.

Interpretation: The mediator should not separately mediate any dispute that already is being mediated. If another mediator has been involved in the case, the mediator should ascertain that this relationship has been terminated before agreeing to become involved.

In cases in which a co-mediation procedure is being used, all the mediators involved should keep each other informed about activities and developments relevant to the case, and the clients should know at the outset that this information sharing will occur. Co-mediators should handle any disagreements they may have in a collaborative manner.

Mediators should respect the involvement of legal, mental health, social services, and other professionals involved in the dispute or with the parties and should work with them in a cooperative and respectful manner.

APPENDIX 6

Resources for Technical Assistance and Training: Written Materials, Training Manuals, Videotapes, Organizations, Mediation Role Plays

Resources for Technical Assistance and Training

Training manuals for program organizers and mediators, videotapes, lists of resources, and training institute schedules are available from the following organizations, which provide services on a nationwide basis.

United States

DM PCM	Academy of Family Mediators 1158 High Street, Suite 202 Eugene, OR 97401 (503) 345-1205	PCM	The Children's Hearing Project Cambridge Family and Children's Service 99 Bishop Richard Allen Drive Cambridge, MA 02139 (617) 661-4700
DM PCM	Association of Family and Conciliation Courts 329 West Wilson Madison, WI 53703 (608) 251-4001	CM MS VOM SM PCM	The Community Board Program Conflict Resolution Resources 1540 Market Street, Suite 490 San Francisco, CA 94102 (415) 552-1250
VOM MS DM CM	Center for Creative Justice 304 Lynn Avenue Ames, IA 50010 (515) 292-3820	ALL	Conflict Resolution International 7101 Hamilton Avenue Pittsburgh, PA 15208 (412) 371-9884
VOM CM PCM SM MS	Center for Restorative Justice and Mediation School of Social Work, University of Minnesota 383 McNeal Hall 1985 Buford St. Paul, MN 55108 (612) 624-3700	DM SM PCM	Family Mediation Services, Northland Plaza 3800 West 80th Street, Suite 850 Minneapolis, MN 55431 (612) 835-3688

Appendix 6

United States Continued

SM	The Grace Contrino Abrams Peace Education Foundation 3550 Biscayne Boulevard Suite 400 Miami, FL 33137 (800) 749-8838	CM SM PCM MS	The New Mexico Center for Dispute Resolution 620 Roma N.W. Albuquerque, NM 87102 (505) 247-0571
ALL	Mediation Center 210 Spruce Tree Centre 1600 University Avenue St. Paul, MN 55104 (612) 644-1453	VOM CM	Office of Criminal Justice Mennonite Central Committee U.S. P.O. Box 500 Akron, PA 17501 (717) 859-3889
CM VOM	National Association for Community Mediation 1726 M Street N.W., Suite 500 Washington, DC 20036-4502 (202) 467-6226	PCM	The PINS Mediation Project The Children's Aid Society 141 Livingston Street, 15th Floor Brooklyn, NY 11201 (718) 625-8300
SM	National Association for Mediation in Education 425 Amity Street Amherst, MA 01002 (413) 545-2462	ALL	Society of Professionals in Dispute Resolution 815 15th Street N.W. Suite 530 Washington, DC 20005 (202) 783-7277
ALL	National Conference on Peacemaking and Conflict Resolution George Mason University 4400 University Drive Fairfax, VA 22030-4444 (703) 934-5140	VOM	Victim Offender Mediation Association c/o PACT Institute of Justice 254 S. Morgan Boulevard Valparaiso, IN 46383 (219) 462-1127
ALL	National Institute for Dispute Resolution 1901 L. Street, NW, Suite 600 Washington, DC 20036 (202) 466-4764		

Mediating Interpersonal Conflicts: A Pathway to Peace

Canada

VOM	Community Justice Initiatives Association 101-20678 Eastleigh Cresecent Langley, B.C. V3A 4C4 (604) 534-5515	VOM	Victim Offender Ministries Program Mennonite Central Committee Canada 50 Kent Avenue Kitchener, Ontario N2G 3R1
DM PCM	Family Mediation Canada 300 840-6 Avenue SW, Atrium II Calgary, Alberta T2P 3E5 (403) 233-7533	ALL	The Network: Interaction for Conflict Resolution Conrad Grebel College Waterloo, Ontario N2L 3G6 (519) 885-0880

United Kingdom

ALL	Mediation UK 82a Gloucester Road Bishopston, Bristol England BS7 8BN (0272) 241234	VOM	Leeds Mediation & Reparation Service Devonshire House 38 York Place Leeds, England L51 2ED (0532) 435932

Note: Code for Types of Mediation: CM=community mediation; DM=divorce mediation; MS=mediation of staff conflict; PCM=parent-child mediation; VOM=victim-offender mediation; SM=school mediation; ALL=all types of mediation.

Community Mediation Role Play

Conflicts between landlords and tenants are frequently referred to community mediation programs. The following role play has been developed by the Dispute Resolution Center in St. Paul, Minnesota, for use in training volunteer mediators.

Divide into groups of four. Three persons in each group select one of the following roles: landlord, tenant, mediator. The fourth person is an observer and provides feedback to the three other individuals in his or her small group, and reports on the experience to the larger group. Spend at least forty-five minutes role-playing this case and discussing it prior to reporting back to the larger group.

Appendix 6

Landlord Role: Terry Johnson

In 1958 you bought a duplex at 19 Elliot Street. It is the only piece of property you own. You and your spouse, Pat, live in the downstairs apartment and you rent out the upstairs apartment. The mortgage is paid off, but you use the income from the rented unit to supplement your pension and social security income. You live a modest but good life on a limited income.

Until last May you had rented the apartment on the second floor to Mary Bennett since 1968. Mary was a friendly, quiet woman who always paid her rent on time. She was forced to move because she broke her hip and could no longer use the stairs.

On June 1 you rented the upstairs unit to Lee Smith and her two children, ages 8 and 11. Lee signed a one-year lease in which she agreed to pay $450 a month. Lee is a single parent who works every day until 6:00 P.M. Until November, Lee was never more than a day or two late with her rent. In November, after waiting ten days for her payment, you approached Lee and requested that the rent be paid immediately. Lee told you that there was an unexpected family emergency and that she would pay as soon as she could.

Overall, you have had no problems with Lee and her children with one exception. Last month, you had surgery, and after several weeks in the hospital you came home with specific orders that you get plenty of bed rest. Unfortunately, Lee's children, who are home alone most of the time, make far too much noise after school and in the early evening, which you believe has caused your health to suffer. You are reluctant to evict your tenants just before Christmas but you don't know what else to do because you are trying to recuperate and you need the money that Lee owes.

You are willing to try mediation, but you would just as soon have Lee move out so you could start over with a new, more responsible tenant.

Tenant Role: Lee Smith

Last June you and your two children moved into the upstairs unit of a duplex at 19 Elliot Street. You signed a one-year lease and pay $450 a month in rent. Your landlords, an older couple named Terry and Pat Johnson, live in the downstairs apartment. You are an employed single parent and your income barely meets your expenses. Your job usually requires you to work until six each evening, and then you come home and make dinner.

In late October your father unexpectedly died of a heart attack. You lent your mother several thousand dollars (all your savings and more) to help pay for funeral and other expenses. Hence, you have been unable to pay the November and December rent. You are now getting back on track and plan to pay everything you owe as soon as you can, but that may not be until March 1.

Since your father's death, you have been visiting your mother for an hour or so every day after work. You know your kids have been home alone, but they are old enough and well-behaved enough to handle it. You want to stay where you are living and would like to work out some kind of payment plan to catch up on your rent. In fact, you are able to pay $200 today and $200 in two weeks as a sign of good faith. You especially don't want to move in the winter. Also, if you are evicted, you have no idea where you and your children can stay until you find new quarters. Your mother's place is too small.

You are not sure what your chances will be in the courtroom so you decide to try mediation.

Mediator Role

You are a trained volunteer mediator with the Dispute Resolution Center in St. Paul. It is December 11 and you are mediating a case referred by the Ramsey County Housing Court. The parties have the option to appear before a mediator or the Housing Court referee. If the parties choose mediation and can't reach an agreement, the case goes to the referee the very same morning. Terry Johnson (landlord) has brought an unlawful detainer (eviction) action against Lee Smith (tenant) because Smith has not paid the November and December rent. Johnson and Smith agreed to try mediation.

School Mediation Role Play

Conflict between students frequently involves rumors and gossip, as well as threats and anger. The following two role plays have been developed by the New Mexico Center for Dispute Resolution Center in Albuquerque for use in the training of mediators.

Divide into groups of four, and three members each select one of the following roles: student #1, student #2, mediator. The fourth person is an observer and provides feedback to the individuals in the group, and reports on the experience to the larger group. Spend at least forty-five minutes role-playing this case and discussing it prior to reporting back to the larger group.

Role Play 1: Rumor and Gossip

Disputants
Lori and Alfred, who recently broke up as boy-and girlfriend.

Background
Lori and Alfred recently broke up. When Lori was talking with two of her friends, Sue and Cassi, she heard some details about her relationship with Alfred that weren't true. Lori got into an argument with Alfred over this while at school and she agreed to go to mediation.
Lori : You are hurt and embarrassed that your friends are talking about your breakup with Alfred. You are sure that Alfred told them some things. At first

you are concerned about going to mediation with Alfred. You are afraid that the things discussed in mediation will get spread around school.

Alfred: You are angry at Lori for attacking and blaming you about "stories" of your breakup. You are especially angry because you and Lori agreed to keep the details of the breakup to yourselves and because the rumors she heard weren't true. When Lori started yelling and not giving you a chance to tell her what happened, you got angry but agreed to go to mediation to try to set things straight. You want to tell Lori that even though you talked to Sue and Cassi, you didn't tell them anything and they became angry with you and walked away.

Student Mediator
The case of Lori and Alfred has been assigned to you. It is your role to mediate this conflict using the techniques that you have learned.

Role Play 2: Threats and Anger

Disputants
Two students, Lee and Kim, who don't get along well.

Background
Lee and Kim have known each other for nine months. A fight started between them as a result of Kim's "mad dogging" (giving dirty looks) to Lee. They were reported and agreed to try mediation.

Lee: You are angry because Kim has been "mad dogging" you for several weeks. You tried to ignore the comments, but they kept coming at you, especially in front of your friends. You decided to put a stop to the comments, so you punched Kim and a fight started.

Kim: You feel that Lee has been giving you "looks" whenever you see each other in school. Some of Lee's friends have threatened you in the past. You threw comments at Lee because Lee acts like a "know-it-all." In your mind, a fight would clear the air if it doesn't get broken up.

Student Mediator
The case of Lee and Kim has been assigned to you. It is your role to mediate this conflict using the techniques that you have learned.

Divorce and Custody Mediation Role Play

The following are exercises for students to learn about family mediation issues. Meet in groups of four and role-play this first meeting. Choose one person to be the mediator; another, the husband; and another, the wife. The

Mediating Interpersonal Conflicts: A Pathway to Peace

fourth person will observe what the mediator says and does that affect the process of this first meeting, and record any agreements made by the couple.

Role Play an Initial Consultation with Divorcing Couple

The most important meeting with clients is the initial consultation, when they first sit with a mediator to inquire and explore the possibilities of mediation for their issues.

Woody and Eleanor have been referred to you by their marriage counselor to mediate their divorce. They have been married for eight years and have been in conflict for the past two years since Woody's five-year high school reunion, when he saw GiGi, whom he had dated for three years in high school. Though nothing came of that meeting, Eleanor began to wonder whether Woody was the right man for her. It was a period of tremendous doubt and questioning for Eleanor. Woody could not satisfy her in any way. Marriage counseling wasn't helping, so Woody moved out of the family home three weeks ago, leaving the children--Alan, age 6, and Will, age 4--with Eleanor. Woody is a mechanic for Northwest Airlines and has earned a good living during the marriage; he also moonlights at Flying Cloud Airport, repairing planes evenings and weekends, when possible. Eleanor was trained in elementary education and taught third grade until Alan was born. Then she dedicated herself entirely to motherhood. They planned that she would return to work when Will began kindergarten, so Woody could quit his moonlighting and spend more time with the boys.

They arrived at the mediation office together today, and filled out the intake forms, which indicated no abuse. You will meet with them together for the initial consultation to explain and offer your services as a divorce mediator.

Role Play Mediating an Initial Parenting Agreement.

Mediating parenting arrangements is a major role of the divorce mediator. Parents look to the mediator for direction, managing their discussions and developing options. Use of a calendar in this exercise may be very helpful. Again divide into groups of four and, as before, choose the mediator, Clara and Martin, and one person to observe.

Clara and Martin have made a decision to divorce and have chosen you as their mediator. They separated two months ago when they rented an apartment for one to reside in while the other is in the house, a parenting arrangement commonly referred to as bird nesting. They have three children from their fifteen years of marriage. Howard, age 6, is very upset about the divorce; Hazel, age 10, likes only one parent in the house at a time because they don't argue as much; and Gilman, age 14, doesn't care what his parents do as long as they leave him alone with his friends. Clara is an accountant with a medium-sized firm in Minneapolis, and Martin teaches writing at the junior college. They have a lot of conflict regarding spending money and child rearing. Clara is organized and wants the children to be neat and pay attention to schedules and how they spend their allowances. Martin is more interested in talking with the children and making up games to play with them so they become more creative in their thinking.

Clara and Martin are worn out with moving in and out of the house. They meet with the mediator to work out some other parenting schedule. They have agreed that Martin will reside in the house and Clara will rent a townhouse nearby, large enough for the children to have their own space. They do not agree, however, on with whom the children should live--each wants them.

The mediator's task is to help Clara and Martin work out a parenting arrangement that will accommodate both of their interests and the needs of the children. Consider a multidimensional approach to mediating this.

Parent-Child Mediation Role Play

The following role play was developed by the Children's Hearing Project in Cambridge, Massachusetts, for use in the training of volunteer mediators.

Divide into groups of five: four persons each select one of the following roles: Joanne, Mrs. Brown, mediator #1, and mediator #2. The fifth person is an observer who provides feedback to the individuals in the small group, and reports on the experience to the larger group. Spend at least forty-five minutes role-playing this case and discussing it prior to reporting back to the larger group.

Background

Thirteen-year-old Joanne lives in a housing project with her mother and two younger brothers, Eric, age 8, and Paul, age 7. An older sister, Marie, left home about a year ago to live in Fall River with her boyfriend and their baby.

Mr. Brown died three years ago in a car accident. Eric is developmentally delayed and attends special classes. Paul is in the second grade, and Joanne is in the seventh grade. She has been absent from school repeatedly this year despite several warnings from teachers and school officials. When she does go to school, she often leaves after a few periods. School personnel have contacted Mrs. Brown from time to time to discuss Joanne's truancy, but this has not made much difference in her attendance. Mrs. Brown works on the 11 p.m. to 7 a.m. shift at the local hospital as a nurse's aide.

Joanne: You used to like school, but this year the work seems too hard and it's confusing to take six subjects and change rooms every period. Your homeroom teacher is really down on you. You particularly hate math and gym, so those are the times you often cut and leave school. You miss Marie a lot, and sometimes sneak off to visit her and play with the baby. You wish your mom and Marie would get along and that Marie could come home and live with the family again. You daydream a lot about getting a job as a nurse and taking care of babies. Then you could have more money and help your mother. You worry about how hard she works and how tired she is all of the time. The school adjustment counselor is always poking around in other people's business, asking questions. You don't want to talk about "why you cut school" or "what do you do when you're not at school." Being home is nice. You can read or watch television while your mom is sleeping and then make lunch and eat together when she gets up in the afternoon. She never hassles you or asks questions. First your dad got killed and then Marie got in trouble and moved out. It seems as if the family is just going to fall apart. Nobody understands what that feels like, even your best friend, because no one else has been through it.

Mrs. Brown: Joanne has always been successful in school and you were stunned to hear about all her absences and cutting of classes. You don't understand what's been going on. You thought she was going to school every day, unless she was sick. Joanne is a good kid. She helps around the house and is like another mother to the little boys. She and Marie really helped you pull through when your husband died. Marie should have finished high school but instead she quit and had a baby and is living on welfare. Nobody in your family ever took any charity or lived the way she's living. You like your job, though working at night isn't the greatest. You are tired a lot of the time, and the only socializing you do is talk on the phone to your girlfriend. Being a widow has cut you off from many old friends. You feel like an outsider anyway, because you came from a different part of the country and New Englanders aren't really friendly. Being taken to court was horrible. You wish Joanne would go to school and you've told her that she has to. What else can you do? Why did the school system act in such a high-handed way? It really isn't fair--there are kids in a lot worse trouble, so why pick on Joanne? Your husband had two years of college, though you only finished high school. You both always hoped at least one of your kids would get to go to college. Marie used to get straight A's and the teachers always said Joanne was just as smart.

Mediators: It is your responsibility to conduct the initial joint session of the mediation and one private session with each party, using the techniques and stages of the parent-child mediation process.

Victim-Offender Mediation Role Play

Several exercises are offered to assist classes or training groups that are examining victim-offender mediation.

Case Selection

One of the most critical issues related to victim-offender mediation is the selection of cases in which the mediation intervention will be effective. Divide into small groups, read the following case scenarios, and select the cases that you believe would be the most appropriate for mediation. Spend about 15 to 20 minutes on this exercise before reporting back to the full group your selection of cases and the specific criteria you used in making the selection.

1. Theft of $300 worth of material form a garage by a young offender with eight prior theft charges. Comments in the police report suggest that the victim might be willing to meet the offender. The offender, on the advice of his public defender, entered a plea of guilty and was placed on probation. He asserts, however, that he did not really commit the crime; it was committed by a friend of his.

2. An elderly woman was assaulted in front of her apartment by an offender who then stole her purse. Pushed to the sidewalk, she sustained a broken hip and a broken arm. She had lived in the neighborhood for twenty years and had always felt safe. She can't understand why anyone would do such a thing, and wonders if the criminal had been watching her movements. The offender had no prior convictions and was placed on probation.

3. While the family was visiting relatives in another city their home was broken into during the middle of the night. The television, stereo, VCR, and personal computer were taken. No vandalism occurred. Entry had been through a rear window, which was broken. The entire family was greatly frightened. The two young children have had nightmares for several weeks following the burglary. Mrs. Jones is afraid to be home alone at night with the children when her husband is out of town on business. They can't understand why they were victimized and have fears about being burglarized again. The offender has one prior conviction of burglary.

4. As he was driving home from work the city engineer was killed by a drunk driver. His wife and two children were in shock when they were notified; they couldn't believe it happened. As the reality sunk in, they experienced severe grief and agony over the loss. When they heard that the offender was convicted of negligent homicide, they felt relieved but wondered about what type of person could be so drunk while driving that his or her actions would result in the death of a totally innocent person. The offender was a middle-aged man with a wife and one teenage child. An alcoholic, he had recently left a treatment program that his wife had insisted upon. More than any other event related to his drinking problem, this incident shook him up and made him feel terrible. He was sentenced to ten weekends in the county jail and placed on probation for three years.

Mediating Interpersonal Conflicts: A Pathway to Peace

Role Play of Mediation

A typical mediation session between a crime victim and an offender begins with an opening statement that includes the following key points:

1. Introduce everyone and arrange seating.
2. Explain your role as a mediator: "I am here to help both of you
    to talk about what happened and to work out a restitution agreement,
    if possible. . . . I am not a court official and will not be requiring you
    to agree to anything, nor will I be taking sides with either of you."
3. Explain ground rules: "No interrupting of each other."
    4. Identify the agenda:
    - Review facts and feelings related to the crime.
    - Discuss losses and negotiate restitution.
    - Emphasize that both parties must feel any restitution agreement
      that is reached must be fair to both of you.
    - Initiate direct communication between victim and offender, who
      are facing each other. "Mrs. Smith, could you tell John what
      happened from your perspective and how you felt about the
      burglary?"

Following the opening statement, each party has some uninterrupted time to tell his or her story; usually the victim begins. After the facts and feelings related to the offense have been discussed, the mediator then facilitates a transition to discussing losses incurred by the victim and the possibility of negotiating a restitution plan.

Divide into groups of four and have each person select one of the roles: victim, offender, mediator, or observer, who provides feedback to the individuals in the small group, and reports the experience to the larger group. Spend at least forty-five minutes role-playing the case and discussing it prior to reporting back to the larger group.

Victim Role

Your home was broken into by a twenty-year-old young who had only one prior conviction for theft, as a juvenile. A television set and $200 in cash were taken. In addition to the financial loss, you were very emotionally upset, feeling a heightened sense of vulnerability. You felt as if you had been personally assaulted.

Offender Role

You are a twenty-year-old man who was drinking with some friends and ran out of money. Your friends convinced you to break into a house. They waited in a car and were never caught by the police. You were very nervous when you entered the house through a broken window, and you stole about $200 and a television set. It didn't seem like any big deal because these people probably had insurance anyway.

Mediator Role

You serve as a mediator in a case that was referred by the local probation department after the offender admitted his guilt in court. As part of his sentence to probation, he is required to make restitution to his victim, preferably through the mediation program. You met with the offender first, and then met separately with the victim. Both were willing to enter the mediation process.

Informal Mediation of Staff Conflict in Human Services

Conflict in the workplace between staff members frequently involves miscommunication or unstated assumptions about work-related responsibilities and rights. The following two role plays are designed to develop greater awareness in recognizing when mediation may be helpful in resolving conflict.

Role Play 1: Conflict with Supervisor over Case Management

Background

Lisa graduated two years ago from college, and was recently hired in child protection services. Although her previous job was working with the elderly, she has had experience in child protection through volunteer work several years ago. Mark was recently promoted to supervisor after working three years in direct case management. He has worked in social services agencies for the past seven years, but has no previous supervisory experience.

Lisa: Lisa feels frustrated at having to push against her supervisor to do what she considers the right thing to do with her cases. She dislikes being constantly second-guessed, especially because she is working directly with the clients, and her supervisor is getting his information secondhand from her or her reports.

Mark: Mark wants to share his wisdom and insight with Lisa, and he also wants to do an outstanding job as a supervisor. He feels frustrated that Lisa resists listening to his advice and sometimes contradicts him with her assessment of the cases. He is beginning to feel that Lisa is not willing to change or adjust to her new work environment, even though he is getting good reports about her work through client feedback surveys and her co-workers.

Rosemary: Rosemary is Mark's direct supervisor, and she has had conversations with both Mark and Lisa; they have individually approached her with their views of the situation. Rosemary has agreed to serve as an impartial mediator at Lisa's request, on the condition that Mark is also willing to try mediation. She has talked to Mark and he is agreeable.

Role Play 2: Conflict between Co-workers

Background

Heidi and Leigh have been working at the same county agency for two years, and recently were assigned to the same office. Since their first meeting, they have not gotten along because of their different work styles. Heidi tends to leave things as they are or in worse shape, figuring that she will clean them up before she uses them the next time. Leigh likes to leave things all cleaned and set up to be used the next time. Two of the biggest problems usually involve the copier or the coffee maker. Previously Leigh and Heidi had been able to avoid confrontations by not working so closely together; however, working in the same office has added much stress to their working relationship. The problems come to a head when Heidi starts leaving case files lying on top of the file cabinets on a daily basis, and Leigh has to spend at least thirty minutes putting them back in order. She talked to the supervisor, who suggested they might want to try mediation, and recommended two staff mediators who work for the county. Leigh contacts one of the mediators, who agrees to mediate if Heidi is also willing to mediate. Heidi agrees to give it a try, and a time and place is set for the meeting.

Heidi: Heidi doesn't know what the big deal is, because she has always worked this way. She thinks things are going just fine, and doesn't know why Leigh is so uptight. She agreed to mediation only to see if it would help Leigh.

Leigh: Leigh feels helpless when trying to make Heidi understand how much extra work she has to do in any place after Heidi has just been there. She has asked Heidi to pick up after herself on numerous occasions, but Heidi just doesn't cooperate. If mediation doesn't work, Leigh is ready to go to county arbitration to have Heidi reassigned to another department.

Mediator: The mediator works for the county agency and does mediation for staff conflicts and with outside clients. The mediator has already met separately with Heidi and Leigh.